PREPARING EFFECTIVE BUSINESS PLANS

AN ENTREPRENEURIAL APPROACH

SECOND EDITION

Bruce R. Barringer, Ph.D.

Oklahoma State University

Boston   Columbus   Indianapolis   New York   San Francisco   Upper Saddle River
Amsterdam   Cape Town   Dubai   London   Madrid   Milan   Munich   Paris   Montreal   Toronto
Delhi   Mexico City   Sao Paulo   Sydney   Hong Kong   Seoul   Singapore   Taipei   Tokyo

Editor in Chief: Stephanie Wall
Acquisitions Editor: Daniel Tylman
Program Management Team Lead: Ashley Santora
Program Manager: Claudia Fernandes
Director of Marketing: Maggie Moylan
Marketing Manager: Erin Gardner
Project Management Team Lead: Judy Leale
Project Manager: Nicole Suddeth
Procurement Specialist: Michelle Klein
Cover Designer: Karen Salzback
Cover Photo: Angelo Cavalli/Digital Vision/Getty Images
Digital Production Project Manager: Lisa Rinaldi
Full-Service Project Management: Prabhu Chinnasamy at Integra Software Services
Composition: Integra Software Services
Printer/Binder: RR Donnelley
Cover Printer: RR Donnelley
Text Font: 10/12, Times Ten LT Std

Credits and acknowledgments borrowed from other sources and reproduced, with permission, in this textbook appear on the appropriate page within text.

Many of the designations by manufacturers and sellers to distinguish their products are claimed as trademarks. Where those designations appear in this book, and the publisher was aware of a trademark claim, the designations have been printed in initial caps or all caps.

Library of Congress Cataloging-in-Publication Data

Barringer, Bruce R.
    Preparing effective business plans: an entrepreneurial approach/Bruce R. Barringer, Ph.D., Oklahoma State University.—SECOND EDITION.
    pages cm
    Includes index.
    ISBN 978-0-13-350697-6 (alk. paper)—ISBN 0-13-350697-5 (alk. paper) 1. Business planning. 2. Entrepreneurship. 3. New business enterprises—Planning. 4. Small business—Planning. I. Title.
    HD30.28.B36837 2015
    658.4'01—dc23

                                                                    2014003022

10 9 8 7 6 5 4 3 V056 15

ISBN 10:   0-13-350697-5
ISBN 13: 978-0-13-350697-6

Dedication

To my wife Jan, my best friend

BRIEF CONTENTS

CONTENTS

PREFACE

THE SURGE IN INTEREST IN ENTREPRENEURSHIP ON COLLEGE CAMPUSES AND BEYOND

There is tremendous interest in entrepreneurship on college campuses and around the world. In academia, some 2,000 colleges and universities in the United States, about two-thirds of the total, now offer a course in entrepreneurship. As a result, a growing number of students are forgoing traditional careers and starting their own business. Ordinary citizens are equally interested in starting entrepreneurial careers. According to the 2012 Global Entrepreneurship Monitor, in the United States a total of 13 percent of the adult population (ages 18–64) either is starting a business or has started a business in the past 3 ½ years. There are regions of the world where the percentage is even higher. For example, in Latin America and the Caribbean 17 percent of the adult population, on average, either is starting a business or has started a business in the past 3½ years.

NEW TO THIS EDITION

- Fresh material that explains the business startup process, from the original inception of a business idea to a fully fleshed-out business plan
- New or updated Business Plan Insight boxed features
- Revised and updated business plan for Prime Adult Fitness, the fictitious fitness center for people 50 years and older, that is completed step-by-step throughout the course of the book
- New and updated Application Questions at the end of each chapter
- New and updated examples, embedded in each chapter, that illustrate the issues that business plan writers grapple with
- An updated Internet Resource Table (Appendix 2.2), which provides students access to online resources to assist them in completing a First Screen analysis and a complete business plan

THE IMPORTANCE OF BUSINESS PLANS

An important tool that helps people who intend to start a new business is a business plan. A business plan is a written document that carefully explains every aspect of a new venture. Although many entrepreneurs and small business people do not write a business plan before they start their business, it's highly recommended. For most businesses, a business plan serves two functions. Inside the firm, the plan helps a company develop a "blueprint" to follow in executing its strategies and plan. Outside the firm, it introduces potential investors and other stakeholders to the business opportunity the firm is pursuing and how it plans to pursue it.

OBJECTIVES OF THE BOOK

The objectives of this book are twofold. The first objective is to help students and others learn how to write a business plan. This book provides step-by-step instructions for writing a plan. Second, the book immerses its reader in the process of thinking through the issues that are important in starting a business. This objective may be the most compelling advantage of the book. A full business plan is written, chapter-by-chapter, as an example through the course of the book. The issues that are considered in writing this plan provide a template for others to use as they consider their own business ventures and write their own business plan.

ORGANIZATION OF THE BOOK

The book is organized into four distinct parts:

Part	Topic	Chapters in the Book
1	Starting the Process	1
2	What to Do Before the Business Plan Is Written	2–3
3	Preparing a Business Plan	4–10
4	Presenting the Business Plan	11

DISTINGUISHING FEATURES

A number of distinguishing features set this book apart from other business plan books that are available.

Focus on the Entire "Front End" of the Entrepreneurial Process

Although the primary purpose of the book is to describe how to write a business plan, the entire "front end" of the entrepreneurial process is discussed and defined. The most effective business plans are part of a comprehensive process that includes (1) identifying a business idea, (2) screening the idea (or ideas) to determine their preliminary feasibility, (3) conducting a full feasibility analysis to see if proceeding with a business plan is warranted, and (4) writing the plan. Each step in this process is explained in the book.

Feasibility Analysis Worksheets

Two worksheets are included to help students and others work through the feasibility analysis process. The first worksheet is called the "First Screen," and helps determine the preliminary feasibility of a business idea. The second worksheet is a full feasibility analysis and is much more comprehensive. Combined, the worksheets represent a sequential way for students to determine the "feasibility" of their business ideas before they enter the business planning process.

Sample Business Plan

A business plan, for a fictitious company named Prime Adult Fitness, is built through the course of the book. Every aspect of the plan is described and discussed. This plan will give students and others a solid point of reference as they build their own business plans.

Presenting a Business Plan

The final chapter in the book provides tips and suggestions for presenting a business plan with confidence and poise. Based on a 20- to 30-minute hypothetical presentation, a 12-slide PowerPoint presentation is provided with suggestions for what to include on each slide.

Business Plan Insight Boxed Features

Each of the first ten chapters includes a boxed feature that provides special insights on writing a business plan or launching a new venture.

SUPPLEMENTS

At www.pearsonhighered.com/irc, the following supplements are available to adopting instructors for download. Registration is simple and gives you immediate access to new titles and new editions. If you ever need assistance, our dedicated technical support team is ready to help with the supplements that accompany this text. Visit http://247.pearsoned.com/ for answers to frequently asked questions and toll-free user support phone numbers.

- Instructor's Resource Manual
- PowerPoint Presentation

COMPANION WEBSITE

A useful companion website, www.pearsonhighered.com/entrepreneurship, offers free access to teaching resources for all books in the Prentice Hall Entrepreneurship Series, including additional activities, links to latest research, sample entrepreneurship curriculum and syllabi, teaching tips, and Web resource links.

COURSESMART ETEXTBOOKS

CourseSmart eTextbooks were developed for students looking to save on required or recommended textbooks. Students simply select their eText by title or author and purchase immediate access to the content for the duration of the course using any major credit card. With a CourseSmart eText, students can search for specific keywords or page numbers, take notes online, print out reading assignments that incorporate lecture notes, and bookmark important passages for later review. For more information or to purchase a CourseSmart eTextbook, visit www.coursesmart.com

ABOUT THE AUTHOR

Bruce R. Barringer is the N. Malone Mitchell, Jr., Chair in the School of Entrepreneurship at Oklahoma State University. He is also the Head of the School of Entrepreneurship. Dr. Barringer obtained his Ph.D. from the University of Missouri and his MBA from Iowa State University. His research interests include feasibility analysis, firm growth, corporate entrepreneurship, and the impact of interorganizational relationships on business organizations. Over the years, he has worked with a number of technology-based incubators and student-led entrepreneurship activities and clubs.

Dr. Barringer's research has been published in *Strategic Management Journal, Journal of Management, Journal of Business Venturing, Journal of Small Business Management, Journal of Developmental Entrepreneurship,* and in several other outlets. Dr. Barringer is the author or coauthor of five books, including *Entrepreneurship: Successfully Launching New Ventures, Preparing Effective Business Plans, The Truth About Starting a Business, What's Stopping You? Shatter the 9 Most Common Myths Keeping You From Starting Your Own Business,* and *Launching a Business: The First 100 Days.*

CHAPTER 1

WHY PLAN

INTRODUCTION

On college campuses and around the world, entrepreneurship garners tremendous interest. More than 2,000 colleges and universities in the United States, about two-thirds of the total, now offer a course in entrepreneurship.[1] Across the United States, interest in entrepreneurship is growing, among all demographic groups. According to the Kauffman Index of Entrepreneurial Activity, 320 out of every 100,000 adults created businesses in the United States in 2011. That number translates into approximately 543,000 new businesses being created each month during the year.[2] Interest in starting a business among young adults is at an all-time high. According to a recent survey, 54 percent of millennials (ages 18–34) either want to start a business or have already started one. That number is even higher for African Americans and Latinos. A total of 63 percent of African Americans and 64 percent of Latinos expressed a desire to start their own company.[3]

An important tool that helps people who intend to start a new business is a business plan. A business plan is a written document that carefully explains every aspect of a new business venture.[4] Although some entrepreneurs simply "wing it" and start a business without the benefits of formal planning, experts recommend preparing a business plan. For most new ventures, the business plan is a dual-purpose document used both inside and outside the firm. Inside the firm, the plan helps the company to develop a "road map" to follow in executing its strategies and plans. Outside the firm, it introduces potential investors and other stakeholders to the business opportunity the firm is pursuing and how it plans to pursue it.

The most effective business plans are part of a comprehensive process that includes (1) identifying a business idea, (2) screening the idea (or ideas) to determine their preliminary feasibility, (3) conducting a full feasibility analysis to see if proceeding with a business plan is warranted, and (4) writing the plan. Many new businesses fail, not because the founders didn't work hard or weren't committed to the venture, but because the idea wasn't a good one to being with. This process sets forth a specific path for investigating the merits of a business idea. Although the primary purpose of this book is to describe how to write an effective business plan, the second section of the book, titled "What to Do Before You Prepare Your Business Plan," focuses on how to identify and screen business ideas (Chapter 2) and how to test their feasibility (Chapter 3).

Although writing a business plan may appear at first glance to be a tedious process, a properly prepared business plan can save an entrepreneur a tremendous amount of time, money, and heartache by working out the kinks in a business concept before rather than after the business is started. A large percentage of entrepreneurs do not write business plans for their ventures. In fact, a 2010–2012 study of 350 entrepreneurs found that of those that had successful exits (i.e., an IPO or sale to another firm), about 70 percent did not start with a business plan.[5] Similarly, in a 2002 study, *Inc.* magazine asked the founders of the firms that comprised the *Inc.* 500 that year whether they had written a formal business plan before they launched their companies. A total of 60 percent had not. These statistics should not deter an entrepreneur from writing a business plan. Ample evidence supports the notion that writing a business plan is an extremely good investment of an entrepreneur's time and money.[6]

REASONS FOR WRITING A BUSINESS PLAN

There are two primary reasons for writing a business plan, as depicted in Figure 1-1. First, writing a business plan forces the founders of a firm to systematically think through each aspect of their new venture. This is not a trivial effort—it normally takes several days or weeks to complete a well-developed business plan—and the founders will usually meet regularly to work on the plan during this period. Writing a business plan is also an immersion experience—many founders work late nights and on weekends to get their plan completed. An example of how much work is sometimes involved, and how a well-planned new business unfolds, is provided by Gwen Whiting and Lindsey Wieber, the cofounders of The Laundress (www.thelaundress.com), a company that sells specially formulated laundry detergents and other fabric care products. Wieber and Whiting met at Cornell University

FIGURE 1-1 Two Primary Reasons for Writing a Business Plan

Internal Reason	External Reason
Forces the founding team to work together to hammer out the details of a business venture	Communicates the merits of a new venture to outsiders, such as investors and bankers

while studying fabrics, and after graduating, the pair decided to start a business together. The following vignette comes from an interview they gave to Ladies Who Launch (www.ladieswholaunch.com), a Web site that highlights the accomplishments of female entrepreneurs:

> *Gwen*: Lindsey and I went to college and studied textiles at Cornell together and always wanted to be in business together. We knew it was going to happen. We always talked about ideas. We were talking about this concept, and it was the right time for us. The first thing we did was the business plan and then a cash flow analysis. We wanted to do as much research as possible before developing the products.
>
> *Lindsey*: We spent Memorial Day weekend (2003) doing our business plan. We spent the Fourth of July weekend doing our cash flow. After we had our ideas on paper, we went back to Cornell, met with a professor there, and had a crash course in chemistry. She worked with us on the formulation of the products.
>
> *Gwen*: I found a manufacturer on Columbus Day. Every piece of free time we had, we dedicated to the business. We weren't at the beach with our friends anymore.[7]

The payoff for this level of dedication and hard work, which involved the preparation of a formal business plan, is that Whiting and Wieber have now had a successful business for 10 years. Their products are sold through their Web site and in many stores.

To provide another indication of the value of writing a business plan for the founders of a firm, Table 1-1 shows the contents of the business plan for a fictitious

TABLE 1-1	Business Plan Format for New Venture Fitness Equipment Inc.	
	Table of Contents	
I.	Executive Summary	1
II.	Company Description	3
III.	Industry Analysis	6
IV.	Market Analysis	10
V.	Marketing Plan	14
VI.	Management Team and Company Structure	18
VII.	Operations Plan	22
VIII.	Product (or Service) Design and Development Plan	25
IX.	Financial Projections	30
	Appendices	
	Summary of Feasibility Analysis, Including Customer Reaction to the Product or Service	
	Supporting Industry Research	
	Resumes of Management Team Members	

company named New Venture Fitness Equipment. This plan is probably similar to the plan that Gwen Whiting and Lindsey Wieber wrote for The Laundress. New Venture Fitness Equipment plans to sell a new generation of fitness machines that will take the boredom out of exercising indoors by equipping its machines (treadmills, stationary bikes, and rowing machines) with flat-panel monitors that will allow exercisers to compete against virtual opponents, in a sort of electronic-game format, on a variety of simulated outdoor courses. Spend a few minutes looking at each of the topics included in Table 1-1, and then imagine the founders of New Venture Fitness Equipment talking through each of these topics. Imagine the debate that will inevitably ensue as the founders grapple with tough issues, such as projecting the size of their industry, specifying their target market, pricing their products, and determining how many machines they will have to sell to break even in each of their first three years. This process forces a team to not only work together but also turn abstract ideas like "these machines are so great they should sell like hotcakes" into concrete realities like "we'll need to sell 9,850 machines each year during our first three years to break even." The benefit of this type of intense analysis before a business is started provides a compelling rationale for writing a business plan. This sentiment is affirmed by Guy Kawasaki, a well-known Silicon Valley entrepreneur and venture capitalist, who wrote:

> All the late-night, back-o'-the envelope, romantic intentions to change
> the world become tangible and debatable once they're put on paper.
> Thus, the document itself is not nearly as important as the process that
> leads to the document. Even if you aren't trying to raise money, you
> should write one (a business plan) anyway.[8]

The second reason a business plan is important is because it is a selling document for a company. It provides a mechanism for a young company to present itself to prospective investors, business accelerators and incubators, suppliers, potential partners, and others. Investors vary in terms of the reliance they place on formal business plans. Initially, many investors ask for an executive summary, which is a 1–2 page overview of a business plan, or they'll ask for a short set of PowerPoint slides (often called a slide deck) describing the merits of a new venture. If their interest is sufficiently peaked, in some cases they'll ask for a full business plan and in other cases they won't. It's still necessary to have a business plan, however. If an investor commits, in most cases a business plan will be required during the due diligence phase. Due diligence refers to the process investors go through after they tentatively commit to an investment. The commitment is based on a thorough investigation of the merits of the venture, whether any legal complications exist, and whether the claims made in the business plan are accurate and realistic.[9]

As a selling document, a business plan also helps a new company build credibility. For example, imagine that you are an investor and have enough money to invest in one new business. You chat informally with several entrepreneurs at a university-sponsored event for startups and decide that there are two new ventures that you want to know more about. You contact the first entrepreneur and ask for a copy of his business plan. The entrepreneur hesitates a bit and says that he hasn't prepared a formal business plan but would love to buy you lunch to talk about his business idea. You contact the second entrepreneur and make the same request. This time, the entrepreneur says that she would be glad to forward you a copy of a 25-page business plan, along with a 12-slide PowerPoint presentation that provides an overview of the plan. Ten minutes later, the PowerPoint presentation is in your e-mail inbox with a note that the business plan will arrive by FedEx the next morning. You look through the slides, which are crisp and to the point and do an excellent job of outlining the business opportunity. The next day, the business plan arrives just as promised and is equally impressive.

Which entrepreneur is likely to get your attention? All other things being equal, the answer is obvious: the second entrepreneur. The fact that the second entrepreneur has a business plan not only provides you with detailed information about the venture but also suggests that the entrepreneur has thought through each element of the business and is committed enough to the new venture to invest the time and energy necessary to prepare the plan.

Another way that a business plan helps establish credibility for a firm is by winning or placing high in a university-, community-, or state-sponsored business plan competition or similar event. In the United States alone, more than 50 universities conduct business plan competitions, awarding up to $10 million in prizes and in-kind services every year. The participants are able to connect with investors and successful entrepreneurs who serve as judges and the winners are typically featured in local newspapers and business publications. Winning or placing high in a competition also sends a message to investors that a startup is worth looking at. For example, when a professor they admired suffered a heart attack, Ray Li, a Rutgers alumnus, and John Vitug, a graduate of Kean University, created an all-natural, low-calorie beverage named Heart Juice that contains ingredients that combat high cholesterol. The two partnered with Shaun Bratton, an MBA candidate at Rutgers Business School, and entered the 2011 Rutgers Business School Business Plan Competition. They were placed second and won $10,000. Commenting on the value of participating in the competition, Ray Li said:

> The Rutgers competition gave us the push to get our product up and running. The award confirmed the belief that we could be successful and win interest from venture capitalists down the road.[10]

Over 300 stores now carry Heart Juice, and the number is growing.

There is an emerging school of thought that opposes the idea of writing a business plan, and advocates experimentation and trial-and-error learning gleaned through customer feedback over formal planning.[11] This approach, which is associated with the Lean Startup movement, espouses many excellent ideas, particularly in the area of solicitation feedback directly from prospective customers prior to settling on a business idea and a business model to execute on the idea. This book differs from this approach by arguing that a business plan represents an important starting point for a new venture and serves many useful purposes. It is not intended to be a static document written in isolation at a desk. Instead, it is anticipated that the research conducted to complete the plan will place the founders in touch with potential customers, suppliers, business partners, and others, and that the feedback obtained from these folks will cause the plan to change as it's being written.[12] It's also anticipated that the business will iterate and change after it is launched, based on additional feedback. Some businesses will change more than others, depending on the quality of their initial feasibility analysis and the newness and volatility of their industry. An example of a startup that has relied on its business plan extensively but iterates frequently is Moxie Trades (www.moxietrades.com), a company started by Marissa McTasney, a woman in the construction industry. Ms. McTasney couldn't understand why tradeswomen had to wear ill-fitting men's work boots and clothes, so she started a company that designs and sells work boots and work apparel designed specifically for women. Writing about how Moxie Trades has benefited by having a formal business plan and how frequently the plan changes, author Melanie Keveles wrote in the book *Scrappy Startups*:

> Marissa found that she was capable of drawing up a business plan, but she also found that her business plan would work for three months and then it would change. Now, not only does she modify her business plan every six months but she completely changes her strategy along the way.[13]

WHO READS THE BUSINESS PLAN AND WHAT ARE THEY LOOKING FOR?

There are two primary audiences for a firm's business plan. Let's look at each of them.

A FIRM'S EMPLOYEES

A clearly written business plan, which articulates the vision and future plans of a firm, is important for both the management team and the rank-and-file employees. As mentioned above, some experts argue that it's a waste of time to write a business plan and favor trial-and-error learning instead. Although trial-and-error learning is valuable, the process of writing a business plan is often as beneficial as the plan itself, as illustrated through the New Venture Fitness Equipment example. Not only is it useful for a management team to hammer out the contents of a business plan together, but also the process of working together on such an important project can help develop a strong, cohesive team. The process can also uncover potential trouble spots in a team. If particular members of a team can't work together to produce a business plan, it is unlikely they will be successful working together after the business is launched.

A clearly written business plan also helps a firm's rank-and-file employees operate in sync and move forward in a consistent and purposeful manner. The existence of a business plan is particularly useful for a new business that has geographically dispersed employees. For example, say you live in Raleigh, North Carolina, and were just hired to be the primary sales rep for the eastern United States for an information technology startup headquartered in California. Imagine how helpful it would be for you to have a copy of your new firm's business plan, so that you could refer to the plan to make sure everything you do and say is consistent with the overall plans and direction of the company.

INVESTORS AND OTHER EXTERNAL STAKEHOLDERS

External stakeholders, such as investors, potential business partners, potential customers, private and government-funded grant awarding agencies, and key employees who are being recruited to join a firm, are the second audience for a business plan. To appeal to this group, the business plan must be realistic and not reflect overconfidence on the firm's part. A good rule of thumb is that a business plan should be written with extreme empathy for the readers, who are typically busy people who like to read plans that are clear, concise, and plainly explain the business. Overly optimistic statements or financial projections undermine a business plan's credibility, so it is foolish to include them. At the same time, the plan must clearly demonstrate that the business idea is viable and offers potential investors financial returns that are greater than lower-risk investment alternatives. The same is true for potential business partners, customers, grant awarding agencies, and key recruits. Unless the new business can show that it has impressive potential, there is little reason for anyone to become involved.

A firm must validate the feasibility of its business idea and have a good understanding of its competitive environment prior to presenting its business plan to others, as will be emphasized throughout this book. Sophisticated investors, potential business partners, and others will base their assessment of the future prospects of a business on facts, not guesswork or speculation. The most compelling facts a company can provide in its business plan are the results of its own feasibility analysis, particularly if the analysis includes feedback from industry experts and prospective customers. A business plan rings hollow if it is based strictly on entrepreneurs' predictions and estimates of what they "think" will happen.

Particularly when writing for an external audience, entrepreneurs must avoid appearing naïve or uninformed, especially about the industry a firm is about to enter or the amount of competition a firm may encounter. To make this point, William A. Sahlman, a Harvard professor and expert on business plans, says that "Business is like chess: To be successful, you must be able to anticipate several moves in advance."[14] What Sahlman means by this statement is that a business plan that is overly optimistic and doesn't seem to anticipate any problems or competitive challenges to its product or service is by definition naïve and stands to lose credibility quickly. All companies have problems and competitors. In addition, a cardinal rule in approaching an investor or a banker with a business plan is to get a personal introduction. Bankers and investors receive many business plans, and most of them end up in a pile on their credenzas. To have your business plan noticed, find someone who knows the banker or the investor, and ask for an introduction.

GUIDELINES FOR WRITING A BUSINESS PLAN

Several important guidelines should influence the writing of a business plan. It is important to remember that a firm's business plan, its executive summary, or a set of PowerPoint slides that summarizes the plan is typically the first aspect of a proposed venture that will be seen by an investor or whomever the plan is presented to. If the full plan, the executive summary or the PowerPoint slides are incomplete or look sloppy, an investor may easily infer that the venture itself is incomplete or sloppy. It is important to be sensitive to the structure, style, and content of a plan before exposing it to a firm's employees or sending it to an outsider. It is also important for the individuals writing the plan to continually measure the type of company that they are envisioning against their personal goals and aspirations. One of the worst things that can happen to an entrepreneur is to write a business plan, raise money, launch the business, and then realize that the business is inconsistent with his or her personal aspirations or preferred lifestyle and wish that the firm hadn't come to fruition.

STRUCTURE AND STYLE OF THE BUSINESS PLAN

To make the best impression, a business plan should follow a conventional structure, such as in the plan outlined earlier in Table 1-1. Although some entrepreneurs are creative and don't want their plans to "look like everyone else's," departing from the basic structure of the conventional business plan is usually a mistake. Typically, investors are very busy people and want a plan that allows them to easily find critical information. If investors have to hunt for something because it is in an unusual place or just isn't there, they might simply give up and move on to the next plan.

One of the most common questions that the writers of business plans ask is, "How long and detailed should it be?" Experts vary on the optimal page length, but most recommendations fall in the 25–35-page range. Many software packages are available that employ an interactive, menu-driven approach to assist in the writing of a business plan. Some of these programs are very helpful; however, entrepreneurs should avoid a boilerplate plan that looks as though it came from a "canned" source. The software package may be helpful in providing structure and saving time, but the information in the plan should still be tailored to the individual business. Some businesses hire consultants or outside advisors to write their business plans. Although there is nothing wrong with getting advice or making sure that a plan looks as professional as possible, a consultant or outside advisor shouldn't be the author of the plan. Along with facts and figures, a business plan needs to project a sense of anticipation and excitement about the possibilities surrounding a new venture, which is a task best accomplished by the creators of the business. Plus, hiring someone to write the plan denies the entrepreneur or team of entrepreneurs the positive benefits of the writing experience, as explained earlier in the chapter.

The appearance of the plan must be carefully thought out. It should look sharp but not give the impression that a lot of money was spent to produce it. Those who read plans know that entrepreneurs have limited resources and expect them to act accordingly. A plastic spiral binder, including a transparent cover sheet and a back sheet to support the plan, is a good choice. When writing the plan, avoid getting carried away with the design elements included in word-processing programs, such as boldfaced type, italics, different font sizes and colors, clip art, and so forth. Overuse of these tools makes a business plan look amateurish rather than professional. Some style-related things can be done that show the amount of care and attention that went into a plan and that aren't overly flashy or costly. For example, if a company has a well-designed logo, it should be placed on the cover sheet of the business plan and on the header for each page. A simple design element such as having the colors in the charts and graphs in the plan match the colors in the logo shows an attention to detail and an eye toward branding that is impressive to most readers.

One important criterion that all business plans should adhere to is to convey a clear, coherent story of what the business plans to accomplish and how it plans to get there. Many entrepreneurs aren't very good at this, which lessens the potential impact of their plans. Robert W. Price affirms this sentiment in a book titled *Roadmap to Entrepreneurial Success*, which reports the observations of two experts on business plans regarding this issue:

> According to David Berkus, a past-president of the Tech Coast Angels, one of the largest angel investment groups in the United States, the first step to writing a business plan is fleshing out your "talking points" and weaving them into a storyline. Storytelling is having the ability to communicate succinctly and precisely what you do, what you want to do, and what you need to do it. Bill Joos at Garage Technology Ventures, who has heard some 100,000 pitches from entrepreneurs, agrees that there is a "big problem with entrepreneurs who have the inability to talk about what they do."[15]

One thing that a new venture can do to help develop a concise description of their business is develop an elevator speech. An elevator speech is a brief, carefully constructed statement, usually 1–2 minutes long that outlines the merits of a business venture. It is explained in more detail in the following Business Plan Insight box. A properly prepared elevator speech can assist in writing a business plan by helping the founders develop a sharp and concise description of their business.

In business plans, savvy investors and others will pick up on several potential "red flags" when certain aspects of a plan are insufficient or miss the mark. These red flags, which are depicted in Table 1-2, not only undermine the credibility of the business plan but of the individuals who wrote the plan. The writers of a plan should work hard to avoid these potential complications.

CONTENT OF THE BUSINESS PLAN

Most business plans are divided into sections that represent the major aspects of a new venture's business, as depicted in the business plan outline shown earlier in Table 1-1. The titles of the sections will vary from plan to plan, although most plans follow a fairly standard format. What varies, of course, from plan to plan,

---

BUSINESS PLAN INSIGHT

Develop an Elevator Speech

A very useful exercise for a new firm is to develop an elevator speech. An elevator speech (or pitch) is a brief, carefully constructed statement that outlines the merits of a business opportunity. Why is it called an elevator speech? If an entrepreneur stepped into an elevator on the 25th floor of a building and found that by a stroke of luck a potential investor was in the same elevator, the entrepreneur would have the time it takes to get from the 25th floor to the ground floor to try to get the investor interested in the business opportunity. Most elevator speeches are 1–2 minutes long.

An elevator speech might come in handy on many occasions. For example, many university-sponsored centers for entrepreneurship hold events that bring investors and entrepreneurs together. Often these events include breaks designed specifically for the purpose of allowing entrepreneurs looking for funding to mingle with potential investors. The other thing an elevator speech does for a young firm is force the founders to develop a very concise, to-the-point description of the business idea.

An outline for a 2-minute elevator speech is provided here. A new venture's elevator speech should be carefully prepared and practiced often.

STEPS IN AN ELEVATOR SPEECH

Step 1: Describe the opportunity or problem that needs to be solved.	45 seconds
Step 2: Describe how your product or service meets the opportunity or solves the problem.	45 seconds
Step 3: Describe your qualifications.	15 seconds
Step 4: Describe your market.	15 seconds
Total:	2 minutes

---

is the quality of the writing, the substance of the plan, and the degree to which the plan convinces the reader that the business opportunity is exciting, feasible, defensible, and within the capabilities of the people launching the firm. Writing a plan that includes all of these elements is not an easy task, but it is a very useful one, as illustrated throughout this book.

The essence of what should be included in each section of a business plan is described in Chapter 4 through Chapter 10 of this book. After the plan is completed, it should be reviewed for spelling and grammar and to make sure that no critical information has been omitted. There are numerous stories about business plans being sent to investors that left out important information. One investor even said that he once received a business plan that didn't include any contact information for the entrepreneur. Apparently, the entrepreneur was so focused on the content of the plan that he or she simply forgot to provide contact information on the business plan itself. This was a shame because the investor was interested in learning more about the business opportunity.[16]

TABLE 1-2 Red Flags in Business Plans

Red Flag	Explanation
Founders with none of their own money at risk	If the founders aren't willing to put their own money at risk, why should anyone else?
A poorly cited plan	A plan should be built on hard evidence and sound research, not guesswork or what an entrepreneur "thinks" will happen. The sources for all primary and secondary research should be cited.
Defining the market size too broadly	Defining the market for a new venture too broadly shows that the true target market is not well defined. For example, saying that a new venture will target the $205 billion per year pharmaceutical industry isn't helpful. The market opportunity needs to be better defined. Obviously, the new venture will target a segment or a specific market within the industry.
Overly aggressive financials	Many investors skip directly to this portion of the plan. Projections that are poorly reasoned or unrealistically optimistic lose credibility. In contrast, sober, well-reasoned statements backed by sound research and judgment gain credibility quickly.
Hiding or avoiding weaknesses	It is foolhardy for a new venture to try to downplay or hide its weaknesses. All firms have weaknesses, and often one of the most important things an investor or banker can do, beyond providing money, is to help a new venture shore up the weaknesses that it has.
Sloppiness in any area	It is never a good idea to make a reader wade through typos, balance sheets that don't balance, or sloppiness in any area. These types of mistakes are seen as inattention to detail and hurt the creditability of the entrepreneur.
Too long of a plan	Most experienced readers of business plans know exactly what they're looking for, and to make them wade through 50 pages of material just gets in the way. Don't include page after page of descriptive information about an industry, for example. Two pages of "to the point" information and analysis is much more valuable than 20 pages cut and pasted from the Internet.

Entrepreneurs vary in terms of how much feedback they solicit during the business planning process. Companies that formulate their business plans in secret, to avoid tipping off potential competitors as to what they're planning, refer to themselves as operating in stealth mode. For example, during the time that Dean Kamer was developing the Segway, the self-balancing, two-wheeled human transporter, the project was code named "Ginger."[17] This approach is the exception rather than the rule. Generally, it's best to get as much input and feedback as possible from potential customers and others while the business plan is being written.

MEASURING THE BUSINESS PLAN AGAINST YOUR PERSONAL GOALS AND ASPIRATIONS

Another guideline for writing a business plan is that as a plan is being written, the people involved should continually measure the type of company that they are hoping to start against their personal goals and aspirations. This consideration is important for two reasons.

First, the old adage "be careful what you wish for" is as true in business as it is in other areas of life. For instance, if an entrepreneur identifies an opportunity that has a large upside potential and decides to write a business plan to solicit funds from a venture capitalist or other investor, the entrepreneur should know what to expect if the business is funded. In the case of venture capital, most venture capitalists shoot for a 30–40 percent annual return over the period of their investment, which is typically four to seven years.[18] This level of expectation forces a firm into a fast-growth model literally from the start, which typically implies a quick pace of activity, a rapidly raising overhead, and a total commitment in terms of time and attention from the founding entrepreneurs. Accepting venture capital also involves surrendering equity in the firm to outsiders (in exchange for their investment) and heavy scrutiny at all levels. The upside is that if the new company is successful, the founders will normally do very well financially.

The point of this description, within the context of this chapter, is that entrepreneurs crafting business plans to try to attract venture capital should know what they are getting into and should make sure that the lifestyle associated with owning and managing a venture capital-funded firm is something that is consistent with their personal goals and aspirations. Those who want to own their own firm but place a high value on leisure time or family time or don't want the pressures associated with a group of investors continually looking over their shoulder are poor choices to launch venture-backed firms. These types of individual are better suited to launch a firm in a target (or niche) market that flies slightly under the radar of large competitors, and they should write business plans that solicit funds from friends, family, or a lender. There are many successful firms, which include clothing boutiques, Web retailers, and service firms, just to name a few, that fit this profile. In contrast, some people thrive in a high-pressure environment and have a high desire to make a large amount of money. An entrepreneur who fits this profile is better suited to launch a venture-backed firm.

The second reason that it is important for an entrepreneur to continually measure a business plan against personal goals and aspirations is that as a business plan evolves, the entrepreneur may find aspects to the business that are not as attractive as originally anticipated. A firm that is envisioned to be a nonprofit, for example, may not be financially viable as a nonprofit when the numbers are crunched and feedback is solicited from potential donors and other stakeholders. The firm may only be viable as a for-profit firm, which may be less appealing to the potential founders of the firm. Similarly, someone may find, through the course of writing the business plan, that the business being contemplated can only be successful if run at a much larger scale than was originally anticipated.

The additional risk associated with the larger operation may be more than the potential entrepreneur is willing to undertake. In both of these instances, the process of writing the business plan may result in the entrepreneur deciding to not launch the business. This outcome should be considered to be a successful outcome of the process if the resulting business would have been inconsistent with the entrepreneur's personal goals and aspirations.

RECOGNIZING THAT ELEMENTS OF THE PLAN MAY CHANGE

A final guideline for writing a business plan, which has been highlighted throughout this chapter, is to recognize that the plan will invariably change as it is being written. The best insights are gained by physically talking to potential customers. A valuable component of the Lean Startup movement, referred to earlier, is that it encourages founders to "get out of the building" and ask potential customers and others feedback on all elements of a business proposal including product features, pricing, distribution channels, and so on. Revisions are then made based on feedback, and the process starts all over again.[19] This approach is very similar to what will be described in Chapter 3 of this book, which focuses on feasibility analysis. Feasibility analysis is the process of determining if a business idea is viable, and is normally conducted prior to writing the business plan. The purpose is to assess the merits of a business idea prior to dedicating the time and effort to write a business plan.

An academic principle called the corridor principle provides another explanation for why business plan change while they're being written. The principle states that once an entrepreneur starts a business, the entrepreneur begins a journey down a path where "corridors" leading to new venture opportunities become apparent.[20] The same principle applies during the preparing of a business plan. As an entrepreneur or team of entrepreneurs starts testing the merits of a business idea and starts writing the plan, new insights will invariably emerge that weren't initially apparent. This process continues throughout the life of a company, and it behooves entrepreneurs to remain alert and open to new insights and ideas. As a result of this phenomenon, experts like to stress that a business plan is a living, breathing document, rather than something that is set in stone. In support of this notion, Guy Kawasaki, the Silicon Valley investor and entrepreneur quoted earlier in the chapter, recommends to the authors of business plans to "Write Deliberate, (but) Act Emergent."[21] What Kawasaki means by this statement is that it is necessary to write a "deliberate" plan that provides a specific blueprint for a new venture to follow, but at the same time, the individuals involved should be thinking "emergent," which is a mindset that is open to change and is influenced by the day-to-day realities of the marketplace.

TYPES OF BUSINESSES

There are four distinct types of business, as shown in Table 1-3. All of these types of businesses are acceptable—there is no value judgment here. This book, however, focuses primarily on lifestyle firms, managed growth firms,

TABLE 1-3 Types of Businesses		
Type of Business	*Explanation*	*Examples*
Survival	A business that provides its owner just enough money to put food on the table and pay bills	Handyman, lawn service, part-time childcare
Lifestyle	A business that provides its owner the opportunity to pursue a certain lifestyle and make a living at it	Home-based eBay business, subshop, single-unit franchise, clothing boutique, personal trainer
Managed Growth	A business that employs 10 or more people, may have several outlets, and may be introducing new products or services to the market	Multiunit franchise, regional restaurant chain, Web retailer (modest scale)
Aggressive Growth	A business that is bringing new products and services to the market and has aggressive growth plans	Computer software, medical equipment, Web retailer (large scale), national restaurant chain

and aggressive growth firms. Not all businesses grow rapidly and make tons of money but may still provide their owners satisfying lives and financial security. This book equally targets this type of business along with more aggressive growth firms.

THE PLAN FOR THE BOOK

This book is divided into four sections as shown in Figure 1-2 and as listed here:

Section 1: Starting the Process
Section 2: What to Do Before the Business Plan Is Written
Section 3: Preparing a Business Plan
Section 4: Presenting the Business Plan to Investors and Others

STARTING THE PROCESS (CHAPTER 1)

As discussed earlier, there are two primary reasons for writing a business plan: The process of writing a business plan forces the founders to systematically think through each aspect of their new venture, and a business plan introduces potential investors and others to the firm and the business opportunity it is pursuing. Although all business plans vary depending on the nature of the new venture, there are certain guidelines, discussed in this chapter, which can increase the odds that a particular plan will be successful. A particularly important consideration, normally unseen to the reader of a plan, is that an individual's business plan should coincide with the individual's personal goals or aspirations.

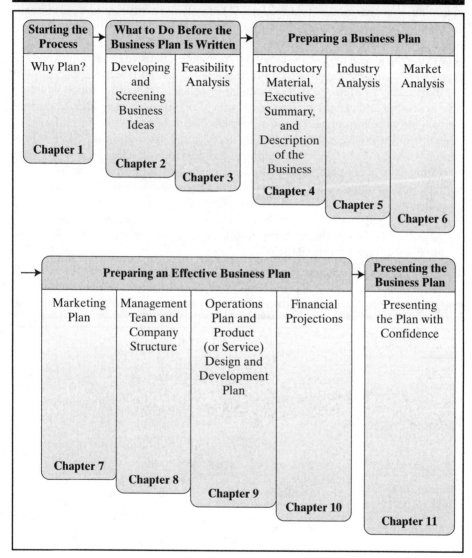

FIGURE 1-2   Steps Involved in Identifying a Business Opportunity, Assessing the Feasibility of the Opportunity, and Preparing an Effective Business Plan

Although writing a business plan can appear to be a tedious process, a well-developed plan can save an entrepreneur a tremendous amount of time and money by working out the flaws in a business idea before rather than after the business is launched. Having a business plan is also an essential document for a firm to have at its disposal, particularly if it plans to reach out to others to try to gain access to resources.

WHAT TO DO BEFORE THE BUSINESS PLAN IS WRITTEN (CHAPTERS 2 TO 3)

As mentioned in the introduction to the chapter, writing a business plan is part of a comprehensive process that includes (1) identifying a business idea, (2) screening the idea (or ideas) to determine their initial feasibility, (3) conducting a full feasibility analysis to determine if proceeding with a business plan is warranted, and (4) writing the plan. These steps, labeled "The Comprehensive Feasibility Analysis/ Business Planning Process," are depicted in Figure 1-3. Although the preparation of a business plan is essential, it is often an insufficient exercise through which to complete a full and candid analysis of the merits of a new business idea. Steps that logically precede the completion of a business plan, which include the preliminary screening of business ideas and feasibility analysis, are also important. Many entrepreneurs make the mistake of identifying a business idea and then jumping directly to writing a business plan to describe and try to gain support for the idea. This sequence often omits or provides little time for the important steps of critically investigating the merits of the idea before the business plan is written.

The sequential nature of the steps shown in Figure 1-3 cleanly separates the investigative portion of thinking through the merits of a business idea from the planning and selling portion of the process. Steps 2 and 3 are investigative in nature and are designed to critique the merits of the business idea. Step 4, the business

FIGURE 1-3 The Comprehensive Feasibility Analysis/Business Planning Process

plan, is focused on planning and selling. The initial steps are important because there is no reason to write a business plan for a business idea that has little chance of succeeding. The reason it is so important to complete the entire process, according to John W. Mullins, the author of a highly regarded book titled *The New Business Road Test*, is to avoid falling into the "everything about my opportunity is wonderful" mode. In Mullin's view, failure to properly investigate the merits of a business idea (Steps 2 and 3) before the business plan is written runs the risk of blinding an entrepreneur to inherent risks associated with the potential business and results in too positive of a plan.[22] A savvy reader is likely to pick up on this lack of awareness and overly positive slant, which undermines the credibility of the plan.

In fairness, some entrepreneurs are able to combine the steps depicted in Figure 1-3 and produce a very well-researched and well-documented plan. On some occasions, however, an entrepreneur might need to move quickly to capture a first-mover advantage or for another reason, so portions of the process depicted in Figure 1-3 need to be done in parallel rather than sequentially. Breaking the process down into the steps shown in Figure 1-3 is a more careful and prudent approach, however, unless this approach isn't practical for a compelling reason.

Chapter 2 in the book focuses on how entrepreneurs identify business opportunities and introduces the preliminary screen, which is a device for rapidly assessing the preliminary feasibility of a business idea (or ideas). Chapter 3 describes how to conduct a complete feasibility analysis.

PREPARING A BUSINESS PLAN (CHAPTERS 4 THROUGH 10)

Chapters 4 through 10 provide an explanation of how to complete each section of a business plan and describe (step-by-step) the business plan for a fictitious company named Prime Adult Fitness. Prime Adult Fitness is a fitness center for people 50 years old and older. The goal is to teach you to write a business plan that is complete, yet concise and to the point.

PRESENTING THE BUSINESS PLAN (CHAPTER 11)

If the business plan successfully elicits the interest of a potential banker or investor, or it is entered into a business plan competition, the next step will be to present the business plan to a small group or audience of individuals. The final chapter of the book provides suggestions and guidelines for presenting a business plan to investors and others. Concrete suggestions are given for how to make effective presentations using PowerPoint slides and how to field questions from an audience effectively.

Chapter Summary

1. A business plan is a written document that carefully explains every aspect of a new business venture.
2. The most effective business plans are part of a comprehensive process that includes (1) identifying a business idea, (2) screening the idea (or ideas) to determine their preliminary feasibility, (3) conducting a full feasibility analysis, and (4) writing the plan.

3. There are two primary reasons for writing a business plan: (1) It forces the founding team to work together to hammer out the details of the business venture, and (2) it communicates the merits of a new venture to outsiders, such as investors or bankers.

4. The process of writing a business plan forces a team to not only work together but also turn abstract ideas into concrete realities.

5. The two primary audiences for a firm's business plan are the firm's employees and investors/other external stakeholders.

6. A firm's business plan, its executive summary, or a set of PowerPoint slides that summarizes the plan is typically the first aspect of a proposed venture that will be seen by an investor (or anyone else who reads the plan), and if the plan is incomplete or looks sloppy, it is easy for an investor to infer that the venture itself is incomplete or sloppy.

7. To make the best impression, a business plan should follow a conventional structure. Typically, the individuals who read business plans are very busy people and want a plan that allows them to easily find critical information.

8. As a business plan is written, the people involved should continually measure the type of company that they are hoping to start against their personal goals and aspirations.

9. There are four types of businesses: survival, lifestyle, managed growth, and aggressive growth. This book focuses on lifestyle, managed growth, and aggressive growth firms.

10. Although the preparation of a business plan is essential, it is often an insufficient exercise through which to complete a full and candid analysis of the merits of a new business venture. Steps that logically precede the completion of a business plan, which include the preliminary screening of business ideas and feasibility analysis, are also important.

Review Questions

1. What is a business plan? What are the advantages to preparing a business plan for a new venture?

2. What are the two most common reasons that entrepreneurs write business plans?

3. Who are the primary consumers of business plans? In what ways do the people who read business plans differ in the information they are looking for?

4. It is often argued that the process of writing a business plan is as important as the plan itself. How is this so?

5. Why is it important for the founders of a firm to continually measure whether the type of company they are envisioning, as described by their business plan, is consistent with their personal goals and aspirations?

6. What are the hazards involved with using a software package to help write a business plan or hiring consultants to write the business plan for you?

7. Describe the general rules of thumb for the length and appearance of a business plan.

8. Why is it important for a firm to test the feasibility of its business idea prior to writing a business plan?
9. Why is it important for entrepreneurs who are writing business plans to "get out of the building" and ask potential customers and others for feedback on all elements of a business proposal?
10. What is an elevator speech? How can developing an elevator speech help a firm write a more effective business plan?

Application Questions

1. Justin Wells is one of three founders of an organic snacks company. The founders have decided to write a business plan to try to obtain funding. In a meeting with his cofounders, Justin said, "I know that we're all very busy, so I'd like to volunteer to write the business plan. My parents have a cabin on a lake about an hour from here, so if it's alright with the two of you, I'd like to take my laptop up to the cabin for a couple of days and hammer out the business plan. Any objections?" If you were one of Justin's cofounders, what would you say? What alternative approach, if any, would you suggest to writing the plan?
2. Melanie Scott is a high school math teacher who is in the process of developing an iPhone app centered on engaging games that require high school students to use math to master the games. Melanie is planning to attend a new business conference in about six weeks that will feature a number of investors. She hopes to make some contacts and schedule follow-up meetings with several investors. Up until now, Melanie has focused primarily on the technical aspects of building the app, and hasn't written a business plan or talked to any potential customers. She's willing to do whatever it takes to get prepared for the conference. What would you tell Melanie to focus on over the next six weeks to get ready for the conference?
3. A year ago, a friend of yours opened an innovative type of fitness center that helps high school athletes improve their fitness and sharpen their skills to the point where they'll be more likely candidates for college scholarships. He recently wrote a business plan seeking $100,000 in funding to expand from one location to three locations. He sent the business plan out to three industry experts for feedback, and was struck by the advice he received. All three experts loved his concept and encouraged him that instead of asking for $100,000 to expand to three locations, he should ask for $1 million to expand to 30 or more locations. What factors should your friend consider before he pursues this advice?
4. Imagine you just received a text message from a friend. The message reads, "Just wanted to share with you some fantastic news. Last Friday, I talked to an investor about my business idea, and he asked me to send him the executive summary from my business plan along with a PowerPoint overview of the plan. I spent the weekend working on his request, and am about to send him an 8-page executive summary and a 42-slide PowerPoint overview. Just thought I

check with you to see if you have any last minute words of advice. I really want to get funding." How would you respond to this request for feedback?

5. Spend some time studying the Web site of Heart Juice (www.heartjuice.com), a healthy beverage company referred to in this chapter. Search for additional information on the company. Write a two minute elevator speech rather than a 60-second elevator speech.

Endnotes

1. J. Cone, "Teaching Entrepreneurship in Colleges and Universities: How (and Why) a New Academic Field Is Being Built," *Kauffman Foundation homepage*, www.kauffman.org (May 29, 2013).

2. R. Fairlie, *Kauffman Index of Entrepreneurial Activity 1996–2011* (Kansas City, MO: Kauffman Foundation, 2012).

3. "An Entrepreneurial Generation of 18- to 34-Year-Olds Wants to Start Companies When Economy Rebounds, According to New Poll," *Kauffman Foundation homepage*, www.kauffman.org (May 29, 2013).

4. A. Burke, S. Fraser, and F. Greene, "The Multiple Effects of Business Planning on New Venture Performance," *Journal of Management Studies*, 47, no. 3 (2012): 391–415.

5. A. Tjan, R. Harrington, and Tsun-Yan Hsieh, *Heart, Smarts, Guts and Luck* (Boston, MA: Harvard Business Review Press, 2012).

6. F. Delmar and S. Shane, "Does Business Planning Facilitate the Development of New Ventures," *Strategic Management Journal*, 24 (2003): 1165–1185.

7. "Lindsey Wieber and Gwen Whiting, Ladies Who Launch Web Site," December 27, 2005, www.ladieswholaunch.com/magazine/lindsey-wieber-and-gwen-whiting/1007 (accessed May 29, 2013).

8. G. Kawasaki, *The Art of the Start* (New York: Portfolio, 2004).

9. B. Barringer and R. D Ireland, *Entrepreneurship: Successfully Launching New Ventures*, 4th ed. (Upper Saddle River, NJ: Prentice-Hall, 2012).

10. "Young Social Entrepreneurs from Rutgers Take on Hearth Health and the Beverage World," *Rutgers Business School Newark and New Brunswick Homepage*. http://business.rutgers.edu (accessed May 29, 2013).

11. S. Blank, "Why the Lean Start-Up Changes Everything," *Harvard Business Review*, 91, no. 5 (2013): 10–112.

12. G. Clydesdale, *Entrepreneurial Opportunity* (New York: Routledge, 2010).

13. M. Keveles, *Scrappy Startups* (Santa Barbara, CA: ABC-CLIO, LLC, 2010).

14. W. A. Sahlman, "How to Write a Great Business Plan," *Harvard Business Review* (July–August, 1997): 98–108.

15. R. Price, *Roadmap to Entrepreneurial Success* (New York: American Management Association, 2004), 11.

16. Personal communication with Michael Heller, January 20, 2003.

17. S. Kemper, *Code Name Ginger* (Boston, MA: Harvard Business Review Press, 2003).

18. "Venture Capital FAQ," *FindLaw*, http://smallbusiness.findlaw.com/starting-a-business/venture-capital-faq.html (accessed May 29, 2013).

19. Blank, "Why the Lean Start-Up Changes Everything."

20. R. Ronstadt, "The Educated Entrepreneur: A New Era of Entrepreneurial Education Is Beginning," *American Journal of Small Business*, 10, 1 (1985): 7–23.

21. Kawasaki, *The Art of the Start*, 72.

22. J. W. Mullins, *The New Business Road Test* (London: Prentice Hall, 2003).

CHAPTER

DEVELOPING AND SCREENING BUSINESS IDEAS

INTRODUCTION

This chapter focuses on how to identify business ideas and how to determine if a specific idea is a good business opportunity. As mentioned in Chapter 1, many new businesses fail, not because the founders didn't work hard or weren't committed, but because the idea wasn't a good one to begin with. What's often missing in the ideas that fail is a lack of simple old-fashioned detective work. Detectives find clues by being curious and alert, by following leads, and by subjecting their ideas and evidence to scrutiny before they form judgments. Similarly, the best new business ideas occur to entrepreneurs who are curious and alert, know where to look for ideas, and are willing to subject their ideas to scrutiny and inspection.

To describe how to develop and screen business ideas, this chapter is divided into two parts. The first part focuses on the three most common sources of new business ideas and the techniques that entrepreneurs use to explore these sources and generate ideas. The second part of the chapter introduces a tool called the First Screen, which allows an entrepreneur to quickly determine whether an idea represents a potentially viable business opportunity. It's called the First Screen because after an idea is chosen, it should be subjected to a more thorough feasibility analysis (Chapter 3) to see if writing a full business plan is warranted. As mentioned in Chapter 1, these preliminary steps are important because there is no reason to write a business plan if an idea has little merit. The First Screen also provides an entrepreneur the flexibility to consider multiple business ideas, rather than settling on a single idea from the outset. As will be explained later in the

FIGURE 2-1 The Comprehensive Feasibility Analysis/Business Planning Process

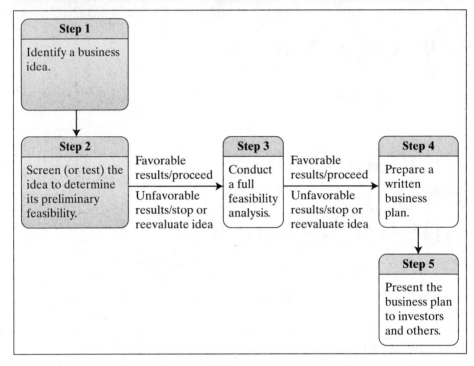

chapter, it shouldn't take more than two to three hours to run an idea through the First Screen worksheet. Hopefully, the expedient nature of this process will encourage a lot of idea generation, so the best possible idea ultimately emerges.

A reminder of the comprehensive feasibility analysis/business planning process introduced in Chapter 1 is provided in Figure 2-1. The highlighted areas show the stages of the process covered in this chapter. Recall that the comprehensive nature of this process is not meant to weigh it down or add extra work but instead to create a context in which only well-researched, well-thought-out, and ultimately realistic and feasible ideas enter the business plan process.

Now let's look at the three most common sources of new business ideas and the specific techniques that entrepreneurs use to explore these sources and generate ideas.

THREE MOST COMMON SOURCES OF NEW BUSINESS IDEAS

The first step in creating an effective business plan is selecting an idea that fills a need and provides unique value to the customer. If a new business provides a product or service that's merely a different version of something that's already available, it has a tough road ahead. It's hard to get people to change their habits

FIGURE 2-2   Three Sources of New Business Ideas

| Changing Environmental Trends | Unsolved Problems | Gaps in the Marketplace |

or behaviors and switch from a product that they're currently using to a new one, even if the new product is better or less expensive. Instead, the most successful new business ideas add value in a unique or compelling way by capitalizing on one of the three sources of business ideas discussed here and shown in Figure 2-2.

CHANGING ENVIRONMENTAL TRENDS

The first source of new business ideas is changing environmental trends. The most important trends to follow are economic trends, social trends, technological advances, and political action and regulatory changes. Changes in these areas often provide the impetus for new business ideas. When looking at environmental trends to discern new business ideas, keep two caveats in mind. First, it's important to distinguish between trends and fads. Startups typically do not have the resources to ramp up quickly enough to take advantage of a fad. Second, even through we discuss each trend individually, they are interconnected and should be considered simultaneously when brainstorming new business ideas. For example, one reason that smartphones, like the Apple iPhone, are so popular is because they benefit from several trends converging at the same time, including teenagers and young adults with increased disposable income (economic trend), an increasingly mobile population (social trend), and the continual miniaturization of electronics (technological trend). If any of these trends weren't present, smartphones wouldn't be as successful as they are.

Table 2-1 provides examples of how changes in environmental trends have provided the impetus for new business ideas. The following is a discussion of each trend and how changes in the trend provide openings for new business and product ideas.

ECONOMIC TRENDS

An understanding of economic trends is helpful in determining areas that are ripe for new business ideas and discerning areas to avoid. When the economy is strong, people are more willing to buy discretionary products and services that enhance their lives. Individual sectors of the economy have a direct impact on consumer buying patterns. For example, a drop in interest rates typically leads to an increase in new home construction, furniture sales, and appliance sales. Conversely, a string of corporate layoffs or a rapid decline in the stock market normally leads to a reduction in the demand for luxury goods.

When studying how economic forces affect opportunities, it is important to evaluate who has money to spend and what they spend it on. For example, an increase in the number of women in the workforce and their related increase

TABLE 2-1   Companies Started to Take Advantage of Changes in Environmental Trends

Changing Environmental Trend	Resulting New Business Opportunities	Resulting Companies
Economic Trends		
Search for ways to use traditional sources of energy more efficiently	Developing technologies, products, and services that help businesses and consumers conserve energy	Noesis Energy, Effortless Energy, Sagewell, eMeter, Nest Labs
Aging of the population	In-home care, health-related products and services, financial services for older people, travel-related service for older people	Comfort Keepers, TenderTree, Adhere Tech, Elder Life Financial Services, Senior Travel Service, Inc.
Social Trends		
Increased interest in different, tastier, and healthier food	Healthy-fare restaurants, food trucks and ethnic packaged foods, craft beer, functional beverages	Naked Pizza, Chobani, Lobsta Truck (Los Angeles), Brooklyn Brewery, Rescue Water
	Healthy-fare restaurants, food trucks and ethnic packaged foods, craft beer, functional beverages	Naked Pizza, Chobani, Lobsta Truck (Los Angeles), Brooklyn Brewery, Rescue Water
Heightened interest in wellness as Americans are increasingly seeking ways to become and stay healthy	Fitness centers, pilates and yoga studios, exercise apps, weight loss programs, and apps	24 Hour Fitness, Yogaview (Chicago), Runkeeper, Noom Weight Loss Coach
Technological Advances		
Smartphones	Smartphone operating systems, smartphone apps, smartphone accessories	Android, Rivio Entertainment (Angry Birds), Instagram, Fitbit, ISkin,
Advances in biotechnology	Biotech-related pharmaceutical products, veterinary products, environmental and food testing	Amgen, Life Technologies, PathSensore, GrayBug
Political and Regulatory Changes		
Increased EPA and OSHA standards	Consulting companies, software to monitor compliance	PrimaTech, Compliance Consulting Services, Inc., SafeSoft
Affordable Care Act (Obamacare)	Electronic medical records, doctor–patient matching services, physician social networks	CareCloud, One Touch EMR, ZocDoc, PracticeFusion, Sermo

in disposable income is largely responsible for the number of boutique clothing stores targeting professional women that have opened in the past several years. Some of the boutiques, such as Ellen Tracey (http://www.ellentracey.com) and

Tory Burch (http://www.toryburch.com), compete on a national scale, whereas others, such as Cha (http://shop-cha.com), in St. Louis, are single-store boutiques that have been opened by one or more individual entrepreneurs. Similarly, as baby boomers reach retirement age, a sizable portion of their spending will be redirected to areas that facilitate their retirement. This trend will invariably spawn new businesses in many areas, largely because baby boomers have greater disposable income relative to previous generations. The most promising areas include health care, finance, travel, housing, and recreation. The high cost of energy, coupled with a desire to be socially responsible, has also spawned a growing number of startups that are developing products and service that help businesses and consumers become more energy efficient. An example is Nest Labs (www.nest.com), a 2010 startup. Nest makes the world's first Learning Thermostat. The thermostat, which can be used in homes or businesses, learns from your temperature adjustments and programs itself to optimize a building's comfort and energy efficiency.[1]

An understanding of economic trends can also help identify areas to avoid. For example, this is not a good time to start a company that sells products or services to public schools. Public schools have been hard hit by local, state, and federal budget cuts. The cuts have significantly reduced their ability to purchase new products or services.

SOCIAL TRENDS

An understanding of the impact of social trends on the way people live their lives and the products and services they need provides fertile ground for new business ideas and opportunities. Often, the reason that a product or service exists has more to do with satisfying a social need than the more transparent need the product fills. For example, the proliferation of fast-food restaurants isn't due primarily to people's love for fast food but rather to the fact that people are busy and often don't have time to cook their own meals. Similarly, social networking sites such as Facebook (www.facebook.com) and Twitter (www.twitter.com) aren't popular because they can be used to post messages and pictures on a Web site. They're popular because they allow people to connect and communicate with each other, which is a natural human tendency.

Changes in social trends alter how people and businesses behave and how they set their priorities. These changes affect how products and services are built and sold. The following list provides a sample of the social trends that are currently affecting how individuals behave and set their priorities:

- Aging of the population
- Growth in the use of mobile devices
- The increasing diversification of the workforce
- Increasing interest in healthy foods and "green" products
- The rise of personal and home entertainment
- Emphasis on alternative forms of energy

- Increasing need for devices that enhance the security of individuals, buildings, public gatherings, and transportation systems
- Continual migration of people from small towns and rural areas to cities
- Desire for personalization (which creates a need for products and services that people can tailor to their own tastes and needs)

Each of these trends in providing the impetus for new business ideas will continue to do so. For example, the aging of the population is spawning business ideas from home health care to devices that remind people to take their medicine on time to fashionable apparel for elderly people with limited mobility. One new company, CareZone.com (ww.carezone.com), was started by Jonathan Schwartz, who was looking for ways to better managing the care of five aging parents and in-laws. CareZone is an app for smartphones, tablets, or computers that allows those involved in a person's care to share and save information in a secure, online setting. Commenting on CareZone's potential market, *Time* magazine reporter Harry McCracken wrote:

> It's not a given that CareZone will take off, but this much is clear: It's potential market is enormous, since almost everyone will join its target audience — people responsible for tending to the medical care of someone else — sooner or later.[2]

CareZone is realizing this potential. Launched in 2012, it has already attracted just under a million users in 100 countries.

TECHNOLOGICAL ADVANCES

Technological advances provide an ongoing source of new business ideas. In most cases, the technology itself isn't the key to recognizing business opportunities. Instead, the key is to recognize how technologies can be used and harnessed to help satisfy basic or changing human needs. For example, the creation of the smartphone is a technological achievement, but it was motivated by an increasingly mobile population that finds many advantages to having the ability to communicate with coworkers, customers, friends, and family from anywhere and everywhere.

Technological advancements also provide opportunities to help people perform everyday tasks in a better or more convenient way. For example, OpenTable.com is a Web site or mobile app that allows users to make restaurant reservations online and now covers most of the United States. If you're planning a trip to Phoenix, for example, you can access OpenTable.com, select the area of the city you'll be visiting, and view descriptions, reviews, customer ratings, and, in most cases, the menus of the restaurants in the area. You can then make a reservation at the restaurant of your choice and print a map of directions to the restaurant. The basic tasks that OpenTable.com helps people perform have always been done — looking for a restaurant, comparing prices and menus, soliciting feedback from people who are familiar with competing restaurants, and getting directions. What OpenTable.com does is help people perform these takes in a more convenient and expedient manner.

Another aspect of technological advances is that after a technology is created, products often emerge to advance it. For example, the creation of the smartphone industry has created related industries that produce smartphone accessories and apps. In fact, according to ABIresearch, the average smartphone owner will spend $56.18 on accessories per device.[3] The value of the app industry is even more promising. The market for paid application downloads reached $8 billion in 2012, up 27% from 2011.[4] An example of a company launched to create apps is BenchPrep (http://benchprep.com), which was started in 2008 by Ashish Rangneikar, who at the time was an MBA student at the University of Chicago, and Ujjwal Gupta, who was working on his PhD at Penn State. BenchPrep creates apps that help students study for standardized tests, such as the GMAT or the GRE. The apps are "smart" in that they give students progress reports to show where they are excelling and where performance needs to improve. According to the company, BenchPrep students increase their scores by an average of 15% on standardized tests by using their apps. This boost in performance leads to high acceptance rates at colleges they are applying to.[5]

POLITICAL ACTION AND REGULATORY CHANGES

Political and regulatory changes also provide the basis for new business ideas. For example, new laws often spur startups which are launched to take advantage of the consequences of the laws. This is currently happening as a result of the Affordable Care Act (Obamacare). The combination of new regulations, incentives for doctors and hospitals to shift to electronic records, and the releasing of massive amounts of data held by the Department of Health and Human Services (on topics such as hospital quality, nursing home patient satisfaction, and regional health care system performance) is motiving entrepreneurs to launch electronic medical records startups, apps to help patients find the best physician for their needs, and similar companies.[6]

On some occasions, changes in government regulations motivate entrepreneurs to start firms that differentiate themselves by "exceeding" the regulation. For example, several years ago, the Federal Trade Commission (FTC) changed the regulation about how far apart the wood or metal bars in an infant crib can be. If the bars are too far apart, a baby can get an arm or leg caught between the bars, causing an injury. An obvious business idea that might be spawned by this type of change is to produce a crib that is advertised and positioned as "exceeding" the new standard for width between bars and is "extra safe" for babies and young children. The change in regulation brings attention to the issue and provides ideal timing for a new company to reassure parents by providing a product that not only meets but exceeds the new regulation.

Political change also engenders new business and product opportunities. For example, global political instability and the threat of terrorism have resulted in individuals, businesses, and communities becoming more security conscious. Each of these groups needs unique new products and services to ensure their safety.

UNSOLVED PROBLEMS

The second approach to new business ideas is unsolved problems. Problems can be experienced or recognized by people through their jobs, hobbies, or everyday activities. Commenting on this issue and how noticing problems can lead to the recognition of business ideas, Philip Kotler, a marketing expert, said:

> Look for problems. People complain about it being hard to sleep through the night, get rid of clutter in their homes, find an affordable vacation, trace their family origins, get rid of garden weeds, and so on. As the late John Gardner, founder of Common Cause, observed: "Every problem is a brilliantly disguised opportunity."[7]

Consistent with this observation, many companies have been started by people who have experienced a problem in their own lives, or observed others struggling with a problem, and created a business to solve the problem. For example after watching countless women walk home barefoot after a long night in heels, New York University finance students Katie Shea and Susie Levitt started a company named CitySlips (www.cityslips.com) to make easily portable comfortable shoes. They created a pair of flats that fold up to fit into a pocket-size zip pouch, which easily fits in most women's purses. When a woman pops on the shoes, the pouch unfurls into a tote bag to carry the high heels. The two began selling CitySlips in 2009, and are now in over 500 stores.[8]

Similarly, Laura Udall invented an alternative to traditional backpacks when her fourth-grade daughter complained daily that her back hurt from carrying her backpack. After conducting research, obtaining feedback from student focus groups, and building several prototypes, Udall invented the ZUCA, a backpack on rollers that strikes the ideal balance between functionality and "cool" for kids. ZUCA (www.zuca.com) is now a successful company, and its rolling backpacks can be purchased online or through a number of retailers.[9]

Some business ideas are gleaned by recognizing problems that are associated with emerging environmental trends. For example, SafetyWeb (www.safetyweb.com) has created a Web site that helps parents protect their children's online reputation, privacy, and safety. It also allows parents to monitor their children's cell phone calls and text messages. The social trends toward more online activity by children and increased cell phone usage and texting have resulted in the need for this service. Similarly, several startups have launched recently to track whether people are taking their medicine as prescribed. AdhereTech (www.adheretech.com), for example, has developed a pill bottle that measures the exact amount of pills or liquid in a bottle in real time, and reminds patients to take their medication via phone calls or text messages. According to the company, simple real-time reminders increase pill taking compliance from 60% up to 90%. Taking medicine on time is particularly important for older patients, who often take multiple medications. The aging of the population is a social trend that has in part spurred the need for startups like AdhereTech.

If you're having difficulty solving a particular problem, one technique that is useful is to find an instance where a similar problem was solved and then apply that solution to your problem. An example is provided by Susan Nichols, the founder of Yogitoes (http://www.yogitoes.com), a company that makes nonslip rugs for yoga enthusiasts. Several yoga positions require participants to strike poses where they balance their weight on their feet at an angle. In this position, it is easy to fall or slip when using a regular rug or mat. Nichols looked for a yoga mat that would prevent her from slipping but found that no one knew how to make one. So she started looking for an example of a product that was designed specifically to prevent it from slipping on a hard floor, to study how it functioned. Eventually, she stumbled upon a dog bowl with rubber nubs on the bottom to prevent it from sliding when a large dog ate or drank from it. Using the dog bowl (of all things) as a model, Nichols found a manufacturer who helped her develop a rug with small PVC nubs that prevents yoga participants from slipping when they perform yoga moves. Nichols started Yogitoes to sell the rugs, and has now been in business for just over 10 years.[10]

Many other colorful examples of people who launched businesses to solve problems are included in Table 2-2. The Business Plan Insight boxed feature provides insight into a rapidly growing group of people starting businesses to solve problems: college students solving problems that college students encounter.

GAPS IN THE MARKETPLACE

The third source of business ideas are gaps in the marketplace. There are many examples of products that consumers need or want that aren't available in a particular location or aren't available at all. Part of the problem is created by large retailers, such as Wal-Mart, Costco, and Kohl's, which compete primarily on price and offer the most popular items targeted toward mainstream consumers. Although this approach allows the large retailers to achieve economies of scale, it leaves gaps in the marketplace. This is the reason that clothing boutiques, specialty shops, and many ecommerce Web sites exist. These businesses are willing to carry merchandise that doesn't sell in large enough quantities for big-box retailers to carry.

Product gaps in the marketplace represent potentially viable business opportunities. For example, Tish Ciravolo realized that there were no guitars on the market made specifically for women. To fill this gap, she started Daisy Rock (www.daisyrock.com), a company that makes guitars just for women and girls. Daisy Rock guitars are stylish, have feminine names (e.g., Powder Pink, Pink Sparkle, and Cosmic Purple), and incorporate design features that accommodate a woman's smaller hands and build. A more common example of a company that filled a gap in the marketplace is provided by Songkick (www.songkick.com), an online company that has created a single place for music lovers to track their favorite bands and buy concert tickets. A gap the founders of Songkick saw is that too often people miss seeing their favorite bands because they didn't realize that the band was in their area. Concert goers try to avoid this prospect by

TABLE 2-2 Companies Started to Solve a Problem

Entrepreneurs	Year	Problem	Solution	Company That Resulted
Ann Scott and Leslie Silverglide	2011	People who are interested to using a personal trainer are often deterred because they don't belong to a gym, have no way of making contact with a personal trainer, or aren't available when the personal trainers are.	Create a Web site that matches personal trainers and clients and allows the sessions to be conducted over live, two-way video.	Wello (www.wello.com)
Greg Goff and Hesky Kutscher	2010	People traveling do not have ready access to their children's' medical records, which may be needed if a child gets injured or sick.	Create an online platform that can be pulled up from any Web browser or on a smartphone that provide access to a child's full medical history.	MotherKnows (www.motherknows.com)
Perry Chen, Charles Adler, and Yancy Strickler	2009	No platform was available online that made it possible for people to raise money for creative projects.	Launch an online crowd funding platform that allows people to raise money for creative projects and new product ideas.	Kickstarter (www.kickstarter.com)
Same Goldman and Ned Tozen	2008	Around 1.5 billion people, living in developing countries, do not have access to electricity. They often use kerosene lanterns to light their homes, which emit harmful fumes and present a fire hazard.	Design and manufacture affordable solar-powered lamps.	d.light (www.delightdesign.com)
Jamie and Ben Heywood	2005	It's difficult for people with life-changing diseases to find people with similar ailments to converse with, share their experiences, and learn techniques to better cope with their disease.	Create a Web-based platform that allows people with serious diseases to find one another, share experiences, and provide each other encouragement and advice.	PatientsLikeMe (www.patientslikeme.com)

Companies Started by College Students Solving Problems that College Students Encounter

Although it's easy to imagine that most of the products and services designed specifically for college students were developed by established companies or experienced entrepreneurs, that's not always the case. A growing number of products and services targeting college students or their parents were developed by college students themselves, first to solve their own problems and then to share the solutions with others.

In 2010, Michael Koetting, a student at the University of Texas, was up late one night trying to complete some calculus homework. He was in the type of class that has several sections and hundreds of students, and it occurred to him that at least 100 of his classmates must be on Facebook at that given moment in time, and if he could connect with them, he could form a study group to tackle the problems. That insight led Koetting, along with cofounders Gaurav Sanghani and Sid Upadhyay, to launch Hoot. me (www.hoot.me), a Facebook application which allows college students to connect with other students, teaching assistants, professors, and others to form study groups to work on homework assignments and class projects. A student can also schedule an appointment with a tutor to get more formalized instruction.

Similarly, as a college student at the University of Colorado, Sarah Schuup invited her parents to visit her a couple of times a year to see the campus and where she was living. Although she enjoyed seeing her parents, one challenge she always encountered was helping them plan their stay and making it enjoyable. As a dormitory resident, she didn't know much about surrounding Boulder-area hotels and shops that were several miles from campus. After muddling through several visits, it occurred to Schuup that what parents needed was a magazine that would provide them a directory of hotels, motels, restaurants, and shops to help them plan their trips to see their kids at college. She felt parents might also be interested in information like how to help their kids apply for scholarships, when tuition payments are due, and where the nearest bank is to a particular location (the guides are now available online as well as in print form). *University Parent* was launched in 2003, and is now available at over 200 colleges and universities.

---

subscribing to venue mailing lists, checking band Web sites, and sifting through generic concert newsletters. This is a clumsy process that often doesn't work. Songkick filled the gap by creating a Web site that allows users to track the bands they like and sends them a personalized concert alert when the bands they are following announce a tour date in their area.

Gaps in the marketplace are commonly recognized when people become frustrated because they can't find a product or service that they need, and they recognize that other people feel the same frustration. This scenario played out for Lorna Ketler and Barb Wilkins, who because frustrated when they couldn't find stylish "plus-sized" clothing that fit. In response to their frustration, they started Bodacious (http://www.bodacious.ca), a store that sells fun and stylish clothing for hard-to-fit women. Ketler and Wilkins' experience illustrates how compelling a business idea can be when it strikes just the right cord by filling a gap that deeply resonates with a specific clientele. Reflecting on the success of Bodacious, Wilkins said:

> It's so rewarding when you take a risk and it pays off for you and people are telling you every single day, "I'm so glad you're here." We've had people cry in our store. It happens a lot. They're crying because they so happy (that they're finding clothes that fit). One woman put on a pair of jeans that fit her, and she called me an hour later and said, "They still look good, even at home!" Sometimes people have a body change that happens, whether they have been ill or had a baby, and there's lots of emotion involved in it. If you can go out and buy clothes that fit, that helps people feel good about themselves.[11]

Gaps in the marketplace can also exist when a geographic area that needs a particular service but doesn't have a large enough population to justify a traditional store or service provider, or the store or provider is not open at night or on weekends. Many rural communities do not have 24-hour pharmacies, for example. This makes it difficult for people who visit an emergency room or an urgent care center at night or on a weekend to quickly fill a prescription. To fill this gap, InstyMeds (www.instymeds.com) developed a vending machine for prescription drugs to be located in rural hospitals and urgent care centers. This is how it works. If you receive a prescription from a doctor in a hospital or urgent care center that has an InstyMeds machine nearby, the prescription will be accompanied by an InstyMeds private code. The code allows you to access the prescription from the machine. If you have insurance, the machine will determine your co-pay for the prescription, and you can pay by cash or credit card. If you don't have insurance, you'll be instructed to pay the full amount. InstyMeds doesn't work for all prescriptions, like those that need to be refrigerated, but does include the 100 or so most common medicines prescribed by emergency and urgent care physicians.

Another approach to filling gaps is to look at existing businesses and determine if a different version of the business is needed as a result of changing environmental trends. This is currently happening in the fitness center industry. There is a growing preference for easily accessible small gyms that cater to a local market and are open 24 hours a day, opposed to large gyms that include swimming pools, racquetball courts, and other amenities. The trend has been motivated by less disposable income, more hectic schedules, and an increase in the number of shift workers in the United States that work odd hours and may not be able to make it to a fitness center that is only open during the morning, day, and evening. Several fitness franchises have launched to fill this gap including Anytime Fitness, Snap Fitness, and 24 Hour Fitness.

Other examples of companies that were launched to fill gaps in the marketplace are included in Table 2-3.

TABLE 2-3 Companies Started to Fill a Gap in the Marketplace		
Gap in the Marketplace	*Resulting New Business Opportunity*	*Companies That Resulted*
No fitness centers open 24 hours per day	Fitness centers that appeal to shift workers, working mothers, and young people who prefer to work out at odd hours rather than during the hours that mainstream fitness centers are open	Anytime Fitness, Snap Fitness, 24 Hour Fitness
Lack of toys that focus on the intellectual development of a child	Toy stores, direct-sales organizations (such as Tupperware), and Web sites that sell educational toys	Modular Robotics, Ubooly, LaunchPad Toys, Kazoo & Company
Shortage in the availability and variety of ethnic food in many parts of the United States	Ethnic food stores, Web sites that sell ethnic food, ethnic food manufacturer, and ethnic restaurants in areas that are underserved	Ethnic Foods Company, International Food Market, Rice King, Senor Sisis
Shortage of clothing stores that sell fashionable clothing for hard-to-fit people	Boutiques and Web sites that sell fashionable clothing for hard-to-fit people, including plus-sized clothes, maternity clothes, or clothing for tall or short people	Casual Male, Fashion to Figure, Motherhood Maternity

TECHNIQUES FOR GENERATING IDEAS

The three sources of new business ideas are used by people in both subtle and overt ways. Some people recognize new business ideas through casual observation, intuition, or even serendipity or luck. Other people are more overt and use the three sources of business ideas to deliberately try to generate new business ideas, whether they have an idea of the type of business they want to start or whether they are starting from scratch. This section of the chapter focuses on three techniques that people use to explicitly try to generate new business ideas.

While considering these techniques, remember that business ideas take time to develop, so it's important to not become discouraged if an idea doesn't come to you quickly. It's also important to realize that the best ideas aren't necessarily the most original. It normally exceeds the budget of a new firm to educate the public about a revolutionary or original idea. The following Business Plan Insight box illustrates the most realistic categories of business ideas for new firms.

BRAINSTORMING

The most common way to generate business ideas is through brainstorming. The term **brainstorming** is a catch phrase that means different things to different people. Technically, a brainstorming "session" is targeted to a specific topic about which a group is instructed to come up with ideas. The leader of the group asks the participants to share their ideas. One person shares an idea, another person reacts to it, another person reacts to the reaction, and so on. A flip chart or whiteboard is typically used to record the ideas. A productive brainstorming session is freewheeling and lively. The session is not used for analysis or decision making—the ideas during a brainstorming session need to be filtered and analyzed, but this is done later.

Brainstorming sessions dedicated to generating new business ideas are often less formal. For example, some business school professors use a tool called the "bug report" to help their students brainstorm business ideas. They instruct their students to list 50–75 things that "bug" them in their everyday lives. A high number is required because if forces students to go beyond thinking about obvious things that bug them (campus parking, roommates, scooping snow in the winter) and think more deeply. On occasion, students actually hold focus groups with their friends to brainstorm ideas and fill out their lists. Another particularly effective approach to brainstorming is to use the three sources for new business ideas as a way of organizing the discussion. Imagine you are part of a small group that is trying to brainstorm ideas for a new type of fitness center. You know the market is too crowded to support another generic center, so you're looking for novel ideas. You create three columns on a whiteboard labeled Changing Environmental Trends, Unsolved Problems, and Gaps in the Marketplace. You then start brainstorming specific ideas, looking at each category individually and then looking at how the categories interact with each other. After brainstorming dozens of ideas in each category, you start grouping the ideas into themes or patterns to create more solid ideas. One pattern jumps out at you: the population is aging, older people are increasingly interested in fitness, many of the exercise machines and classes taught in traditional fitness centers aren't suitable for older people, and there are no fitness centers designed specifically for the 50+ demographic. Based on this pattern, your first solid idea is to create a fitness center designed specifically for people 50 years old and older.

Focus Groups

A **focus group** is a gathering of 5 to 10 people who are selected because of their relationship to the issues being discussed. Although focus groups are used for a variety of purposes, they can be used to help generate new business ideas.

Focus groups typically involve a group of people familiar with a topic, who are brought together to respond to questions and shed light on an issue through the give-and-take nature of a group discussion. Focus groups usually work best as a follow-up to brainstorming, when the general idea for a business has been formulated, such as opening a fitness center for the 50+ demographic, but further refinement of the idea is needed. Usually, focus groups are conducted by trained moderators. The moderator's primary goals are to keep the group "focused" and to generate lively discussion. Much of the effectiveness of a focus group session depends on the moderator's ability to ask questions and keep the discussion on track. For example, to further explore the idea of opening a fitness center designed specifically for older people, a focus group might be assembled that consists of 10 people who are 50 years old or older and are members of generic fitness centers. The moderator might ask, "What is it that you don't like about your fitness center?" A 71-year-old man might say, "I don't like the classes that are offered. They include various types of aerobics and spinning, which I don't mind, but the music is too loud, the pace is too quick, and they are always taught by guys and gals in their twenties who have no idea of what I'm going through in life." The moderator may then ask the group, "How many of you would feel more comfortable if the classes in your fitness center were taught by people your own age?" If 7 out of the 10 hands shot up, you might have just discovered one refinement for your business idea.

LIBRARY AND INTERNET RESEARCH

A third approach to generate new business ideas is to conduct library and Internet research. A natural tendency is to think that an idea should be chosen, and the process of researching the idea should then begin. This approach is too linear. Often, the best ideas emerge when the general notion of an idea, like opening an innovative type of fitness center, is merged with extensive library and Internet research, which may provide insights into the best type of innovative fitness center to pursue.

Libraries are often underused as a source of information for generating business ideas. The best approach to using a library is to discuss your general area of interest with a reference librarian, who can point you to useful resources, such as industry-specific magazines, trade journals, and industry reports. Simply browsing through several issues of a trade journal on a topic can spark new ideas. Very powerful search engines, databases, and industry reports are also available through university libraries, which would cost hundreds or thousands of dollars to access on your own. An example is IBISWorld (www.ibisworld.com), a company that publishes full industry reports on all major industries and subcategories within industries. IBISWorld is a fee-based site but is normally free if accessed through a university or large city library. For example, if you wanted to study the fitness industry, IBISWorld has a current, comprehensive report titled "Gym, Health & Fitness Clubs in the United States." Spending time reading through the report could spark new ideas for fitness centers or help affirm an existing idea. Spending just a few minutes reading IBISWorld's report bodes well for the idea of opening a fitness center for the 50+ demographic. According to the report, fitness center memberships have increased considerably over the past 10 years, rising from 46.4 million in 2003 to more than 52.6 million in 2013. Households with higher incomes and more leisure time are more likely to belong to fitness clubs, which fits the 50+ demographic. A full 20% of people who belong to fitness centers are now 55 years or older. Particularly encouraging is a statement contained in the "Industry Outlook" portion of the report. According to the report:

> Over the next five years and beyond, population growth and
> demographic change will significantly influence industry revenue.
> It is estimated that the mature market (people aged 55 and older)

will maintain a more active lifestyle and continue to focus on physical appearance and weight. By 2014, the retiring baby boomer generation will likely create strong opportunities for gyms and health and fitness clubs to focus on this massive potential market segment.[12]

This analysis bodes extremely well for the idea of a fitness center focused exclusively on people 50 years old and older.

Internet research is also important. If you're starting from scratch, simply typing "new business ideas" into Google or Bing will produce links to newspaper and magazine articles about the "hottest" and "latest" new business ideas. Although these types of articles are general in nature, they represent a starting point if you're trying to generate new business ideas from scratch. If you have a specific idea in mind, like the fitness center concept we've been discussing, a useful technique is to set up a Google or Yahoo! "alert" using keywords that pertain to your topic of interest. Google and Yahoo! alerts are e-mail updates of the latest Google or Yahoo! results (i.e., Web site updates, press releases, news articles, blog postings) based on your topic. This technique, which is available free, will feed you a daily stream of news article and blog postings about a specific topic.

FIRST SCREEN

After a business idea, or several ideas, have been chosen, it is important to have a way to quickly assess the merits of the idea, before subjecting it to full feasibility and business planning. The First Screen provides a mechanism for quickly assessing the merits of a business idea.[*] As mentioned earlier, it is called the First Screen because it is an entrepreneur's (or group of entrepreneurs') first pass at assessing the feasibility of a business idea. If a business idea cuts muster at this stage, and the decision is made to pursue it, it will be subjected to a full feasibility analysis (Chapter 3), which includes talking to potential customers, before a full business plan is written. Recall, these early steps are necessary to make sure that only ideas with sufficient potential enter the full business planning process. The First Screen template is provided in Appendix 2.1 at the end of this chapter.

Although completing the First Screen does take some research and analysis, it is not meant to be a lengthy process. It is also not meant to be a shot in the dark. The best ideas are the ones that emerge from analysis that is based on facts and good information, rather than speculation and guesses. Appendix 2.2, at the end of this chapter, contains an Internet Resource Table that may be particularly helpful in completing a First Screen analysis. Several of the most valuable resources, such as IBISWorld, Factiva, LexisNexis Academic, and ProQuest, are fee based but are typically free if accessed through a university or major public library. It is well worth your time to learn how to use these resources—they are rich in terms of their content and analysis.

---

[*] Copies of the First Screen worksheet, in both MS Word and PDF format, can be obtained from the author's Web site at www.prenhall.com/entrepreneurship.

The First Screen contains 25 items and should be able to be completed in two to three hours. A mental transition needs to be made when completing the First Screen from thinking of a business idea as just an idea to thinking of it as a business. The First Screen is an assessment of a *business* idea rather than strictly a *product* or *service* idea. The mechanics of filling out the First Screen Worksheet are straightforward. The final section of the worksheet, "Overall Potential," includes a section that allows for suggested revisions to a business idea to improve its potential or feasibility. For example, a business might start out planning to manufacture its own product, but through the process of completing the worksheet, learn that the capital needed to set up a manufacturing facility is prohibitive in terms of both the money that would need to be raised and the extended time to break even for the business. As a result, two of the five items in Part 5, "Initial Capital Investment" and "Time to Break Even," might be rated "low potential." This doesn't need to be the end of the story, however. In the column labeled "Suggestions for Improving the Potential," the founders of the business might write, "Consider contract manufacturing or outsourcing as an alternative to manufacturing the product ourselves." The value of the First Screen worksheet is that it draws attention to issues like this one and forces the founders to think about alternatives. If this particular suggestion is realistic and is determined to be a better way to proceed, a revised version of the First Screen might rate the two factors referred to previously, "Initial Capital Requirements" and "Time to Break Even," as "high potential" rather than "low potential" because of the change in the business concept that was made. Business ideas should always be seen as fluid and subject to change. Little is lost if several versions of the First Screen are completed for the same business idea, however, there is much more to be lost if a startup gets halfway through writing a business plan and concludes that the business isn't feasible, or actually launches a business without having all the kinks worked out.

A brief explanation of each section of the First Screen Worksheet follows.

PART 1: STRENGTH OF THE BUSINESS IDEA

High-potential ideas are typically drawn from one of the three sources of business ideas discussed in this chapter and are timely in terms of market introduction. In regard to timeliness, for an entrepreneur to capitalize on an idea, its window of opportunity must be open.[13] The term *window of opportunity* is a metaphor describing the time period in which a firm can realistically enter a new market. Once the market for a new product is established, its window of opportunity opens. As the market grows, firms enter and try to establish a profitable position. At some point, the market matures, and the window of opportunity closes. An important judgment call is whether the window of opportunity for a particular business idea is open or closed.

A new idea must "add value" for its buyer or end user in some appreciable way, like the ZUCA (backpack on rollers) adds value by allowing school kids to pull rather than carry their backpacks and InstyMeds' vending machines add value by providing people in rural areas access to prescription medications at night or on holidays when local pharmacies are closed. Value refers to worth, importance, or utility. A related topic is the extent to which consumers are already reasonably satisfied. If consumers, in general, are satisfied with the products or services that are similar to the ones you're thinking about producing, your job will be much harder than if people are ambivalent or dissatisfied. In addition, investors and others tend to be skeptical of ideas that require meaningful changes in behavior, and they shy away from them as a result.

Several online resources, such as the Bizminer, Mintel, and IBISWorld, provide information on industry trends. These discussions provide data on the most promising trends in an industry, which often helps affirm or refute the attractiveness of a potential business idea. Two particularly powerful search engines, ProQuest (sometimes listed under ABI/Inform) and LexisNexis Academic, are useful for gathering more general information about a product or service idea. Often, simply querying a product or service idea via one of these search engines produces magazine and newspaper articles that provide important insight.

PART 2: INDUSTRY-RELATED ISSUES

The industry that a company enters is extremely important. In various studies, researchers have found that 8 to 30 percent of the variation in firm profitability is directly attributable to industry factors. Among the most important factors for an industry are the number of competitors, the stage it's at in its life cycle, and its growth rate. Industries that are growing, are not crowded, and are in the emergence or growth stages of their life cycles and more receptive to new entrants than industries with the opposite characteristics. An important caveat to this set of heuristics is the target market that a new firm selects. There are markets within older, crowded, slow-growth industries that defy the industry's norms and provide attractive opportunities for new firms.

The average net profit for the firms in an industry is also important. Table 2-4 shows the average net profits for firms organized as subchapter-S Corporations for several industries. If you're looking for net profit estimates for an industry you're interested in, BizStats, Bizminer, and IBISWorld are the best bets. BizStats is more limited than Bizminer and IBISWorld in terms of the number of industries that it follows, but narrows its reporting to firms that are organized as C-corporations, subchapter-S corporations, or sole proprietorships.

PART 3: MARKET- AND CUSTOMER-RELATED ISSUES

The identification of the target market in which the firm will compete is extremely important. A target market is a place within a larger industry or market segment that represents a narrower group of customers with similar interests. Most new firms do not start by selling to broad markets. Instead, most start by identifying an emerging or underserved niche within a larger market. The ability to create "barriers to entry" is an important aspect of any firm's potential competitive advantage. A barrier to entry is a condition that creates a disincentive for

TABLE 2-4 Average Net Profit for Firms in Certain Industries	
Industry	*Average Net Income*
Agriculture, Forestry, Fishing	0.77 (%)
Accommodation, Food Service	5.95 (%)
Construction	6.32 (%)
Professional, Scientific, Technical Services	11.36 (%)
Arts, Entertainment, Recreation	11.67 (%)
Health, Social Services	12.66 (%)

Source: BizStats, www.bizstats.com, June 7, 2013.

another firm to enter a company's niche market. Barriers to entry can be created through a number of means, such as economies of scale, product differentiation, unique access to distribution channels, and intellectual property protection, such as patents and trademarks.

Mintel publishes periodic reports that describe the purchasing power of various age and demographic groups, along with their spending patterns. In terms of the purchasing power of people in a specific geographic area, American Factfinder, drawing on census data, provides access to the medium household income for any city, county, or ZIP code in the United States. Similar, and often more current, information is provided by City-Data.com. The ease of making customers aware of a new product or service is another important consideration. A new firm typically does not have the resources to educate the public about a revolutionary new product or service, unless the firm is particularly savvy at using the blogosphere and other means to get the word out for free.

Another important issue is the growth potential of a firm's target market. Because a startup's target market is normally a small slice of a larger market, it's usually harder to get a feel for the growth potential of a target market than it is for a broader industry. For example, if you were interested in the growth rate of the pet food and supplies industry, that number would be fairly easy to get from IBISWorld, Mintel, or Standard and Poor's NetAdvantage. But if you planned to produce high-end organic pet food, the growth rate for that slice (or segment) of the industry isn't as easy to find. The best approach in this type of circumstance is to first read through the applicable industry reports through the sources mentioned previously to see if organic pet food is mentioned and discussed. The next step is to search articles on "organic pet food" through LexisNexis Academic, ProQuest, Google, and other search services you are familiar with. Another excellent potential source of information is an industry trade association. This pursuit is somewhat of a scavenger hunt. For instance, in the organic pet food example just discussed, there are pet food trade associations, such as the American Pet

Products Association (www.americanpetproducts.org) and organic products trade associations, such as the Organic Trade Association (www.ota.com). Both associations may have useful information on the growth rate of organic pet food sales, either on their Web sites or by contacting them directly. Industry trade journals are another potential source of information.

If you're thinking about producing a product or service that doesn't exist, such as AdhereTech's automated pill bottle, your task is harder. The ability to produce the AdhereTech bottle has only recently become possible due to advances in sensor technology, which enables the bottle to discern how many pills or how much liquid remains is in the bottle at any given point in time. In this instance, you have to be somewhat creative. Markets do exist for pill bottles and for less sophisticated products that help people remember when to take their medication. Using the approaches suggested earlier, you would try to learn as much as you could about the market for pill bottles and the market for medication compliance products, and then make an informed judgment.

PART 4: FOUNDER- (OR FOUNDERS-) RELATED ISSUES

This portion of the First Screen requires the potential founder or founders of the business to complete a self-assessment, so it is important to be honest and fair. Few firms, particularly if they are being started by younger people, will score high on each of the five dimensions. Still, the strength of the founding team is extremely important. An often-repeated phrase among investors is that they would rather invest in a strong founding team with a weak product idea than a weak founding team with a strong product idea. The attributes that make for a strong founder (or founding team) is experience in the industry the new venture is entering, skills as they relate to the new venture's product or service, and broad social and professional networks in the industry the firm will be entering. It is also important that the new firm is consistent with the founder's (or founding team's) personal goals and aspirations.

A particularly important issue is the likelihood that a firm will be able to put together a team to launch and grow the new venture. As one expert has put it, "People are the one factor in product...that animates all the others."[14] A good start is for a firm to assemble an advisory board, which will assist in future recruitment and selection efforts.

PART 5: FINANCIAL ISSUES

The initial capital investment needed to start a firm is important. Although an exact estimate is not needed at this point, it is important to have a sense of the magnitude of the investment. For a retail or service business, it is fairly easy to put together a good-faith estimate of the capital that will be needed. For a business that is developing a new product, it is much harder to estimate the development costs that will be incurred and the costs associated with securing distribution for the product. The best way to approach this task is to talk to industry experts, read industry-specific blogs and trade journals, and read through industry-specific reports available through the resources mentioned earlier. A directory of trade magazines, sorted by industry, is available by typing "trade show directory" into any major search engine.

If you're unsure of the capital requirements necessary to enter an industry, IBISWorld provides a discussion of the overall "cost structure" associated with owning firms in the industries that it follows. Other reporting services provide similar information. The information contained in these reports is often quite insightful. For example, IBISWorld reports that many firms in the fitness industry rent rather than own their facilities and often lease rather than purchase the exercise equipment they feature, such as treadmills and rowing machines. These factors lower the capital requirements necessary to enter the fitness club industry, which in part explains the large number of participants in the industry.

The number of revenue drivers that a business has is also important. For example, most electronics stores have several revenue drivers, which include selling electronics products, selling extended warranties, servicing and repairing electronic products, and installing products, such as car stereos. Some of the revenue drivers may be loss leaders, such as a $699 52-inch TV to get people in the store. Other items, like car stereos, may make very little money, but large margins might be available through an installation service. Startups don't want to lose focus by creating multiple revenue drivers, but typically the financial potential of a firm is greater if it has several ways of generating sales.

The time it takes a firm to break even or recoup its initial investment is also important. Businesses that have a fairly low initial investment break even fairly quickly, as the income generated by the business pays back the initial investment. The time to break even is lengthier and the risk is higher for businesses with high capital investments or lengthy product development cycles.

The next issue to consider for this part of the First Screen is to assess the financial performance of businesses similar to the one you are contemplating to get a feel for the type of sales and financial returns to anticipate. Both ReferenceUSA and the "Build a List" feature in Hoover's premium service provide estimates of the sales of privately owned firms, which are more likely to be similar to your startup than publicly traded firms. Of course, you'll need to make adjustments based on the initial size of your firm compared to firms you're looking at and on other factors. Another approach is to search for newspaper and magazine articles on firms that are similar to the one you're thinking about starting. Often, the articles will comment on the sales and profitability of the firms they are focusing on.

The final item in Part 5 refers to your ability to fund the initial product (or service) development and initial startup expenses for your venture from personal funds or via bootstrapping. The salience of this item depends on how far along a firm is at the time it is preparing its business plan. If all a company has is an idea, it will be tough to get financing or funding. Normally, investors and lenders like to see a working prototype of an idea with customer feedback and preferably initial sales before they invest. As a result, a firm is much better off if it can self-fund and/or bootstrap its initial product development and startup costs before it tries to raise investment capital or borrow money.

Chapter Summary

1. The three most common sources of new business ideas include changing environmental trends, unsolved problems, and gaps in the marketplace.
2. The most important environmental trends to follow, in the context of discovering new business ideas, are economic trends, social trends, technological advances, and political action and regulatory changes.
3. Many companies have been started by people who have experienced a problem in their lives and then realized that the solution to the problem represented a business opportunity.
4. Gaps in the marketplace exist when there are products or services that consumers want but that aren't available through larger firms or aren't available at all.
5. Three techniques that entrepreneurs use to generate new business ideas include brainstorming, focus groups, and library and Internet research.
6. The most common way to identify business ideas quickly is through brainstorming. Technically, a brainstorming "session" is targeted to a specific topic about which a group is instructed to come up with ideas.
7. A focus group is a gathering of 5 to 10 people who are selected because of their relationship to the issues being discussed. Although focus groups are used for a variety of purposes, they can be used to help generate new business ideas.
8. Often, the best new business ideas emerge when the general notion of an idea is merged with extensive library and Internet research.
9. Once a business idea, or several ideas, have been chosen, it is important to have a way to quickly assess the merits of the idea before subjecting the idea to a full feasibility analysis. The First Screen provides a mechanism for quickly assessing the merits of a business idea.
10. Although completing the First Screen does take some research and analysis, it is not meant to be a lengthy process. It contains 25 items and should be able to be complete in two to three hours.

Review Questions

1. What are the three most common sources of new business ideas? Briefly describe how each of the sources spawns potential business ideas.
2. What four environmental trends provide the richest sources of new business ideas? List each environmental trend and provide an example of the type of business idea that it might create.
3. Explain how "unsolved problems" can create a business idea. Provide an example that was not mentioned in the chapter of a business that was created by solving an unsolved problem.
4. Explain how finding a gap in the marketplace can lead to new business ideas.
5. Describe the four categories of new business ideas and the most realistic categories for new firms.

6. Describe the brainstorming process. How can brainstorming be used to generate new business ideas?
7. Describe how a focus group is set up and how it can be used to generate new business ideas?
8. Explain how library and Internet research can be used to generate new business ideas?
9. Why is it necessary to quickly assess the merits of a business idea before conducting a feasibility analysis and writing a business plan?
10. Describe the makeup and the purpose of the First Screen.

Application Questions

1. Study the Web site of InstyMeds (www.instymeds.com), one of the startups mentioned in the chapter. Imagine you were part of InstyMeds' founding team, and in meetings with investors it was your job to #1 describe the problem that InstyMeds had identified and #2 describe how the InstyMeds service solves the problem. Write out what you would have said to address points #1 and #2 above.
2. Calab Holms just finished reading this chapter and was struck by the idea of developing products to help older people remember to take their medicine on time. He has an idea for an iPhone app that will not only remind people to take their medicine on time, but will require the user to verify when the medicine has been taken and will send a text alert to a caregiver if the medicine isn't being taken on time. Calab is ready to run with the idea, but first wants to make sure that it is consistent with changing economic trends, social trends, and technological advances. Make a table that lists these three environmental trends and the changes in these trends that work for and work against this idea.
3. Think about the problems that you encounter in your everyday life. Select one problem, and describe how solving the problem might represent the basis for a new business idea.
4. Identify three startups, other than those mentioned in the chapter or included in Table 2-3, that were started to fill a gap in the marketplace. Identify the gap and how the startup is filling the gap in the marketplace.
5. Complete the First Screen for the business idea you selected to answer Question #3. Which areas of the First Screen were the easiest to complete and which areas were the most difficult? Was the result the one you expected?

Endnotes

1. Nest Labs Homepage, www.nest.com (June 4, 2013).
2. H. McCracken, "CareZone, a Private Service for People Who Take Care of People," *Time*, February 15, 2012, p. 39.
3. ABIresearch, "Smartphone Accessory Revenues Valued at $20 Billion in 2012," *AIBresearch*, June 18, 2012, www.abiresearch.com/press/smartphone-accessory-revenues-valued-at-20-billion (accessed June 6, 2013).

4. R. Empson, "Report: Market for Paid Apps Hits $8B in 2012, While Average Revenue Per App Drops 27%," *Techcrunch*, Techcrunch Homepage, www.tech crunch.com (accessed June 6, 2013).
5. BenchPrep Homepage, www.benchprep.com, June 6, 2013.
6. T. Friedman, "Obamacare's Other Surprise," *The New York Times*, May 25, 2013, p. 45.
7. P. Kotler, *Marketing Insights from A to Z* (New York: John Wiley & Sons, 2003), 128.
8. CitySlips Homepage, www.cityslipe.com, June 6, 2013.
9. Zuca Homepage, www.zuca.com, June 7, 2013.
10. Yogitoes Homepage, http://yogitoes.com, June 7, 2013.
11. Lorna Ketler, "Lorna Ketler and Barb Wilkins," *Women Who Launch*, April 15, 2006.
12. D. Schmidt, *IBIS World Industry Report 71394 Gym. Health & Fitness Clubs in the US*, May 2013.
13. D. N. Snull, "The Three Windows of Opportunity," *Harvard Business Review Working Knowledge,* June 6, 2005.
14. C. Read and others, *eCFO* (Chichester, UK: John Wiley & Sons), 117.

First Screen

PART 1: STRENGTH OF BUSINESS IDEA

For each item, circle the most appropriate answer and make note of the (-1), (0), or $(+1)$ score.

	Low Potential (-1)	Moderate Potential (0)	High Potential $(+1)$
1. Extent to which the idea: • Takes advantage of an environmental trend • Solves a problem • Addresses an unfilled gap in the marketplace	Weak	Moderate	Strong
2. Timeliness of entry to market	Not timely	Moderately timely	Very timely
3. Extent to which the idea "adds value" for its buyer or end user	Low	Medium	High
4. Extent to which the customer is satisfied by competing products that are already available	Very satisfied	Moderately satisfied	Not very satisfied or ambivalent
5. Degree to which the idea requires customers to change their basic practices or behaviors	Substantial changes required	Moderate changes required	Small to no changes required

PART 2: INDUSTRY-RELATED ISSUES

	Low Potential (−1)	*Moderate Potential* (0)	*High Potential* (+1)
1. Number of competitors	Many	Few	None
2. Stage of industry life cycle	Maturity phase or decline phase	Growth phase	Emergence phase
3. Growth rate of industry	Little or no growth	Moderate growth	Strong growth
4. Importance of industry's products and/or services to customers	"Ambivalent"	"Would like to have"	"Must have"
5. Industry operating margins	Low	Moderate	High

PART 3: TARGET MARKET AND CUSTOMER-RELATED ISSUES

	Low Potential (−1)	*Moderate Potential* (0)	*High Potential* (+1)
1. Identification of target market for the proposed new venture	Difficult to identify	May be able to identify	Identified
2. Ability to create "barriers to entry" for potential competitors	Unable to create	May or may not be able to create	Can create
3. Purchasing power of customers	Low	Moderate	High
4. Ease of making customers aware of the new product or service	Low	Moderate	High
5. Growth potential of target market	Low	Moderate	High

PART 4: FOUNDER- (OR FOUNDERS-) RELATED ISSUES

	Low Potential (−1)	Moderate Potential (0)	High Potential (+1)
1. Founder or founders experience in the industry	No experience	Moderate experience	Experienced
2. Founder or founders skills as they relate to the proposed new venture's product or service	No skills	Moderate skills	Skilled
3. Extent of the founder or founders professional and social networks in the relevant industry	None	Moderate	Extensive
4. Extent to which the proposed new venture meets the founder or founders personal goals and aspirations	Weak	Moderate	Strong
5. Likelihood that a team can be put together to launch and grow the new venture	Unlikely	Moderately likely	Very likely

PART 5: FINANCIAL ISSUES

	Low Potential (−1)	Moderate Potential (0)	High Potential (+1)
1. Initial capital investment	High	Moderate	Low
2. Number of revenue drivers (ways in which the company makes money)	One	Two to three	More than three
3. Time to break even	More than two years	One to two years	Less than one year
4. Financial performance of similar businesses	Weak	Modest	Strong
5. Ability to fund initial product (or service) development and/or initial startup expenses from personal funds or via bootstrapping	Low	Moderate	High

OVERALL POTENTIAL

Each part has five items. Scores will range from −5 to +5 for each part. The score is a guide—there is no established rule of thumb for the numerical score that equates to high potential, moderate potential, or low potential for each part. The ranking is a judgment call.

	Score (−5 to +1)	Overall Potential of the Business Idea Based on Each Part	
Part 1: Strength of Business Idea		High potential	☐
		Moderate potential	☐
		Low potential	☐
Part 2: Industry-Related Issues		High potential	☐
		Moderate potential	☐
		Low potential	☐
Part 3: Target Market and Customer-Related Issues		High potential	☐
		Moderate potential	☐
		Low potential	☐
Part 4: Founder- (or Founders-) Related Issues		High potential	☐
		Moderate potential	☐
		Low potential	☐
Part 5: Financial Issues		High potential	☐
		Moderate potential	☐
		Low potential	☐
Overall Assessment		High potential	☐
		Moderate potential	☐
		Low potential	☐

Summary—briefly summarize your justification for your overall assessment:

Internet Resource Table

Resource to Help Complete the First Screen

Source	Description	Applicable Parts of First Screen	Cost/Availability
American Factfinder (http://factfinder2.census.gov)	An easy-to-use portal for obtaining census data. You can find facts about a specific community, such as population, medium household income, demographic breakdown (age, gender, race), and other information by using the "Community Facts" search engine on the site.	Part 3	Free
A-Z Index of Trade Associations (www.usa.gov/directory/tradeassc/index.shtml)	Directory provides access to the phone numbers and Web site addresses of trade associations in all industries. Trade associations can be contracted to obtain information on all areas of feasibility.	Parts 1, 2, 3, 4, and 5	Free
BizMiner (www.bizminer.com)	Detailed reports available on hundreds of industries, including industry financial reports, micro-firm profit–loss reports, micro-market industry reports, and competitive market analyzer.	Parts 1, 2, 3, and 5	Fee based; Typically free if accessed through a university library
BizStats (www.bizstats.com)	Has a variety of detailed financial data on various industries. On the site, a user can type in the projected income of a firm, by industry, and receive a mock income statement in return.	Parts 2 and 5	Free

Source	Description	Applicable Parts of First Screen	Cost/Availability
City-Data.com (www.city-data.com)	Contains detailed information on cities, including median resident age, median household income, ethnic mix of residents, and aerial photos.	Part 3	Free
County Business Patterns (www.census.gov/econ/cbp/)	Good resources for looking at business activity, including the number of competitors, at a city, county, or state level. For example, you can find the number of accommodation and food service businesses in a specific zip code or city.	Parts 2 and 3	Free
Factiva (www.factiva.com)	Robust search engine that aggregates content from more than 36,000 sources such as newspapers, magazines, journals, photos, and radio and television transcripts.	Parts 1, 2, 3, 4, and 5.	Fee based; typically free if accessed through a university library
Hoovers Online (www.hoovers.com)	Brief histories and financial information on companies, industries, people, and products. Premium service provides access to detailed financial information and 10-K reports for publicly traded firms.	Parts 2, 3, and 5	Fee based; typically free if accessed through a university library
IBISWorld (www.ibisworld.com)	Detailed reports available on hundreds of industries, including industry stats, trends, buyer behavior, and expected returns.	Parts 1, 2, 3, and 5	Fee based; typically free if accessed through a university library
LexisNexis Academic (www.lexisnexis.com)	Provides access to sales data for public and private firms, which can be searched in a number of useful ways. Helps startups estimate the financial performance of similar businesses. Go to "Business" and then "Company Financial."	Part 5	Fee based; typically free if accessed through a university library

Source	Description	Applicable Parts of First Screen	Cost/Availability
MagPortal.com (www.magportal.com)	Search engine and directory for finding online magazine articles. Helps startups by providing access to magazine articles about their product/ service and industry of interest. This information may be helpful in all areas of feasibility analysis.	Parts 1, 2, 3, 4, and 5	Free
Mergent Online (www.mergentonline.com)	Provides near instant access to financial data, including income statements, balance sheets, and cash flows, on more than 10,000 U.S. public corporations.	Parts 2 and 5	Fee based; typically free if accessed through a university library
Market Research.com	Allows anyone to search for market research reports on an industry or demographic. Reports cost from $199 to several thousand dollars.	Parts 1, 2, 3, and 5	Free
Mintel (www.mintel.com)	Detailed reports available on hundreds of industries, including industry stats, trends, buyer behavior, and expected returns.	Parts 1, 2, 3, and 5	Fee based; typically free if accessed through a university library
ProQuest (www.proquest.com); Sometimes listed under ABI/Inform on a library's Web site	Very robust search engine for searching publications such as the *Wall Street Journal* and the *New York Times*. Useful for all areas of feasibility analysis.	Parts 1, 2, 3, 4, and 5.	Fee based; typically free if accessed through a university library
Quickfacts (http://quickfacts.census.gov)	A very quick way to access census bureau data, including population, median household income, census breakdowns by age and other demographic characteristics, and so on.	Parts 2 and 3	Free

Source	Description	Applicable Parts of First Screen	Cost/Availability
ReferenceUSA (http://www.referenceusa.com)	Provides contact information, estimated annual sales, credit rating score, year established, news, and other information on both public and private companies. Contains more information on private firms than many similar sites. Helps start-ups estimate the financial performance of similar businesses.	Part 5	Free
Salary.com (www.salary.com)	Useful resources for determining salary ranges for positions (such as a computer programmer) in a specific city or zip code.	Part 5	Free
Standard & Poor's NetAdvantage (http://www.netadvantage.standardpoors.com)	Detailed reports available on hundreds of industries, including industry stats, trends, buyer behavior, and expected returns.	Parts 1, 2, 3, and 5	Fee based; typically free if accessed through a university library
Thomas Register of American Manufacturers (www.thomasregister.com)	Search engine for sourcing components, equipment, raw materials, and custom manufacturing services. Helpful in determining how much it will cost to manufacture a product.	Part 5	Free
Yahoo! Industry Center (http://biz.yahoo.com/ic)	Provides a directory of industries, along with a list of the companies in each industry, the latest industry-related news, and performance data on the top companies in an industry.	Parts 2, 3, and 5	Free

FEASIBILITY ANALYSIS

INTRODUCTION

This chapter focuses on assessing the feasibility of a business idea. Feasibility analysis is the process of determining if a business idea is viable. In Chapter 2, we introduced the First Screen, which is a tool for quickly assessing the merits of business ideas. A feasibility analysis is a more stringent test designed to take the best ideas that emerge from the First Screen and more fully assess their feasibility.

As mentioned in Chapter 1, the most effective business plans are part of a comprehensive process that includes (1) identifying a business idea, (2) screening the idea (or ideas) to determine their preliminary feasibility, (3) conducting a feasibility analysis to see if proceeding with a business plan is warranted, and (4) writing the plan. A visual reminder of the comprehensive nature of this process and where feasibility analysis fits in is provided in Figure 3-1. Recall the sequential nature of the steps shown in Figure 3-1 cleanly separate the investigative portion of thinking through the merits of a business idea from the planning and selling stage of the process. Steps 2 to 3, which focus on feasibility analysis, are investigative in nature and are designed to critically assess the merits of a business idea. Step 4, the business plan, focuses on planning and selling. A properly conducted feasibility analysis lays the foundation for a well-reasoned and well-researched business plan. The most compelling facts a company can include in a business plan are the results of its own feasibility analysis, particularly if the analysis includes feedback from industry experts and prospective customers.

This chapter presents a template for completing a feasibility analysis and describes each of the four steps in the feasibility analysis process.

FIGURE 3-1   The Comprehensive Feasibility Analysis/Business Planning Process

Step 1

Identify a business idea.

Step 2

Screen (or test) the idea to determine its preliminary feasibility.

Favorable results/proceed

Unfavorable results/stop or reevaluate idea

Step 3

Conduct a full feasibility analysis.

Favorable results/proceed

Unfavorable results/stop or reevaluate idea

Step 4

Prepare a written business plan.

Step 5

Present the business plan to investors and others.

Note: Shaded step is covered in this chapter.

TEMPLATE FOR COMPLETING A FEASIBILITY ANALYSIS

The template for completing a feasibility analysis is shown in Table 3-1. It includes an introduction, the four parts of feasibility analysis (product/service feasibility, industry/market feasibility, organizational feasibility, and financial feasibility), and a summary and conclusion. A fuller version of the template, with instructions and assessment tools, is provided in Appendix 3.1 at the end of this chapter. It may be helpful to refer to Appendix 3.1 periodically when reading through the descriptions of each of the four forms of feasibility to visualize how the various parts of the feasibility analysis fit together and see what the assessment instruments look like.*

The template shown in Table 3-1 represents a full feasibility analysis. Whereas the First Screen should take only two to three hours to complete, completing a full feasibility analysis is a lengthier process. It requires both primary

---

* Copies of the feasibility analysis shown in the Appendix, along with each of the assessment tools mentioned in the chapter, can be obtained from the publisher's Web site at http://www.prenhall. com/barringer.

TABLE 3-1   Full Feasibility Analysis

Introduction
A.   Name of the proposed business
B.   Name of the founder (or founders)
C.   One paragraph summary of the business

Part 1: Product/Service Feasibility
A.   Product/service desirability
B.   Product/service demand

Part 2: Industry/Target Market Feasibility
A.   Industry attractiveness
B.   Target market attractiveness
C.   Market timeliness

Part 3: Organizational Feasibility
A.   Management prowess
B.   Resource sufficiency

Part 4: Financial Feasibility
A.   Total startup cash needed
B.   Financial performance of similar businesses
C.   Overall financial attractiveness of the proposed venture

Summary and Conclusion

(Circle correct response.)

Product/service feasibility	Not feasible	Unsure	Feasible
Industry/market feasibility	Not feasible	Unsure	Feasible
Organizational feasibility	Not feasible	Unsure	Feasible
Financial feasibility	Not feasible	Unsure	Feasible
Overall assessment	Not feasible	Unsure	Feasible
Suggestions for improving feasibility in one or more areas			

and secondary research. Primary research is original research that is collected by the person or persons completing the analysis. It normally includes talking to industry experts, obtaining feedback from prospective customers, and administering surveys. Secondary research probes data that are already collected. The data generally include industry studies, Census Bureau data, company reports, and other pertinent information gleaned through library and Internet research.

It should be emphasized that while a feasibility analysis tests the merits of a specific idea, it allows ample opportunity for the idea to be revised, altered, and changed as a result of the feedback that is obtained and the analysis that is conducted. The whole idea behind the feasibility analysis process is to take an abstract concept, like the idea of opening a fitness center for the 50+ demographic (introduced in Chapter 2), and put it to the test—by talking to industry experts, surveying prospective customers, studying industry trends, thinking through the financials, and scrutinizing it in other ways. These types of activities not only help determine whether an idea is feasible but also help shape and mold the idea. The importance of this notion is affirmed by R.G. Cooper, a widely published author in the area of new product development, who wrote:

> New product success is largely decided in the first few plays of a game— in those critical steps and tasks that precede the actual development of a product. The upfront homework defines the product and builds the business case for development.[1]

Although Cooper was referring specifically to developing new products, the same can be said for developing new companies. The most critical steps are the early ones, where the upfront homework (i.e., feasibility analysis and preparing a business plan) defines the business and provides sufficient evidence to build a compelling case for moving forward.

An integral part of the feasibility analysis described in this chapter is the set of assessment tools that helps organize the thinking of the people completing a feasibility analysis and helps them make final judgments regarding each area of feasibility. The assessment tools are referred to in the chapter and are shown in their entirety in Appendix 3.1 at the end of this chapter.

Now let's look at each of the four components of feasibility analysis and how each of the four components should be evaluated and assessed.

PRODUCT/SERVICE FEASIBILITY ANALYSIS

Product/service feasibility is an assessment of the overall appeal of the product or service being proposed. Although there are many important things to consider when launching a new venture, nothing else matters if the product or service itself doesn't sell. There are two key issues to consider at this point: product desirability and product demand.

PRODUCT/SERVICE DESIRABILITY

The first component of product/service feasibility is to affirm that the proposed product or service is desirable and serves a need in the marketplace. The following questions speak to the basic appeal of the product:

- Does it make sense? Is it reasonable? Is it something that a specific group of consumers will get excited about?
- Does it take advantage of an environmental trend, solve a problem, or fill a gap in the marketplace?
- Is this a good time to introduce the product or service to the market?
- Are there any fatal flaws in the product's basic design or concept?

The proper mindset at the feasibility analysis stage is to get a general sense of the answers to these and similar questions, rather than to try to reach final conclusions. One way to achieve this objective is to administer a concept test.

Concept Test.   A concept test involves showing a preliminary description of a product or service idea, called a concept statement, to industry experts and prospective customers to solicit their feedback. It is normally a one-page document, which includes the following:

- A description of the product or service
- The intended target market
- The benefits of the product or service
- A description of how the product or service will be positioned relative to competitors
- A description of how the product or service will be sold
- A brief description of the company's management team (for purposes of completeness)

After the concept statement is developed, it should be shown to 5 to 10 people who are familiar with the industry that the firm hopes to enter and who can provide informed feedback and to 5 to 10 potential customers. The temptation to show it to family members and friends should be avoided because these people are predisposed to give positive feedback. Instead, it should be distributed to people who will provide candid and informed feedback and advice. A short survey should be attached to the statement that asks the participants to (1) tell you three things that they like about the product or service idea, (2) provide you three suggestions for making it better, (3) tell you whether they think the product or service idea is feasible, and (4) share additional comments or suggestions. The information gleaned from the statements should be tabulated and carefully read. If time permits, the statement can be used in an iterative manner to strengthen the product or service idea. For example, you might show the statement to a group of potential customers, get feedback, tweak the idea, show it to second group for additional feedback, tweak the idea some more, and so on.

The concept statement for a fictitious company, named Prime Adult Fitness, is provided in Figure 3-2. The fitness center, as alluded to several times in the book, will target consumers who are 50 years old and older and will be the main focus of the business plan, discussed in Chapters 4 through 10. Prime Adult Fitness will feature exercise machines, classes, and workouts that are specifically designed for older people. It will also offer massage therapy and physical therapy services on site and will feature classes that focus on its members' mental fitness to complement the activities that focus on physical fitness. To help facilitate this goal, the company will maintain a well-stocked game room and will facilitate small groups that meet to play Sudoku and similar games.

There are many variations on how entrepreneurs solicit feedback on their business ideas. Rather than developing a formal concept statement, some entrepreneurs conduct product/service feasibility analysis by simply talking through their ideas with potential customers and others and gathering informal feedback. For example, during the development of Proactiv (www.proactiv.com), a popular acne medication, Dr. Katie Rodan, one of the company's cofounders, hosted dinner

FIGURE 3-2   Concept Statement: Prime Adult Fitness

Product

Prime Adult Fitness will be a fitness center for people 50 years old and older. The center will be two-thirds the size of an average Bally Fitness Center or Gold's Gym and will feature exercise machines, classes, and workouts that are especially designed for its clientele. It will also feature access to massage and physical therapy services.

Prime Adult Fitness will provide an atmosphere that encourages older people to exercise and stay fit. Substantial evidence suggests that older people prefer to exercise with people their own age. In fact, according to one study, many older people would rather exercise alone than in a mixed group that includes younger people. As a result, there may be a large untapped market of older people who would like to join a fitness center but aren't interested in their current choices. Prime Adult Fitness will provide older people a fitness center designed specifically for them.

Target Market

Prime Adult Fitness will be located in Central Florida, one of the fastest growing areas for people 50 years old and older in the country. It will limit its membership to people 50 years old and older. Although the fitness industry itself is on a steady growth curve, we believe that existing fitness centers are not able to offer the environment, programs, or mix of classes that are optimal for older people. As shown by Curves International (just for women) and others, focusing on a single demographic is a viable and potentially profitable way of carving out a distinct target market in the fitness industry.

How Prime Adult Fitness Will Be Positioned Relative to Competitors

Prime Adult Fitness will be the only fitness center in Central Florida exclusively focused on people 50 years old and older. Its amenities will be equal to the major competitors in its target market, which include Life Time Fitness, LA Fitness, and the YMCA. The company's approach will free it to focus exclusively on the needs of its clientele.

Management Team

Prime Adult Fitness is led by its cofounders, Jeremy Ryan and Elizabeth Sims. Jeremy started a successful fitness center in South Florida and grew it to 38 units in 3 years before selling it to a major chain. Elizabeth Sims worked with Jeremy in his last venture and has 19 years experience as a certified public accountant.

parties at her house to solicit feedback from guests about her product idea. The guests included business executives, market researchers, an FDA regulatory attorney, the chief financial officer of a major company, and others.[2] Similarly, Sharelle Klause, the founder of Dry Soda (http://www.drysoda.com), a company that makes an all natural soda that's paired with food the way wine is in upscale restaurants, tested her idea by first talking to her husband's colleagues, who were in the food industry, and then tapped into the professional network of a friend, who owned a bottled water company. Through this process, she met a chemist who was instrumental in helping her develop the initial recipes for her beverage. Klause also went directly to restaurant owners and chefs to ask them to sample early versions of her initial four flavors: Rhubarb, Kumquat, Lavender, and Lemongrass.[3]

On other occasions, feasibility analysis is used to help entrepreneurs gain insight on certain aspects of their product idea. For example, Tom Patterson, who started a men's undershirt company named Tommy John's (www.tommyjohnwear.com), was particularly interested in how men's undershirts are bought. As a result, he went to stores and literally spent hours watching people buy undershirts. One thing he found out is that men only buy undershirts for about 17 years of their life. From age 0 to 17 their mothers buy their undershirts, and from age 34 (or whenever they get married) on their wives buy it. As a result of this insight, he designed a box with very feminine colors, chocolate brown and Tiffany blue, specifically to catch the eye of a woman. The box was designed to slide open easily, so a shopper could touch the undershirt, a distinct attribute of his boxes that also appeals to female purchasers.[4]

Although not a complete approach, there is merit to the give-and-take that entrepreneurs like Rodan, Klause, and Patterson experienced by talking with (and observing) prospective customers rather than just handing them a concept statement and asking them to complete a survey. A catchy phrase that champions the idea of soliciting feedback from potential customers and others to validate the merits of a business idea is "Get Out of the Building." The meaning of the phrase "Get Out of the Building" and how it applies to product/service desirability is described in the following Business Plan Insight boxed feature.

PRODUCT/SERVICE DEMAND

The second component of product/service feasibility analysis is to determine if there is demand for the product or service. A useful technique to gain a preliminary sense of the demand for a product or service is to administer a buying intentions survey.

Buying Intentions Survey. A buying intentions survey is an instrument that is used to gauge customer interest in a product or service. It consists of a concept statement (or a similar description of a product or service) with a short survey attached. The statement and the survey should be distributed to 25 to 50 potential customers (do not include any of the people who completed the concept statement test). Each participant should be asked to read the statement and complete the survey. The survey typically features a question that looks something like this:

How likely would you be to buy a product (or service) like this, if we make it?

_____ Definitely would buy
_____ Probably would buy
_____ Might or might not buy
_____ Probably would not buy
_____ Definitely would not buy

The number of people who indicate that they *definitely* would buy is typically combined with the number of people who indicate that they *probably* would buy to gauge customer interest.

One caveat is that people who say that they intend to purchase a product or service don't always follow through, so the numbers resulting from this activity are almost always optimistic. The survey also doesn't normally tap a scientifically random sample. Still, the results give a potential entrepreneur a general sense of the degree of customer interest in the product or service idea.

BUSINESS PLAN INSIGHT

Get Out of the Building

A staple concept of the lean startup movement, pioneered by Steve Blank and others, is the idea that you cannot make something people will love without making something people want. And the best way to find out if anyone will actually buy what you're making is to Get Out of the Building. What the phrase "Get Out of the Building" refers to is that it's impossible to really understand customers and to fully assess the merits of a business idea from your office, apartment, classroom, or dorm. Instead, you have to "Get Out of the Building" and interact with potential customers and others in their offices, stores, factories, homes, or wherever they are to get a true sense of the veracity of a business idea.

Once you "Get Out of the Building" the idea is to observe, interview, probe, ask follow-up questions, and so forth to not only validate but also to improve upon your idea. Here's an example. Say you're thinking about opening a pet supply store. You've done tons of library and Internet research and think you've come up with a concept that will set you apart from the big-box pet supply stores like PetSmart and Petco. But from the desk in your office how do you really know? The key to validate what you believe to be true is to "Get Out of the Building" and talk to people who can give you informed feedback. In the pet supply store example, here's how it works. Imagine how much you'd learn about what people want from pet stores, if your idea resonates with them, and suggestions you will get for improving on your idea if you conducted the following "Get out of the Building" research:

- Interview 25 people who shop once a month or more at a pet supply store.
- Visit 12 pet supply stores and spend 60 minutes per store observing people shopping, taking note of what they purchase (and the combination of things that they purchase), listening to them ask store personnel questions, and approaching them with questions of your own if something sparks your interest.
- Contact five vendors who supply products to pet supply stores and interview them in person or over the phone.
- Contact five veterinarians and ask them for interviews.

After you hear from potential customers and others, you'll have a much better sense of whether your idea is a good one. You'll also learn things that will invariably help you improve on and strengthen your idea. The key is to Get Out of the Building and test your ideas.

Additional questions are often added to the buying intentions survey, depending on the nature of the product or service involved. Examples of the types of questions that are added include the following:

- How much would you be willing to pay for the product or service? This provides insight into pricing.
- Where would you expect to find this product or service for sale? This may provide insight into sales and distribution.

The survey should be kept short to maximize participation.

To find people to talk through a product or service idea or to react to a concept statement, entrepreneurs should contact industry trade associations and attend industry trade shows. A Web site that provides a directory of the trade associations in an industry and displays a schedule of trade show dates and locations are included in the Internet Resources Table (Appendix 2.2) at the end of Chapter 2. Another online resource, Trade Show News Network (http://www.tsnn.com), provides a searchable database of more than 25,000 trade shows, conferences, and seminars for various industries. For example, if you were launching a Web site to help engaged couples better plan their weddings, you could go to the Trade Show News Network Web site (www.tsnn.com), type the word "wedding" in the search box, and obtain a complete list of wedding related trade shows and conferences including dates, descriptions and links to their Web sites. Attending a trade show or conference that is related to the industry your business will be entering is an excellent way to make contacts with industry experts and potential business partners.

To supplement the techniques discussed above, there are a growing number of tools available online for all facets of feasibility analysis, as shown in Table 3-2. The tools range from open-ended Q&A sites, like Quora (www.quora.com), to sites that will conduct usability tests of Web sites and applications. A particularly useful and affordable tool is Google Consumer Surveys (www.google.com/consumersurveys), where you can create a survey and obtain responses for as little as 10 cents per respondent. In addition to providing raw data, Google Consumer Surveys produces charts summarizing responses and highlighting interesting differences among respondents, which can be segmented by age, gender, location, and other demographic categories.

INDUSTRY/TARGET MARKET FEASIBILITY ANALYSIS

Industry/target market feasibility is an assessment of the overall appeal of the industry and the target market for the product or service being proposed. There is a distinct difference between a firm's industry and its target market, which should be clearly understood. An industry is a group of firms producing a similar product or service, such as fitness centers, smartphones, elderly home care, or online education. A firm's target market is the limited portion of the industry that it goes after or tries to appeal to. Most firms do not try to service their entire industry. Instead, they select or carve out a specific target market and try to service that market very well. Prime Adult Fitness's target market is people 50 years and older within the broader fitness center industry.

It's important to assess both the broad industry you will be entering and your specific target market. If you want more detailed information on either of these topics, you can skip ahead to Chapters 5 and 6 of this book, which focus on the industry analysis and market analysis sections of the business plan.

INDUSTRY ATTRACTIVENESS

Industries vary in terms of their overall attractiveness. In general, the most attractive industries for startups are large and growing, are young rather than old, are early rather than late in their life cycle, are fragmented rather than

TABLE 3-2 Online Tools Available for Completing Feasibility Analysis

Tool	Source	Cost
A/B testing—meaning respondent is given two options (i.e., which logo is more appealing? which product idea is best)	Pick-fu (http://pickfu.com)	$20 for a single test
Consumer trends (shows how often a particular search terms is entered, which is a proxy for how much interest there is in a particular topic)	Google Trends (www.google.com/trends)	Free
Feedback on product ideas	Quirky (www.quirky.com)	Free
Feedback on ideas or designs	Conceptshare (www.conceptshare.com)	Free 15-day trial; tiered pricing system based on level of feedback.
Q&A sites—open-ended questions	Quora (www.quora.com)	Free
	Startup Nation (www.startupnation.com)	Free
Survey	SurveyMonkey (www.surveymonkey.com)	Free for basic survey; fee based for more extensive surveys
	Ask Your Target Market (www.aytm.com)	About $1 per respondent; pricing varies depending on the nature of the survey.
	Google Consumer Surveys (www.google.com/consumersurveys)	Starts at 10 cents to 50 cents per respondent depending on how tightly focused the survey audience is
Web site usability tests	UserTesting (www.usertesting.com)	$49 for video of a visitor speaking their thoughts as they use your Web site
	Loop 11 (www.loop11.com)	Flat fee of $350 for user testing project
	OpenHallway (www.openhallway.com)	Tiered pricing system starting at $49 per month

concentrated, and have high rather than low operating margins. You also want to pick an industry that's structurally attractive—meaning startups can enter the industry (in various target markets) and compete. Some industries are characterized by such high barriers to entry or the presence of one or two dominant players that potential new entrants are essentially shut out.

Other factors are also important. For example, the degree to which environmental and business trends are moving in favor rather than against the industry
is important for the industry's long-term health and its capability to spawn new
target or niche markets. For example, an increased awareness of the benefits of
exercise is an extremely positive trend for the fitness industry. Another factor is
how important the products or services an industry sells are to its customers. One
of the reasons the pharmaceutical industry is so profitable is because there are
no good substitutes for its products. Compare that to the movie theater industry,
which is struggling. How many options do we have for watching movies at home
(i.e., Netflix, Hulu.com, cable, DVD rentals) and how many alternatives do we
have for spending our free time and money other than going to a movie theater?

The assessment tool provided in the feasibility analysis in Appendix 3.1
enables you to assess the industry you're thinking about entering. As you fill out
this assessment tool, make sure to stick strictly to an assessment of your industry,
not the specific portion of the industry you plan to target. Refer to the Internet
Resources Table in Appendix 2.2 at the end of Chapter 2 to identify sources that
will help you make your assessments. IBISWorld, Bizminer, and Mintel are particularly useful resources for this section of the feasibility analysis.

TARGET MARKET ATTRACTIVENESS

As mentioned, a target market is a place within a larger market segment
that represents a narrower group of customers with similar needs. Most startups
simply do not have the resources needed to participate in a broad market, at
least initially. Instead, by focusing on a smaller target market, a firm can usually
avoid head-to-head competition with industry leaders and can focus on serving a
specialized market very well.

The challenge in identifying an attractive target market is to find a market
that's large enough for the proposed business but is yet small enough to avoid
attracting larger competitors. An example of a company that has targeted a
market that meets these criteria is Songkick (www.songkick.com), the Web-
based startup introduced in Chapter 2 that allows users to "follow" their favorite
bands and sends them an alert when one of the bands they're following is in
their area. The company, which launched in 2007, has five million unique visitors to its site every month and lists over 100,000 upcoming concerts on its site.[5]
Although Songkick operates in the $16.5 billion global music industry, it has
carved out a specialized target or niche market (connecting concert goes with
concerts in their area) for itself and is gaining traction. As the company gains
momentum and financial resources, it may grow beyond this specialized market,
but has gotten off to a good start largely because it has remained laser focused on
a clearly defined target market within a larger industry.

Although it's generally easy to find good information to assess the attractiveness of an industry, discerning the attractiveness of a small target market
is tougher, particularly if the firm is pioneering the market. Often, under these
circumstances, information from more than one industry and/or market must
be collected and synthesized to make an informed judgment. For example,

RunKeeper (www.runkeeper.com) is a smartphone app that launched in 2008 and was the first app that allowed runners to track runs on smartphones and view the results on a Web site that provided analytics, running-related tips, and social support. The question for a product like this is what market to assess? There are no Standard Industrial Classification (SIC) or North American Industry Classification System (NAICS) codes for the "smartphone running app" industry or market. Obviously, a combination of markets must be studied, including the smartphone market, the app market, and the market for running-related products. It would be important to know not only how well smartphones and apps are selling but also what the current trends in running are. If running was gaining in popularity, as it was at the time, then that would be a positive sign for RunKeeper's market. If smartphone and apps were selling like hotcakes, but running was on a sharp decline, the niche market that RunKeeper was pioneering would be much less attractive.

Google Trends (www.google.com/trends) is a useful tool for assessing whether the popularity of a particular topic or product is gaining or losing momentum. In short, Google Trends shows how often a particular search term is entered relative to the total search volume. Here's how it works. Go to Google Trends (www.google.com/trends) and type the term "running app" into the search box. If you see a trend line that's sloping upward to the right, it means that a steadily increasing number of people are searching for the term "running app" on Google. You can also use Google Trends to compare the volume of searches between two or more terms, which may provide insight into which is the better of two product ideas. For example, enter the terms "running app" and "biking app" (separated by a comma) into Google Trends. You'll probably see a much more promising trend line for running apps than biking apps.

A tool for assessing the validity and attractiveness of a target market is provided in the full feasibility analysis in Appendix 3.1. Again, make sure to focus this analysis strictly on the portion of your industry you plan to target.

MARKET TIMELINESS

The final step in industry/market feasibility analysis is to evaluate the timeliness of the introduction of the proposed product or service. There are two important considerations. The first consideration is to determine if the window of opportunity for the product or service is open or closed. As explained in Chapter 2, the term "window of opportunity" is a metaphor describing the time period in which a firm can realistically enter a new market. After the market for a new product is established, its window of opportunity opens. As the market grows, firms enter and try to establish a profitable position. At some point, the market matures, and the window of opportunity closes. An important judgment call is whether the window of opportunity for a particular business idea is open or closed.

The second consideration regarding market timeliness is to study the simple economics of the industry the firm plans to enter to determine whether the timing is right for a new entrant. For example, over the past several years, the Formal Wear and Costume Rental Industry has experienced a perfect storm of trends working against future growth. The trends include inexpensive imports (making it as inexpensive to buy as rent), lower disposable income, and a general societal leaning toward dressing more casually, even for traditionally formal events like weddings and proms. These trends, which aren't expected to change anytime soon, suggest that now is not a good time to launch a Formal Wear and Costume Rental startup.[6] A tool for assessing market timeliness for any startup is provided in the full feasibility in Appendix 3.1.

Firms that do not conduct a thorough industry and target market analysis and enter a small part of an industry without knowing its size or potential, often find that the market is not large enough to maintain and grow the business. In these instances, firms must often scramble to find a complementary niche to expand the size of their business.

ORGANIZATIONAL FEASIBILITY ANALYSIS

Organizational feasibility analysis is conducted to determine whether a proposed business has sufficient management expertise, organizational competence, and resources to successfully launch its business. There are two primary issues to consider in this area: management prowess and resource sufficiency.

MANAGEMENT PROWESS

A startup should assess the prowess, or ability, of its initial management team, whether it is a sole entrepreneur or a larger group. This task requires the individuals starting the firm to be honest and candid in their self-assessments. Two of the most important factors in this area are the passion that the sole entrepreneur or management team has for the business and the extent to which the people involved understand the markets in which the firm will compete. There are no practical substitutes for strengths in these areas.

A collection of additional factors help define management prowess, including prior entrepreneurial experience,[7] the depth of the professional and social networks of the people involved,[8] the degree of creativity among the members of the group, the extent of experience that the team has in cash flow management, and the extent to which the sole entrepreneur and members of the team have college degrees.[9] In most instances, not all of these qualities will be present. This is the reason that many startups fairly quickly add an industry veteran or an experienced entrepreneur to their team, or place one or more individuals with these credentials on their board of advisors. The prowess, or strength, of a startup's management team is normally given disproportionate weight when outsiders evaluate the desirability of a new venture, and most entrepreneurs know this.

A tool for assessing management prowess is provided in the full feasibility analysis in Appendix 3.1.

RESOURCE SUFFICIENCY

The second step in organizational feasibility analysis is to determine whether the proposed venture has or is capable of obtaining sufficient resources to move forward. The focus in organizational feasibility analysis is on nonfinancial resources because financial feasibility is considered separately. It is not necessary to develop an exhaustive list of nonfinancial resources. The objective is to identify the 8 to 12 most important and potentially problematic nonfinancial resources and assess whether they are available. An example is a startup that will require one or more wet labs to produce its products or perform its service. A wet lab is a space where chemicals, drugs, or other material or biological matter is tested or analyzed, and requires water, direct ventilation, and specialized piped utilities. Most wet labs are in buildings that are specifically designed to house them. If a firm plans to rent its wet labs, but no wet lab rental space is available in the community where the firm plans to locate, a serious resources sufficiency problem exists. Other nonfinancial resources, which often become issues due to concerns regarding their affordability or availability, include office space, light manufacturing space, key management employees, key support personnel, and support from state and local governments if applicable.

One important but easily overlooked resource sufficiency issue that new firms should consider is their proximity to similar firms. There are well-known clusters of high-tech firms, for example, in the Silicon Valley of California, on Route 128 around Boston, and in Austin, Texas. Clusters arise because they increase the productivity of the firms participating in them. Because these firms are located near each other, it is easy for their employees to network with each other, and it is easy for the firms to gain access to specialized suppliers, scientific knowledge, and technological expertise native to the area.[10] For example, there is a cluster of medical device companies in the Twin Cities area of Minnesota. As a result, a medical device firm that decided to locate in Des Moines, Iowa, for example, may have a decided disadvantage over a similar startup located in Minneapolis, which is just 240 miles to the north. Researchers have found that small manufacturing firms benefit more than larger firms by being physically close to a cluster of similar firms.[11]

An instrument to assess resource sufficiency is provided in the full feasibility analysis in Appendix 3.1.

FINANCIAL FEASIBILITY ANALYSIS

Financial feasibility analysis is the final stage of a comprehensive feasibility analysis. For feasibility analysis, a preliminary financial analysis is normally sufficient. More rigor at this point is typically not required because the specifics of the business will inevitably evolve, making it impractical to spend a lot of time early on preparing detailed financial statements. Still, it is important to have more than a cursory sense of the financial feasibility of a proposed business.

The most important issues to consider at this stage are total startup cash needed, financial performance of similar businesses, and the overall financial attractiveness of the proposed venture. If a proposed new venture moves beyond the feasibility analysis stage, more complete financial projections will be included in the business plan.

TOTAL STARTUP CASH NEEDED

The first issue refers to the total cash needed to prepare the business to make its first sale. An actual budget should be prepared that lists all the anticipated operating expenses and capital purchases that will be needed to get the business up and running. After a total figure is arrived at, an explanation of where the money will come from should be provided. Avoid cursory explanations such as "I'll borrow the money" or "I plan to bring equity investors on board." Although you may ultimately involve lenders or investors in your business, a more thoughtful account is required of how you'll provide for your initial cash needs.

If the money will come from friends and family or is raised through other means, such as credit cards or a home equity line of credit, a reasonable plan should be stipulated to repay the money. Showing how a new venture's startup costs will be covered and repaid is an important issue. Many new ventures look promising as ongoing concerns but have no way of raising the money to get started or are never able to recover from the initial costs involved. When projecting startup expenses, it is better to overestimate rather than underestimate the costs involved. Murphy's Law is prevalent in the startup world—things will go wrong. It is a rare startup that doesn't experience some unexpected expenses during the startup phase.

A form for estimating total startup expenses is included in the full feasibility analysis in Appendix 3.1.

FINANCIAL PERFORMANCE OF SIMILAR BUSINESSES

The second component of the financial feasibility analysis is estimating a proposed startup's potential financial performance by comparing it to similar, already-established businesses. Obviously, this effort will result in approximate rather than exact numbers. There are several ways of doing this, all of which involve a little ethical detective work. First, substantial archival data are available online, which offer detailed financial reports on thousands of individual firms. The easiest data to obtain are on publicly traded firms through Hoovers, Yahoo! Industry Center or a similar source. These firms are typically too large, however, for meaningful comparisons to proposed new ventures. The trick is to find the financial performance of small, more comparable firms. A listing of Web sites that are helpful in this regard are provided in the Internet Resources Table in Appendix 2.2 at the end of Chapter 2. Both Bizminer and Bizstats, for example, provide revenue, expense, and income estimates for firms in specific industries. Bizstats (www.bizstats.com), which is free, allows an entrepreneur to type in the projected revenue of his or her firm, by industry classification, and receive a mock income statement in return that shows the average profitability and expense percentages of U.S. small businesses in the same category. Bizminer (www.bizminer.com) provides a printout of the average sales and profitability for firms in the industries they follow, which provides more detail than similar reports. Bizminer's reports cost between $69 and $99, unless accessed for free through a large public or university library. IBISWorld provides data on the average sales and profitability for the firms in the industries they track. It also normally provides a chart of the average expenses (as a percentage of net sales) for major items like wages, rent, and utilities for firms in the industries they follow. There are additional ways to obtain financial performance data on smaller firms. Some industry trade associations publish data on the sales and profitability of the firms in their industries. If the data can't be easily found, you can call or e-mail a trade association to ask if the data are available. Similarly, if startup entrepreneurs identify a business that is similar to the one they want to start, and the business isn't likely to be a direct competitor, it's not inappropriate to ask the owner or manager of the business to share sales and income data. Even if the owner or manager is only willing to talk in general terms (i.e., "our annual sales are in the $2 million range, and we're netting between $150,000 and $200,000 per year"), that information is certainly better than nothing.

Simple Internet searches are also often helpful. If you're interested in the fitness industry, simply typing "fitness industry sales" and "fitness industry profitability" in the Google or Bing search bar will invariably result in links to stories about fitness companies that will discuss sales and profitability data.

A final way to obtain sales data for similar businesses is through simple observation and legwork. This approach works in some cases, and in some cases, it doesn't. For example, if you were proposing to open a smoothie shop, you could gauge the type of sales to expect by estimating the number of people, along with the average purchase per visit, who patronize similar smoothie shops in your area. A very basic way of doing this is to frequent these stores and count the number of customers who come in and out of the stores during various times of the day.

The assessment tool associated with this topic is included in the full feasibility analysis that appears in Appendix 3.1.

OVERALL FINANCIAL ATTRACTIVENESS OF THE PROPOSED VENTURE

A number of other factors are associated with evaluating the financial attractiveness of a proposed venture. Again, at the feasibility analysis stage, the extent to which a proposed business appears positive relative to each factor is based on an estimate or forecast rather than actual performance. Important factors in this category include the extent to which sales can be expected to grow during the first one to two years of the venture, the percentage of recurring revenue to anticipate (it's cheaper to serve a small number of loyal customers than to continually have to find new customers), the likelihood that internally generated funds will be available within two years to finance growth, and the availability of exit opportunities for investors if applicable.

An instrument to assess the overall financial attractiveness of the proposed venture is provided in the full feasibility analysis in Appendix 3.1.

In summary, feasibility analysis is a vital step in the process of both validating and developing business ideas. Although the process described in this chapter will not give an entrepreneur a final answer regarding the potential feasibility of a business idea, it should provide substantial clarity and insight. The ultimate goal of the process is that only well-researched, well-thought out, and potentially feasible ideas enter the business planning process.

Chapter Summary

1. Feasibility analysis is the process of determining if a business idea is viable.
2. Primary research is original research that is collected by the person or persons completing the analysis. It normally includes talking to industry experts, obtaining feedback from prospective customers, and administering surveys.
3. Secondary research probes data that are already collected. The data generally include industry studies, Census Bureau data, company reports, and other pertinent information gleaned through library and Internet research.
4. Product/service feasibility is an assessment of the overall appeal of the product or service being proposed. Its two components are product/service desirability and product/service demand.
5. A concept test involves showing a preliminary description of a product or service idea, called a concept statement, to industry experts and prospective customers to solicit their feedback.
6. A buying intentions survey is an instrument used to gauge customer interest in a product or service. It consists of a concept statement (or a similar description of a product or service) with a short survey attached.
7. Industry/target market feasibility is an assessment of the overall appeal of the industry and market for the product or service being proposed. Its three components are industry attractiveness, target market attractiveness, and market timeliness.
8. Organizational feasibility analysis is conducted to determine whether a proposed business has sufficient management expertise, organizational competence, and resources to successfully launch its business. Its two components are management prowess and (nonfinancial) resource sufficiency.
9. Clusters of firms arise because of the increase in the productivity of the firms participating in them. Because the firms are located near each other, it is easy for the employees to network with each other, and it is easy for the firms to gain access to specialized suppliers, scientific knowledge, and technological expertise native to the area.
10. Financial feasibility analysis is conducted to determine if a new venture is feasible from a financial perspective. Its three components are total startup cash needed, financial performance of similar businesses, and overall financial attractiveness of the proposed venture.

Review Questions

1. What is a feasibility analysis? How does a feasibility analysis differ from a business plan?
2. What are the four individual components of a full feasibility analysis?
3. What is the difference between primary research and secondary research? Are both types of research necessary to complete a full feasibility analysis?

4. Describe the purpose of product/service feasibility analysis. Briefly describe its two components.
5. Describe the purpose of a concept test and how it should be executed. Also, describe the purpose of a buying intentions survey and how it should be distributed and assessed.
6. Explain the purpose of industry/target market feasibility analysis. Briefly describe its three components.
7. What is a target market? Why do most startups start in target markets rather than broader markets that have more customers?
8. Describe the purpose of organizational feasibility analysis. Briefly describe its two components.
9. What is an industry "cluster?" Why might a semiconductor startup, for example, decide to launch in a geographic area where there are other semiconductor firms, rather than another area?
10. Describe the purpose of a financial feasibility analysis. Briefly describe its three components.

Application Questions

1. Kendall Ryan just applied for a bank loan to finance a Greek-style restaurant he plans to open near a large Midwestern university campus. The banker asked Kendall if he conducted any primary research to assess the feasibility of the restaurant. Kendall replied that he spent countless evenings and weekends in the library and on the Internet collecting data on the feasibility of Greek-style restaurants, and he is confident that his restaurant will be successful. He said that he even did careful research to make sure that Greek-style restaurants do well near large Midwestern university campuses. If you were the banker, how would you react to Kendall's statements?
2. Three recent startups, CareZone, BenchPrep, and CitySlips were mentioned in Chapter 2. Pick one of these companies and write a concept statement for it.
3. InstyMeds, another company introduced in Chapter 2, developed a vending machine for prescription drugs to be located in rural hospitals and urgent care centers. Describe how you would have conducted an industry/target market feasibility analysis for this startup.
4. Jane Robinson has developed a software product that helps elementary school teachers better prepare their lesson plans and more accurately assess their students' progress. Jane is now wondering whether this is a good time to launch the product. What factors should Jane consider in making this determination?
5. Using one or more of the resources included in the Internet Resources Table in Appendix 2.2 at the end of Chapter 2, investigate the health and growth potential of the spa industry in the United States.

Endnotes

1. R. G. Cooper, *Product Leadership: Creating and Launching Superior New Products* (Reading, MA: Perseus Books, 1998), 99.
2. B. R. Barringer and R. Duane Ireland, *Entrepreneurship: Successfully Launching New Ventures* (Upper Saddle River, NJ: Prentice-Hall, 2012).
3. G. Galant and S. Klause, "VV Show #35" (Venture Voice), http://www. venturevoice.com (March, 2006).
4. B. Fried and T. Patterson, "Tom Patterson, Inventor & Founder of Tommy John," *Got Invention Radio Podcast*, http://gotinvention.com/, originally posted on July 15, 2012 (accessed on June 9, 2013).
5. M. Butcher, "Songkick Secures Sequoia's First Ever UK Investment With a $10M B Round," *Techcrunch*, www.techcrunch.com, March 8, 2012 (accessed June 9, 2013).
6. S. Lerman, "IBIS World Industry Report 53222 Formal Wear & Costume Rental in the US," June 2013.
7. D. Politis, "The Process of Entrepreneurial Learning: A Conceptual Framework," *Entrepreneurship Theory and Practice*, 29 (2005): 399–424.
8. D. M. DeCarolis and P. Saparito, "Social Capital, Cognition, and Entrepreneurial Opportunities: A Theoretical Framework," *Entrepreneurship Theory and Practice*, 30 (2006): 41–56.
9. NFIB, *National Small Business Poll*, Volume 12, no. 2 (Washington, D.C.: NFIB Research Foundation, 2012).
10. B. Feld, *Startup Communities* (New York, NY: Wiley, 2012).
11. M. Rogers, "Networks, Firm Size and Innovation," *Small Business Economics*, 22, no. 2 (2004): 141–153.

Full Feasibility Analysis

Note: All fields can be expanded to provide additional space to respond to the questions. A copy of this template, along with each of the assessment tools, is available in MS Word and PDF format at the authors' Web site at http://www.bus.ucf.edu/barringer.

INTRODUCTION

A. Name of the proposed business
B. Name of the founder (or founders)
C. One paragraph summary of the business

PART 1: PRODUCT/SERVICE FEASIBILITY

ISSUES ADDRESSED IN THIS PART

A. Product/service desirability
B. Product/service demand

ASSESSMENT TOOLS

Concept Statement Test

- Write a concept statement for your product/service idea. Show the concept statement to 5 to 10 people who are familiar with the industry your startup will be entering and 5 to 10 potential customers. Select people who will give you informed and candid feedback.

- Attach a blank sheet to the concept statement, and ask the people who read the statement to (1) tell you three things they like about your product/service idea, (2) provide three suggestions for making it better, (3) tell you whether they think the product or service idea is feasible (or will be successful), and (4) share any additional comments or suggestions.

- Summarize the information you obtain from the concept statement into the following three categories:

  - Strengths of the product or service idea—things people who evaluated your product or service concept said they "liked" about the idea

  - Suggestions for strengthening the idea—suggestions made by people for strengthening or improving the idea

  - Overall feasibility of the product or service concept—report the number of people who think the idea is feasible, the number of people who think it isn't feasible, and any additional comments that were made

  - Other comments and suggestions

Buying Intentions Survey

- Distribute the concept statement to 25 to 50 prospective customers (do not include any of the people who completed the concept statement test) with the following buying intentions survey attached. Ask each participant to read the concept statement and complete the buying intentions survey. Record the number of people who participated in the survey and the results of the survey here.

- Along with the raw data recorded here, report the percentage of the total number of people you surveyed who said they would probably buy or definitely would buy your product or service if offered. This percentage is the most important figure in gauging potential customer interest.

- One caveat is that people who say that they intend to purchase a product do not always follow through, so the numbers resulting from this activity are almost always optimistic. Still, the numbers provide you with a preliminary indication of how your most likely customers will respond to your potential product or service offering.

How likely would you be to buy the product or service described above?

_____ Definitely would buy
_____ Probably would buy
_____ Might or might not buy
_____ Probably would not buy
_____ Definitely would not buy

Additional questions may be added to the buying intentions survey.

Conclusion (expand fields and report findings, in discussion form, for each area)

A. Product/service desirability
B. Product/service demand
C. Product/service feasibility (circle the correct response)
   Not Feasible   *Unsure*   *Feasible*
D. Suggestions for improving product/service feasibility

PART 2: INDUSTRY/MARKET FEASIBILITY

ISSUES ADDRESSED IN THIS PART

A. Industry attractiveness
B. Target market attractiveness
C. Timeliness of entry into the target market

ASSESSMENT TOOLS

Industry Attractiveness

- To the extent possible, assess the industry at the five-digit NAICS code level your potential business will be entering. Use a broader industry category (less NCICS digits) if appropriate (www.census.gov/eos/www/naics/concordances/concordances.html).

- Assess the attractiveness of the industry the potential business plans to enter on each of the following dimensions.

Industry Attractiveness Assessment Tool
(used to assess the broad industry, rather than the specific target market, you plan to enter)

	Low Potential	Moderate Potential	High Potential
1. Number of competitors	Many	Few	None
2. Age of industry	Old	Middle aged	Young
3. Growth rate of industry	Little or no growth	Moderate growth	Strong growth
4. Average net income for firms in the industry	Low	Medium	High
5. Degree of industry concentration	Concentrated	Neither concentrated nor fragmented	Fragmented
6. Stage of industry life cycle	Maturity phase or decline phase	Growth phase	Emergence phase
7. Importance of industry's products and/or services to customers	"Ambivalent"	"Would like to have"	"Must have"
8. Extent to which business and environmental trends are moving in favor of the industry	Low	Medium	High
9. Number of exciting new product and services emerging from the industry	Low	Medium	High
10. Long-term prospects	Weak	Neutral	Strong

Target Market Attractiveness

- Identify the portion or specific market within your broader industry that you plan to target.
- Assess the attractiveness of the target market on each of the following dimensions.

Target Market Attractiveness Assessment Tool
(used to assess the specific target market, rather than the broader industry, you plan to enter)

	Low Potential	Moderate Potential	High Potential
1. Number of competitors in target market	Many	Few	None
2. Growth rate of firms in the target market	Little to no growth	Slow growth	Rapid growth
3. Average net income for firms in the target market	Low	Medium	High

	Low Potential	Moderate Potential	High Potential
4. Methods for generating revenue in the industry	Unclear	Somewhat clear	Clear
5. Ability to create "barriers to entry" for potential competitors	Unable to create	May or may not be able to create	Can create
6. Degree to which customers feel satisfied by the current offerings in the target market	Satisfied	Neither satisfied or dissatisfied	Unsatisfied
7. Potential to employ low-cost guerrilla and/or buzz marketing techniques to promote the firm's product or services	Low	Moderate	High
8. Excitement surrounding new product/service offerings in the target market	Low	Medium	High

Market Timeliness

- Determine the extent to which the "window of opportunity" for the proposed business is open or closed based on the following criteria.
- Determine the timeliness of entering a specific target market based on other criteria.

Market Timeliness Assessment Tool

	Low Potential	Moderate Potential	High Potential
1. Buying mood of customers	Customers are not in a buying mood	Customers are in a moderate buying mood	Customers are in an aggressive buying mood
2. Momentum of the market	Stable to losing momentum	Slowly gaining momentum	Rapidly gaining momentum
3. Need for a new firm in the market with your offerings or geographic location	Low	Moderate	High
4. Extent to which business and environmental trends are moving in favor of the target market	Low	Medium	High
5. Recent or planned entrance of large firms into the market	Large firms entering the market	Rumors that large firms may be entering the market	No larger firms entered the market or are rumored to be entering the market

Conclusion (expand fields and report findings, in discussion form, for each area)

A. Industry attractiveness
B. Target market attractiveness
C. Market timeliness
D. Industry/market feasibility (circle the correct response)
   Not Feasible   *Unsure*   *Feasible*
E. Suggestions for improving industry/market feasibility.

PART 3: ORGANIZATIONAL FEASIBILITY

ISSUES ADDRESSED IN THIS PART

A. Management prowess
B. Resource sufficiency

ASSESSMENT TOOLS

Management Prowess

- Use the following table to candidly and objectively rate the "prowess" of the founder or group of founders who will be starting the proposed venture.

Management Prowess Assessment Tool

	Low Potential	*Moderate Potential*	*High Potential*
1. Passion for the business idea	Low	Moderate	High
2. Relevant industry experience	None	Moderate	Extensive
3. Prior entrepreneurial experience	None	Moderate	Extensive
4. Depth of professional and social networks	Weak	Moderate	Strong
5. Creativity among management team members	Low	Moderate	High
6. Experience and expertise in cash flow management	None	Moderate	High
7. College graduate	No college education	Some college education but not currently in college	Graduated or are currently in college

Resource Sufficiency

- The focus in this section is on nonfinancial resources. Use the following table to rate your "resource sufficiency" in each category.
- The list of resources is not meant to be exhaustive. A list of the 6 to 12 most critical nonfinancial resources for your proposed business is sufficient.

An explanation of the rating system used in the first portion of the table is as follows:

- ① Available
- ② Likely to be available: will probably be available and will be within my budget
- ③ Unlikely to be available: will probably be hard to find or gain access to, and may exceed my budget
- ④ Unavailable
- ⑤ NA: not applicable for my business

Resource Sufficiency Assessment Tool

Ratings	Resource Sufficiency
① ② ③ ④ ⑤	Office space
① ② ③ ④ ⑤	Lab space, manufacturing space, or space to launch a service business
① ② ③ ④ ⑤	Contract manufacturers or outsource providers
① ② ③ ④ ⑤	Key management employees (now and in the future)
① ② ③ ④ ⑤	Key support personnel (now and in the future)
① ② ③ ④ ⑤	Key equipment needed to operate the business (computers, machinery, delivery vehicles)
① ② ③ ④ ⑤	Ability to obtain intellectual property protection on key aspects of the business
① ② ③ ④ ⑤	Support of local and state government if applicable for business launch
① ② ③ ④ ⑤	Ability to form favorable business partnerships
① ② ③ ④ ⑤	Availability of online tools that lower the cost of doing business

Ratings: Strong, Neutral, or Weak

_____	Proximity to similar firms (for the purpose of knowledge sharing)
_____	Proximity to suppliers
_____	Proximity to customers
_____	Proximity to a major research university (if applicable)

Conclusion (expand fields and report findings, in discussion form, for each area)

A. Management prowess
B. Resource sufficiency
C. Organizational feasibility (circle the correct response)
   Not Feasible   *Unsure*   *Feasible*
D. Suggestions for improving organizational feasibility

PART 4: FINANCIAL FEASIBILITY

ISSUES ADDRESSED IN THIS PART

A. Total startup cash needed
B. Financial performance of similar businesses
C. Overall financial attractiveness of the proposed venture

ASSESSMENT TOOLS

Total Startup Cash Needed

- The startup costs (which include capital investments and operating expenses) should include all the costs necessary for the business to make its first sale. New firms typically need money for a host of purposes, including the hiring of personnel, office or manufacturing space, equipment, training, research and development, marketing, and the initial product rollout.

- At the feasibility analysis stage, it is not necessary for the number to be exact. However, the number should be fairly accurate to give an entrepreneur an idea of the dollar amount that will be needed to launch the firm. After the approximate dollar amount is known, the entrepreneur should determine specifically where the money will come from to cover the startup costs.

- The total startup cash needed can be estimate using the following table.

Total Startup Cash Needed (to Make First Sale)

Capital Investments	Amount
Property	_____
Furniture and fixtures	_____
Computer equipment	_____
Other equipment	_____
Vehicles	_____

Operating Expenses	*Amount*
Legal, accounting, and professional services	
Advertising and promotions	
Deposits for utilities	
Licenses and permits	
Prepaid insurance	
Lease payments	
Salary and wages	
Payroll taxes	
Travel	
Signs	
Tools and supplies	
Starting inventory	
Cash (working capital)	
Other expense 1	
Other expense 2	
Total Startup Cash Needed =	

Comparison of the Financial Performance of Proposed Venture to Similar Firms

- Use the following tables to compare the proposed new venture to similar firms in regard to annual sales (Year 1 and Year 2) and profitability (Year 1 and Year 2).

Comparison of the Financial Performance of Proposed Venture to Similar Firms Assessment Tool

Annual Sales

Estimate of Proposed Venture's Annual Sales—Year 1	*Explanation of How the Estimate Was Computed*
Estimate of Year 1 Sales _____	
Summary: How proposed annual sales, on average, compares to similar firms (circle one)	
Below Average *Average* *Above Average*	
Estimate of Year 2 Sales _____	
Summary: How proposed annual sales, on average, compares to similar firms (circle one)	
Below Average *Average* *Above Average*	

Net Income

Estimate of Proposed Venture's Net Income—Year 1	Explanation of How the Estimate Was Computed
Estimate of Year 1 Net Income _____	_____
Summary: How proposed net income, on average, compares to similar firms (circle one)	_____
Below Average *Average* *Above Average*	_____
Estimate of Year 2 Net Income _____	_____
Summary: How proposed net income, on average, compares to similar firms (circle one)	_____
Below Average *Average* *Above Average*	_____

Overall Financial Attractiveness of the Proposed Venture

- The following factors are important in regard to the overall financial attractiveness of the proposed business.
- Assess the strength of each factor in the following table.

Overall Financial Attractiveness of Proposed Venture Assessment Tool

	Low Potential	*Moderate Potential*	*High Potential*
1. Steady and rapid growth in sales during the first one to three years in a clearly defined target market	Unlikely	Moderately likely	Highly likely
2. High percentage of recurring income—meaning that once you win a client, the client will provide recurring sources of revenue	Low	Moderate	Strong
3. Ability to forecast income and expenses with a reasonable degree of certainty	Weak	Moderate	Strong
4. Likelihood that internally generated funds will be available within two years to finance growth	Unlikely	Moderately likely	Highly likely
5. Availability of exit opportunity for investor if applicable	Unlikely to be unavailable	May be available	Likely to be available

Conclusion (report finding for each area)

A. Total startup cash needed
B. Financial performance of similar businesses
C. Financial feasibility (circle the correct response)
   Not Feasible   *Unsure*   *Feasible*
D. Suggestions for improving financial feasibility

OVERALL FEASIBILITY: SUMMARY AND CONCLUSION

	Overall Feasibility of the Business Idea Based on Each Part		*Suggestions for Improving the Feasibility*
Product/Market Feasibility	Not feasible	☐	_____
	Unsure	☐	_____
	Feasible	☐	_____
Industry/Market Feasibility	Not feasible	☐	_____
	Unsure	☐	_____
	Feasible	☐	_____
Organizational Feasibility	Not feasible	☐	_____
	Unsure	☐	_____
	Feasible	☐	_____
Financial Feasibility	Not feasible	☐	_____
	Unsure	☐	_____
	Feasible	☐	_____
Overall Assessment	Not feasible	☐	_____
	Unsure	☐	_____
	Feasible	☐	_____

Conclusion—briefly summarize your justification for your overall assessment.

C H A P T E R

INTRODUCTORY MATERIAL, EXECUTIVE SUMMARY, AND DESCRIPTION OF THE BUSINESS

INTRODUCTION

As discussed throughout the book, a business plan is a written document (usually 25 to 35 pages) that carefully explains every aspect of a new business venture. An entrepreneur provides the business plan to an investor or other interested party to describe why the business is starting and how it will make money. If properly prepared, the business plan also relays the passion and energy that the individuals who wrote the plan have for the proposed business venture.

This chapter begins our discussion of how to write a business plan. Although experts vary on the order of the topics in a business plan, most plans follow a fairly standard format. The first two steps in a business plan, the executive summary and the company description, will be discussed in this chapter, along with the title page, the table of contents, and how to select a name for a business. The executive summary and the company description are arguably the most important sections of a business plan because if the reader's interest isn't captured early on, the plan won't get read. The title page, the table of contents, and the name of a business are also important issues. A new venture's name is often the first thing that someone associates with the business, and the title page and table of contents are the first things people observe in a business plan. As a result, to get off to a good start, all of these items should be given careful consideration.

Two quick points before we get started. First, as mentioned in Chapter 1, a business plan should be written with extreme empathy for the reader. Most of the people who will read your plan are extremely busy, so it's important that the plan is clear, concise, and easy to follow. It should also be interesting—a topic that we'll stress throughout the book. If the plan is dull, contains too much jargon, or simply plods along, it's unlikely to get completely read. Second, remember that as your readers evaluate your plan, they're not only evaluating the plan, but they're forming judgments about you. If the plan looks sharp, reads well, is backed up by solid research, and has a professional and upbeat tone, it's easy for the reader to associate those same attributes with you. In contrast, if the plan has the opposite qualities, it may not matter how good the business idea is or how sharp you really are, the reader may simply tune out. Never underestimate the importance of this latter set of points. Even though a business plan explains how a new business will be set up, most readers realize that the plan will change and evolve and that the business may look very different a year from now than it does today. As a result, what's more important than the specific details of the plan, which will invariably change, is the sense of competence, passion, and attention to detail that it projects.

Now let's begin by looking at the cover page and table of contents.

COVER PAGE AND TABLE OF CONTENTS

As mentioned in Chapter 1, to make the best impression, a business plan should follow a conventional format. This advice starts with the cover page and the table of contents.

COVER PAGE

The cover page should include the name of the company, its street address, its e-mail address, its phone number (land based and cell), the date, the contact information for the lead entrepreneur, and the company's Web site address if it has one. This information should be centered at the top of the page. The bottom of the page should include information alerting the reader to the confidential nature of the plan. If the company already has a logo or trademark, it should be placed somewhere near the center of the page. If you have a Facebook page or Twitter account, you can place the applicable addresses near the top of the cover page, if they reflect positively on your potential business.

It may also be appropriate to place a sketch or photo of your product or service on the cover page if you have one and it looks sharp. In some instances, a generic stock photo will do. If you don't have one, many Web sites, such as INMAGINE, (www.inmagine.com), provide access to photos that can be downloaded for as less as $5.00. For example, if you plan to open a dance studio, many digital photos of ballerinas and other dancers are available at the INMAGINE site. Placing an image on your cover page that depicts the type of dancer your studio will train may make a valuable contribution to the plan.

The single most important item on the cover page is the contact information for the authors of the plan. You want to make it extremely easy for anyone reading the plan to be able to contact you.

TABLE OF CONTENTS

A table of contents should follow the cover page. It should list the main sections, subsections, and appendices to the plan along with their corresponding page numbers. The goal is to make it easy to find anything in the plan. Some plans include tabs, which makes it easier to go directly to a section. A carefully developed table of contents can draw attention to areas of the plan you want to emphasize. For example, if your business plan is for a restaurant, and you have several attractive sketches of what the exterior and interior of the restaurant will look like, creating a subsection labeled "artist depiction of what the restaurant will look like" under the appropriate section of the plan may cause someone who is glancing at the table of contents to turn directly to that part of the plan. These types of items are often overlooked in a quick perusal of a plan.

The table of contents for the Prime Adult Fitness business plan, which represents the format of the business plan described in this book, is provided in Figure 4-1. It's always a good idea to double-check the page numbers included in the table of contents to make sure they correspond with the page numbers in the plan before you send it out. It's easy to forget last-minute additions to the plan that can throw off the page numbers in the table of contents.

EXECUTIVE SUMMARY

The executive summary is the first item that appears in a business plan. This short overview of the entire plan provides a busy reader with everything that needs to be known about the new venture's distinctive nature. In many instances, an investor will first ask for a copy of the executive summary and will request a copy of the full business plan only if the executive summary is sufficiently convincing. The executive summary, then, is arguably the most important section of the business plan.[1] If it doesn't interest and excite the reader, it's unlikely that the reader will look any further.

The most important thing to remember when writing an executive summary is that it's not an introduction or a preface to the business plan. Instead, it is meant to be a summary of the plan itself. After reading the executive summary, the investor or other interested party should have a good sense of the entirety of the plan. The executive summary for Prime Adult Fitness is shown in Figure 4-2.

FORMAT

An executive summary shouldn't exceed two single-spaced pages. The cleanest format for an executive summary is to provide an overview of the business plan on a section-by-section basis, as shown previously in Figure 4-2. The topics should

FIGURE 4-1 Table of Contents (Prime Adult Fitness Business Plan)

be presented in the same order as they are presented in the plan. Two identical versions of the executive summary should be prepared—one that's part of the business plan and one that's a stand-alone document. The stand-alone document is used to accommodate people who ask to see the executive summary before they decide whether they want to see the full plan. Make sure to place your contact information on any stand-alone executive summaries that you send out.

FIGURE 4-2   Executive Summary (Prime Adult Fitness Business Plan)

Introduction
The fitness industry grew to over $25.9 billion in 2012, up substantially from 2007. The industry's growth has been driven largely by middle-aged and older people, who are increasingly concerned about their health and fitness. A gap in the industry is the lack of fitness centers that focus exclusively on people 50 years old and older, who prefer a different type of fitness experience than younger people. Prime Adult Fitness will fill that gap in Center Florida by opening a fitness center that focuses exclusively on that clientele.

Company Description
Prime Adult Fitness is proposing to operate a 21,600 square foot facility in Oviedo, Florida, a suburb of Orlando. Oviedo is an ideal community for the center—it has a higher percentage of older people with a higher income than national averages. The center will feature a carefully selected assortment of fitness machines, classes, and programs, all tailored specifically for people 50 years old and older. There will also be seminars and workshops on nutrition, sleep, neurobics (brain exercises), and similar topics.
    Designing and operating a fitness center for older people is a unique challenge. It requires an extreme sensitivity to their needs, both physical and emotional. As a result, the operations of the center will be geared to (1) providing an uplifting environment for the members, (2) providing high-quality classes and equipment, and (3) encouraging people to socialize and make Prime Adult Fitness one of the centerpieces of their lives.

Industry Analysis
Prime Adult Fitness will compete in the "Fitness and Recreational Sports Centers" industry (NAICS 71394). The $25.9 billion industry is in the growth stage of its life cycle. Growth is being driven primarily by an increased awareness of the importance of fitness and exercise. The industry's biggest challenge is competing for the leisure time of its customers.
    The industry is competitive. Fitness centers, on average, earn a net profit of 7.0 percent to 10.0 percent (IBISWorld, May, 2013). The key success factors are a good location, effective product promotion, providing appropriate equipment and maintaining it regularly, skilled employees that can demonstrate how to use the equipment, and a management team that can turn a profit.

Market Analysis
Prime Adult Fitness's trade area will be Seminole County, Florida, which is the county in which Oviedo is located. According to latest census bureau data, Seminole County, Florida has 425,000 residents, 37 percent of whom are 50 years old or older (157,250 people). A total of 75 percent of the county is in Prime Adult Fitness's trade area. That means that there are approximately 117,900 people (rounded to the nearest 100) 50 years old or older in Prime Adult Fitness's trade area. Nationwide, approximately 15 percent of people 50 years or older belong to a fitness center. This means that roughly 17,685 people in Prime Adult Fitness's trade area 50 years old or older currently belong to a fitness center.
    Prime Adult Fitness's membership and income goals are as follows:

Year	Membership Goal	Total Projected Income
2014	2,100 units	$1,690,398
2015	2,226 units	$2,416,514
2016	2,360 units	$2,561,955
2017	2,502 units	$2,716,124

The company, through focus groups and a study conducted by its Customer Advisory Board, believes that 50 percent of its membership will come from people who already

FIGURE 4-2 (continued)

belong to a fitness center, and 50 percent will be new members, drawn in by its unique concept. If 50 percent of its members come from the existing market, that means Prime Adult Fitness will need to enroll 1,113 people 50 years old or older who currently belong to another fitness center (6.29 percent of the total) and 1,113 people 50 years old or older who do not currently belong to a fitness center (based on 2015 projections). The company is confident that its membership goals are achievable.

Marketing Plan
The overall objective of Prime Adult Fitness's marketing strategy will be to make people 50 years old and older aware of the benefits of exercise, and to sell them on the idea of Prime Adult Fitness as the best place for them to either start or to continue exercising.
    The company's points of differentiation are as follows:

- Only fitness center in its target market exclusively for people 50 years old and older
- Strong emphasis placed on the social aspect of belonging to a fitness center
- Well-trained staff that cares about the needs and lives of older people

The company's promotional activities will include a mixture of traditional and grassroots marketing techniques. The company has established cobranding relationships with Central Florida Health Food and Oviedo Doctor's and Surgeon's Medical practice. Talks are currently under way to solidify the specifics of these relationships.

Management Team and Company Structure
A five-member management team is in place, led by cofounders Jeremy Ryan, age 46, and Elizabeth Sims, age 49. Ryan started a fitness franchise in South Florida and grew it to 38 units before selling to a larger company. He has 14 years of additional experience in the industry. Elizabeth Sims, who worked with Ryan in his former venture, is a CPA with more than 19 years of experience.
    Prime Adult Fitness has a five-member board of directors, a four-member board of advisors, and a 10-member customer advisory board.

Operations and Development Plan
Prime Adult Fitness has signed a seven-year lease, subject to funding, for the 21,600 square foot facility it plans to occupy. The lease includes an option to buy the facility at the end of the term.
    The 21,600 square foot building will require $1 million in retrofitting. Preliminary plans for the retrofitting have been developed by an architect experienced in designing buildings suitable for an older clientele. The retrofitting of the building will be done with extreme sensitivity to the company's target market.

Financial Projections
The business plan includes a full set of pro forma income statements, balances sheets, and cash flows (five years income statements and balance sheets, and four years cash flows). The company projects an operating loss for 2014 (its initial year of operations) and steady gains from that point forward. Projected ROS is 13.1 percent in 2015, 10.5 percent in 2016, and 11.3 percent in 2017. Net income is projected to be $317,740 in 2015 and $269,670 in 2016. The company will remain cash flow positive throughout its startup period.

Funding Sought
The company is seeking $515,000 in investment capital.

BUSINESS PLAN INSIGHT

Write the Pitch and Then Write the Plan

Guy Kawasaki, a well-know investor and entrepreneur, has an interesting theory about business plans and PowerPoint presentations (or pitches). Kawasaki says that the pitch should come before the plan. Here's what he means.

Many people, according to Kawasaki, write their business plan and then put together a PowerPoint presentation that's an abbreviated version of the plan. He sees that sequence as backward. Kawasaki thinks that it's best to put the PowerPoint presentation together first and then use it as a guide in writing the plan. Here's the rationale. Kawasaki is a big believer in trying things out. He tells entrepreneurs to develop a pitch, whether it's a PowerPoint presentation or another format, of their business idea and try it out in front of as many groups as possible before they write their business plan. Why? Because it's easier to revise a 15-slide PowerPoint presentation than a 25- to 35-page business plan. And you get immediate feedback on a pitch, whereas you're unlikely to get feedback on a business plan until it's finished.

Kawasaki makes a good point. Although you shouldn't let the pitch dictate your plan, any feedback you can get before the plan is written is a good idea. By putting together the first cut of your PowerPoint presentation before you write the plan, you have an ideal tool to solicit feedback and try out your plan before it's written. You'll also have a head start on preparing a polished PowerPoint overview of your plan when it's finished.

Guy Kawasaki writes a blog titled "How to Change the World," which is very colorful and focused on entrepreneurship and related issues. The blog is available at http://blog.guykawasaki.com.

Source: Guy Kawasaki Blog, "The Zen of Business Plans," posted January 21, 2006. The blog is available at http://blog.guykawasaki.com.

One thing, as mentioned in Chapter 1, to be prepared for is that an increasingly common practice among investors and others is to ask for a short PowerPoint overview of a business plan rather than an executive summary. Investors do this because clicking through a dozen or so slides is an even quicker way to size up a business idea than reading an executive summary. In these instances, the executive summary should be boiled down to the 10 to 15 slides that are usually requested. Tips for how to prepare PowerPoint slides to send or present to an investor are provided in Chapter 11. More information about the value of developing a PowerPoint overview of your business plan is provided in the following Business Plan Insight box.

Even though the executive summary appears at the beginning of the business plan, it should be written last. The plan itself will evolve as it's written, so not everything is known at the outset. In addition, if you write the executive summary first, you run the risk of trying to write a plan that fits the executive summary rather than thinking through each piece of the plan independently.[2]

CONTENT

Each section of the executive summary should contain a short synopsis of the material that's provided in the same section of the broader plan. To fit all of the material into two pages, each section must be crisp and concise. The section headings should be labeled in boldfaced type to allow them to stand out from the text.

The primary goal of an executive summary is to capture the reader's attention. To do this, the tone should be businesslike yet convey a sense of excitement and anticipation. Each section should be factual and well written and should show that you have conducted research to ensure that your assumptions are correct. You should avoid using a lot of technical or industry-specific jargon, unless you're writing for a very specific audience, such as a group of angel investors specializing in your industry. You should also try to connect with your readers on both an objective and an emotional level, if possible. For example, in the executive summary shown in Figure 4-2, we quote a 71-year-old man who participated in the buying intentions survey that we administered as part of our feasibility analysis. The heartfelt statement made by the man illustrates the value that he sees Prime Adult Fitness playing in his life. Statements like this can cause a reader to pause and think, "I bet there are a lot of people out there that think like that. Prime Adult Fitness just might be a hit."

It's also important that the first section of the executive summary, which covers the company description, begins by describing the opportunity and then shows how the proposed business meets the opportunity. For example, it's not very effective to start by saying something like "Prime Adult Fitness, incorporated in the state of Florida, will open a fitness center for people 50 years old and older. The center will feature exercise machines, classes, and other activities that are specifically designed for its clientele." This type of statement invites a "so what?" sort of response. It doesn't say anything about the fitness industry or the opportunities that exist. It only says what you want to do. A better way to start is to say something like, "The fitness center industry grew to over $25.9 billion in 2012, and is expected to continue to grow at a rate of 2.9% per year through 2018.[3] The industry's growth has been driven largely by middle-aged and older people, who are increasingly concerned about their health. A gap in the industry is a lack of fitness centers that focus exclusively on people 50 years and older, who prefer a different type of fitness center experience than younger people. Prime Adult Fitness will fill that gap in Central Florida by opening a fitness center that focuses exclusively on people 50 years old and older." This opening creates a better tone. It first describes the opportunity and then shows how Prime Adult Fitness will meet the opportunity.

Most experts recommend that if a new venture is seeking financing or funding, the executive summary should state the amount of funds being requested. Some plans will state how much equity a business is willing to surrender for a certain amount of investment capital. In these instances, the executive summary will conclude with a section labeled "Status and Offering" as shown earlier in the executive summary in Figure 4-2. The Prime Adult Fitness executive summary indicates that the firm is prepared to offer a 20 percent ownership position in exchange for a $515,000 investment. Some entrepreneurs are more leery about how much equity they are willing to surrender and leave their plans intentionally vague on this point.

COMPANY DESCRIPTION

The main body of the business plan begins with a general description of the company. Although at first glance this section may seem less critical than others, it is extremely important. It demonstrates to your reader that you know how to translate an idea into a business. There are also issues within this section that take a lot of thought and planning, such as your company's mission and its legal form of business ownership.

A company description for Prime Adult Fitness is provided in Figure 4-3. The description shows the major headings that are included in the section. The headings are labeled in boldfaced type to make them stand out from the text.

The company description should start with a brief introduction, which provides an overview of the company and reminds the reader of the reason it is starting. Demographic information should be also provided, including the names of the founders, the address of the company's headquarters, and contact information for the lead entrepreneur.

There are two important points to be mindful of as you start writing this section and prepare to tackle the rest of the plan. First, a business plan is at its core a story about an opportunity and how a person (or group of people) plans to start a business to take advantage of the opportunity. It's also about how the business plans to deliver value to its customers, compete in the marketplace, and make money. This basic storyline should be evident throughout the plan. If the story isn't consistent, or the plan is a hodgepodge of loosely related material, it will be ineffective. Second, you build credibility with your readers by backing up assumptions with facts and research. The Internet resources suggested in Chapter 2, along with the results of your feasibility analysis, should provide you ample information to validate your claims. For instance, there is no reason to make a statement like "the fitness industry is large and growing." This statement may be true, but it is insufficient. Exactly how big is the fitness industry? How much is it growing? What are industry experts saying about its future? Including this type of information strengthens your statements and builds credibility in your plan.

The following is a discussion of each of the five individual elements of the company description.

COMPANY HISTORY

The "Company History" section should be brief, but should explain where the idea for the company came from and the driving force behind its inception. If it is a startup, simply mention that the company is in its startup stage. If the story of where the idea for the company came from is interesting or heartfelt, tell it.

FIGURE 4-3 Company Description (Prime Adult Fitness Business Plan)

Introduction

Prime Adult Fitness is proposing to operate a 21,600 square foot fitness center, specifically for people 50 years old and older, in Oviedo, Florida, a suburb of Orlando. The center will pioneer a new concept in fitness—it will be for exclusively for people 50 years old and older.

Prime Adult Fitness's cofounders are Jeremy Ryan, age 46, and Elizabeth Sims, age 49. The company is located at 1990 Palm Drive, Oviedo, Florida. Jeremy Ryan can be reached by phone at 407-760-6325 or via e-mail at Jeremy@primeadultfitness.com

Company History

In the summer of 2012, Jeremy Ryan, a cofounder of Prime Adult Fitness, was making a presentation at a fitness industry conference in Atlanta. During the Q&A period following his presentation, a member of the audience asked, "Why isn't there a fitness center concept designed specifically for older people? Curves created a successful chain of fitness center just for women. Why not a fitness center just for older people?"

That question changed Jeremy Ryan's life. A longtime fitness industry veteran and advocate of fitness for older people, he had never thought of opening a fitness center exclusively for older people. In October, November, and December of 2012, a feasibility analysis was completed, which validated the idea for the center. On January 8, 2013, Prime Adult Fitness was incorporated.

Mission Statement

The mission of Prime Adult Fitness is to make exercise and fitness a vibrant and satisfying part of the lives of people who are 50 years old and older.

Tagline

The company's tagline, which will be an important part of its branding strategy, is "Meet Your Dreams." The tagline, which emerged from a focus group session, captures the essence of what fitness ultimately accomplishes for people of all ages. It helps people feel better, live longer, and lead more satisfying lives.

Product and Services

The design of the Prime Adult Fitness offering has been guided by the results of its feasibility analysis. To properly determine the interests and preferences of its potential clientele, in November 2012, the company distributed its concept statement and a questionnaire to a random sample of 196 people 50 years and older in its trade area. It has also conducted three focus groups.

Based on the results of these efforts and its ongoing research, Prime Adult Fitness will offer its members the following mix of programs and amenities:

- *Exercise Machines*. A full complement of exercise machines selected specifically for our clientele.
- *Fitness Classes and Programs*. Fitness classes and programs will be offered at various times during the day. The classes will include water aerobics, low impact land aerobics, yoga, Pilates, body sculpting, and several others. Nontraditional classes will also be offered, such as outdoor "walking" classes where members will walk in classes throughout Central Florida neighborhoods.
- *Seminars and Workshops*. Seminars and workshops will be offered on nutrition, sleep, neurobics (brain exercises), avoiding back and neck pain, aging with dignity, and other topics.
- *Massage and Physical Therapy*. Massage and physical therapy services, by fully certified personnel, will be offered at the center.

FIGURE 4-3 (continued)

- *Safety.* Attention to detail in regard to safety and support for the needs of older people will be evident throughout the center.
- *Emotional Support.* Prime Adult Fitness will feature a caring staff that is dedicated to meeting the needs of its older clientele in an uplifting, motivating, and fun atmosphere.

Current Status
Prime Adult Fitness is poised to commence operations on January 1, 2014. Since it was incorporated on January 8, 2013, the following milestones have been completed, and the following milestones remain to be completed for the company to start operations.

Milestones Completed:

- Feasibility analysis, prospect survey, and three focus groups completed
- Business plan completed
- Five-member management team in place
- Board of directors, general advisory board, and customer advisory board in place
- Seven-year lease, subject to funding, signed on 21,600 square foot building
- $325,000 invested by management team
- $175,000 invested by angel investor
- $60,000 grant obtained from Healthy After 50, an organization supportive of the mission and goals of Prime Adult Fitness

Milestones Remaining to Be Completed:

- Obtain additional funding (see specifics below)
- Retrofit building
- Select exercise equipment, plan programs and classes, hire personnel
- Prepare for grand opening

Funding Sought
As described in detail in the business plan, Prime Adult Fitness is seeking $515,000 in investment capital.

Legal Status and Ownership
Prime Adult Fitness is a Limited Liability Corporation incorporated in the state of Florida. It is currently owned by its management team and angel investor. A detailed schedule of ownership is provided in the "Management Team and Company Structure" section of the plan.

For example, in Chapter 2, we introduced Laura Udall, the mother who created the ZUCA, a backpack on rollers that provides an alternative for school-aged kids who carry heavy backpacks to school every day. Ms. Udall created the company after her fourth-grade daughter complained daily that her back hurt from carrying her backpack. Udall's story is interesting and is one that anyone can relate to. It might even cause the person reading the plan to pause and think, "When I leave for work in the morning, I frequently see kids in my neighborhood walking to the bus stop and often notice the huge backpacks they're carrying. I imagine the backpack do hurt kids' backs. I bet moms and dads would go for an alternative to that!" By telling a story, you place a human face on the business plan and potentially connect with readers on an emotional level.

If you don't have an interesting story to tell, you can talk briefly about how your idea will meet a compelling need. If the company has been in business for a while, you should provide a brief timeline in narrative form and talk about its major achievements. You should also talk about its history of revenues, net income, and sales growth.

MISSION STATEMENT

A mission statement defines why a company exists and what it aspires to become.[4] If carefully written and used properly, a mission statement can define the path a company takes and act as its financial and moral compass. For a business plan, a well-written mission statement demonstrates that your business is focused and you can articulate its purpose clear and distinctly.

The trick to writing an effective mission statement is to articulate the mission or purpose of the company in as few words as possible. A short mission statement is easier to remember than a longer one and is usually more effective. The mission statement should also be more than empty words. It should be the driving force behind the company and the major decisions that it makes. Many resources are available on the Internet and elsewhere that provide advice for how to write an effective mission statement. Several rules of thumb for writing an effective mission statement are as follows. Your mission statement should

- Not be a mini-overview of the business
- Describe what makes your company different
- Be honest—don't claim to be something you aren't
- Convey passion and stick in the mind of the reader
- Define your "reason for being"
- Be risky and challenging but achievable
- Use a tone that best reflects your company's culture
- Be something that everyone involved with the firm can relate to
- Involve everyone on your team in its creation

Examples of several mission statements are shown in Table 4-1.

Along with a mission statement, some companies have mottos or taglines that are effective in conveying their purpose and building the brand. Examples of famous mottos or taglines include Google—"Don't be evil"; Nike—"Just do It!"; and Nokia—"Connecting people." Some companies, such as Nike and Nokia, have built their entire branding campaigns around their taglines. If your company has a motto or tagline, it should be mentioned in this section of the plan.

TABLE 4-1 Examples of Mission Statements

Facebook

Facebook's mission is to make the world more open and connected.

Starbucks

Our mission is to inspire and nurture the human spirit—one person, one cup, and one neighborhood at a time.

New Balance

New Balance aims to become recognized as the world's leading manufacturer of high-performance footwear and apparel, by conducting our internal and external relationships to three core values—Teamwork, Total Customer Satisfaction, and Integrity.

Amazon.com

We seek to be Earth's most customer-centric company for four primary customer sets: consumers, sellers, enterprises, and content creators.

Twitter

To instantly connect people everywhere to what's most important to them.

There is no set procedure for how to come up with a mission statement or tagline. Often, the founders and early employees of a company get together and simply brainstorm ideas. The following anecdote about how Google came up with the motto "Don't be evil" may be helpful to you in thinking about how to come up with a mission statement or motto for your company. In July 2001, as Google was becoming larger, and the founders were worried that it might lose its corporate identity, Stacy Sullivan, the head of Google's HR department, rounded up a cross section of employees with the mission of clarifying Google's core values. According to a well-regarded book on the early history of Google, titled "The Search: How Google and Its Rivals Rewrote the Rules of Business and Transformed Our Culture" by John Battelle, the meeting sputtered some, as the people in the room suggested generic clichés like "treat everyone with respect" and "be on time for meetings." The following picks up the description of the meeting directly from the book:

> The engineers in the room were rolling their eyes. Patel (a Google employee) recalls: "Some of us were very anticorporate, and we didn't like the idea of all of these specific rules. And engineers in general like efficiency—there had to be a way to say all these things in one statement, as opposed to being so specific." That's when Paul Buchheit, another engineer in the group, blurted out what would become the most important three words in Google's corporate history. Paul said, "All of these things can be covered by just saying, Don't be evil," Patel recalls. "And it just kind of stuck."[5]

The story goes on to explain that to reinforce the phrase, Patel scribbled "Don't be evil" in the corner of nearly every whiteboard in the company. The phrase caught on and became the rallying cry for Google's employees. Commenting on the importance of "Don't be evil," which is still prominent at Google today, Larry Page, one of the company's cofounders, said, "When you are making a decision, it causes you to think. I think that's good."[6]

PRODUCTS AND SERVICES

The "Products and Services" section should include an explanation of your product or service, beyond what you said in the executive summary. Include a description of how your product or service is unique and how you plan to position it in the marketplace. A product or service's position is how it is situated relative to its rivals. If you plan to open a new type of coffee shop, for example, you should explain how your coffee shop differs from others and how it will be positioned in its market in terms of the products it offers, its location, and its price range. You should also identify who your clientele will be and why they would patronize your coffee shop instead of Starbucks or another existing chain.

The product/service description is the ideal place for you to start reporting the results of your feasibility analysis. If the concept test and buying intentions survey produced meaningful results, they should be reported here. It's appropriate to allow your reader insight into how you shaped the ideas for your product or service and how you determined its positioning strategy. For example, in the coffee shop example, you might report, "A concept statement that outlined the company's initial business concept was distributed to 10 industry experts and 10 potential customers. The feedback suggested that we should broaden our product line in select areas. As a result, we plan to complement our menu of coffee, tea, specialty coffees, lattes, and desserts with bottled drinks such as Honest Tea and Jones Soda and a limited line of smoothies. To affirm our revised business concept, we queried a new set of 5 industry experts 10 potential customers and who responded very favorably to our expanded product mix for our upscale target market."

You should explain any proprietary aspects to your product or service and the extent to which you have protected your intellectual property. If your product is patentable, at the minimum, you should seek the advice of a patent attorney about filing a provisional patent application, which grants "provisional rights" for up to one year. If there is nothing proprietary about your product or service, you should briefly mention how you will create barriers to entry to prevent it from being quickly copied. Without adequate barriers to entry, it will be easy for a larger competitor to copy what you are doing. This later point raises an important issue. The realization that your product or service idea can be copied by a larger competitor, absent any intellectual property protection, will be recognized by a savvy reader of the plan. At exactly this type of juncture, your business plan either gains or loses credibility. If you duck the issue and say nothing, you'll lose credibility. The reader of the plan will know that a lack of barriers to entry could be a huge problem for your firm and will notice that you didn't address it. In contrast, if you confront the issue head-on and offer a plausible explanation or say that an inability to create barriers to entry is a major risk, you'll gain credibility. You should also think creatively about risk. In some cases, introducing a product or service that is likely to attract the interest of larger firms is just what you want. It may make your company an attractive acquisition target and provide a liquidity event for your investors. The overarching point is that you must confront difficult issues head-on and offer plausible explanations or disclose major risks. If you don't, your business plan will lose credibility quickly.

CURRENT STATUS

The "Current Status" section should reveal how far along your company is in its development. A good way to frame this discussion is to think in terms of milestones. If you have selected and registered your company's name, completed a feasibility analysis, written a business plan, and established a legal entity, you have already cleared several important milestones. Any similar activities that you have accomplished or about to accomplish should be mentioned.

Three issues are particularly important for this section: the current composition of your management team, early customer reaction to your product or service, and your company's financial status. In regard to your management team, if you're an early-stage venture, and the company consists of just you or a small group of people, that's okay, but you should mention your future staffing plans. If you've put together or are putting together a board of advisors, you should mention that. In regard to your product or service, if you have conducted a feasibility analysis and have feedback from potential customers, you should summarize any results that indicate how enthused people are about your product idea and how close it is to being marketable. Similarly, if you have attended trade shows or have solicited feedback on your product or service idea in a similar way, you should report the results.

Finally, in regard to the financial status of your company, your readers will want to know how the company has been funded up to this point, and if you have any debt or have surrendered any equity in the firm. If you are seeking funding, briefly indicate how much funding you are seeking and for what purpose. You'll be able to expand on all of these points in the financial section of the plan.

LEGAL STATUS AND OWNERSHIP

The "Legal Status and Ownership" section should indicate who owns the business, how the ownership is split up if more than one individual is involved, and whether a founder's agreement has been set up. A founders' agreement (or shareholders' agreement) is a written document that deals with issues such as the relative split of the equity among the founders of the firm, how individual founders will be compensated for the "sweat equity" they put into the firm, and how long the founders will have to remain with the firm for their shares to be vested. If you don't have a founders' agreement (and more than one founder is involved), you should indicate that this step is pending to alert the reader that you are thinking about it and recognize its importance.

You should also indicate what your current form of business ownership is. If you've done nothing in this regard, you're a sole proprietorship or a general partnership by default, which is an untenable position for any length of time. A much better choice is to form a subchapter S corporation, a C corporation, or a Limited Liability Company (LLC). You should retain an attorney to help you resolve this manner. Again, if you haven't selected a form of business ownership, you should at the minimum state that this matter is pending to alert your reader that you understand the importance of this task.

The next section of the chapter deals with selecting the name for a business. This discussion is included here because selecting a name for a business is an activity that often goes hand in hand with feasibility analysis and the early stages of preparing a business plan. It is also an issue that makes a lot of difference for a firm, so should be considered carefully.

SELECTING THE NAME FOR A BUSINESS

Although selecting a name for a business isn't part of the formal business planning process, it's an important activity. A company's name is normally the first thing that people associate with a business, and it's the term they'll type into their computer, smartphone, or GPS if they want to find you. It is also an integral part of a company's branding strategy. A company's brand is the unique set of attributes that allow consumers to separate it from its competitors. As a result, it is important for a business to choose its name carefully so that it will facilitate rather than hinder how the business plans to differentiate itself in the marketplace. You don't want someone mentally questioning the wisdom of your company's name before they even start reading the business plan.[7]

PRIMARY CONSIDERATION IN NAMING A BUSINESS

The primary consideration in naming a business is that the name should complement the type of business the company plans to be. It is helpful to divide companies into four categories to discuss this issue.

CUSTOMER-DRIVEN COMPANIES

If a company plans to focus on a particular type of consumer, its name should reflect the attributes of its clientele. For example, an online store that sells clothing for big and tall men and boys is named Big and Tall Guys (www.bigandtallguys.com). Similarly, a company that installs cameras in day care centers and allows parents to log on to a password-protected Web site to see their children during the day is called ParentWatch (www.parentwatch.com). These companies have names that were chosen to appeal specifically to their target market or clientele.

PRODUCT- OR SERVICE-DRIVEN COMPANIES

If a company plans to focus on a particular product or service, its name should reflect the advantages that its product or service provide. Examples include 1-800-FLOWERS, SiriusXM Radio, Whole Foods Markets, and Jiffy Print. These companies have names that were chosen to reflect the distinctive attributes of the product or service the company offers, regardless of the clientele.

INDUSTRY-DRIVEN COMPANIES

If a company plans to focus on a broad range of products or services in a particular industry, its name should reflect the category it is participating in. Examples include General Motors, Linens N Things, Kraft Foods, and Home Depot. These companies have names that are intentionally broad and are not limiting in regard to a target market or a product selection.

PERSONALITY- OR IMAGE-DRIVEN COMPANIES

Some companies are founded by individuals who put such an indelible stamp on the company that it may be smart to name the company after its founder. Examples include Ben & Jerry's Homemade, Charles Schwab, Dell Inc., Liz Claiborne, and Magic Johnson Enterprises. These companies have names that benefit from a positive association with a popular or distinctive founder. Of course, this strategy can backfire if the founder falls out of favor in the public eye.

LEGAL ISSUES

Many legal issues are involved in naming a business, and these should be addressed before the business plan is finalized. The general rule for business names is that they must be unique. In other words, in most instances, there may not be more than one business per name per state. In addition, a new business may not adopt a name that is confusingly similar to an existing business. This regulation prevents a new overnight delivery company from naming itself FedExtra, for example, which FedEx would undoubtedly claim is confusingly similar to its name.

There are three steps that must be taken to make sure that the name you select hasn't already been taken and is available for use. These steps are shown in Table 4-2. There are consequences for now following proper procedures. If a business selects a name and finds out that it's already been legally taken, the business may have to (1) amend its articles of incorporation, (2) change its Internet domain name, (3) obtain new listings in telephone and other directories, (4) redo signage, advertising copy, stationary, and business cards, and (5) incur the expense and potential embarrassment of introducing a new name to its customers.

The process of finding a name for a business can be frustrating because the most obvious names are often already taken. For example, if you wanted to start a quick printing company, almost every possible combination of the names "quick" and "print" are taken. These combinations include quick-print, jiffy-print, instant-print, swift-printing, fast-print, and so on. A complicating factor is getting an Internet domain name that is the same as a company's name. Because no two domain names can be exactly the same, frustrations often arise when a company tries to register its domain name, and the name has already been taken. Still, a little imagination goes a long way in selecting a company name and an Internet domain name. For instance, the Internet domain name for Prime Adult Fitness (www.primeadultfitness.com) was available so we registered it on Godaddy.com.

TABLE 4-2 How to Find out if a Name for Business is Already Taken

1. Go to the United States Patent and Trademark (USPTO) Web site at www.uspto. gov. Click on the link labeled "Trademark Search." Enter the name you've picked for your business. If the name has already been taken, you'll have to select another name.

2. Visit the secretary of state's Web site for the state in which you'd like to register your business. Find the area labeled Business Services, Business Filing Center, or something similar to that. Type in the name of your business. If the name has already been taken, you'll have to find another name.

3. In some states, there is not a statewide search engine for business names. If this is the case for your state, check with your municipal government (if you live in a city or town) or your county government (if you live in the country) to make sure your business name hasn't already been taken.

Source: Adapted from B. Barringer, *Launching a Business The First 100 Days* (New York: Business Expert Press, 2013).

You must also be careful to pick a name that won't be a problem in a foreign culture if your business expands. The classic example of this is the Chevy NOVA. After much advertising and fanfare, the car received a very cool reception in Mexico. It turned out that the phrase *No Va* in Spanish means "Doesn't go." Not surprisingly, the NOVA didn't sell well in Mexico.

A brief mention should be made in the business plan that a company's name has been registered and trademarked, and that the Internet domain name has been secured. If these activities have not been completed, you should mention that they are pending so the reader of the plan knows you are aware of their importance.

Chapter Summary

1. The executive summary and the company description are arguably the most important sections of a business plan because if the reader's interest isn't captured early on, the plan is unlikely to get read.

2. The cover page should include the name of the company, its street address, its e-mail address, its phone number (land based and cell), the date, the contact information for the lead entrepreneur, and the company's Web site address if it has one. It can also include the company's logo and Facebook address and Twitter account if applicable.

3. The table of contents should follow the cover page and should list the main sections, subsections, and appendices to the plan along with their corresponding page numbers.

4. The executive summary is the first item that appears in a business plan. It is a short overview of the entire plan that provides a busy reader with everything about the new venture's distinctive nature.

5. The most important thing to remember when writing an executive summary is that it's not an introduction or a preface to the business plan. Instead, it is meant to be a summary of the plan itself.

6. Even though the executive summary appears at the beginning of the business plan, it should be written last. The plan itself will evolve as it's written, so not everything is known at the outset.

7. The main body of the business plan begins with a general description of the company. Although at first glance this section may seem less critical than others, it is extremely important. It demonstrates to your reader that you know how to translate an idea into a business.

8. The subsections under the Company Description category are Company History, Mission Statement, Products and Services, Current Status, and Legal Status and Ownership. It is best to follow this order.

9. A mission statement defines why a company exists and what it aspires to become.

10. The primary consideration in naming a business is that the name should complement the type of business the company plans to be.

Review Questions

1. Why is it important for a business plan to have a cover page? What information should the cover page contain?

2. What is it important for a business plan to have a table of contents? What are the attributes of an effective table of contents?

3. What is an executive summary? Why is it often called the most important part of a business plan?

4. At what point in the process of putting together a business plan should the executive summary be written?

5. Why would in investor ask for a PowerPoint overview of a business plan rather than an executive summary or the full plan?

6. Explain the statement "the primary goal of an executive summary is to capture the reader's attention."

7. What are the subsections that are included under the company description section of a business plan?

8. What is the purpose of a mission statement? Why is it important to include a mission statement in a business plan?

9. To what extent should the results of a company's feasibility analysis be reported in its business plan?

10. Why is selecting a company's name a critical issue?

Application Questions

1. Sarah Austin, who has worked with disabled children all of her professional career, is in the final stretch of developing an iPhone app that will help parents with disabled children better cope with their disabilities. She has put a considerable amount of time and effort into the project, and believes the app can make a meaningful difference in the lives of those who use it. Sarah has a dilemma. She had planned to spend the next three weeks completing

a feasibility analysis and incorporating the results of the feasibility analysis into her business plan, which she thinks will take an additional two weeks. An alternative is to move forward with the business plan and complete the feasibility analysis later. Sarah has heard that several competing apps are in various stages of development, and fears that if she doesn't get her business plan completed quickly and out for review she may get beat to the punch. What would you tell Sarah if she asked you for your advice?

2. Write a mission statement for ZUCA (www.zuca.com), the backpack (and suitcase) on wheels company mentioned in several chapters of this book. How can this statement help define the path that ZUCA takes and act as the company's financial and moral compass?

3. Suppose you have been asked by your local newspaper to write a 400-word article about the importance of writing a business plan and how to start the process. Please write a 400-word article about the importance of writing a business plan and how to begin the process.

4. Scott and Rebecca Wheeler's youngest daughter, Emily, has struggled with asthma since she was born. In caring for Emily over the years, Rebecca designed and made a variety of cards, posters, notes, and even decorated lunch bags that encouraged Emily, educated her about her condition, and reminded her to take her medicine on time. Scott and Rebecca are in a support group for parents with asthmatic children, and many of the parents have encouraged Rebecca to start a company to make the items she made for Emily available to other parents. Rebecca has decided to go for it and is writing a business plan for the company. One thing she's unsure about is how much of her personal story to include in the plan. Should she talk about how she developed the items for her own daughter, Emily, or should she stick to the facts? If Rebecca asked you for your advice, what would you tell her?

5. Suggest an alternative name for the fictitious fitness club, Prime Adult Fitness, discussed in the chapter. The Internet domain name must be available for the alternative name that you suggest. Explain the rationale for the name you choose.

Endnotes

1. B. Barringer and R. D. Ireland, *Successfully Launching New Businesses*, 4th ed. (Upper Saddle River, NJ: Pearson, 2012).
2. B. Ford, J. Bornstein, and P. Pruitt, *The Ernst & Young Business Plan Guide*, 3rd ed. (New York: John Wiley & Sons, 2007).
3. D. Schmidt, *IBISWorld Industry Report 71394 Gym, Health & Fitness Clubs in the US*, May 2013.
4. J. Barney and W. Hesterly, *Strategic Management and Competitive Advantage* (Upper Saddle River, NJ: Prentice Hall, 2006).
5. J. Battelle, *The Search How Google and Its Rivals Rewrite the Rules of Business and Transformed Our Culture* (New York: Portfolio, 2005), 138.
6. Ibid.
7. P. Pakroo, *The Small Business Start-Up Kit*, 7th ed. (Berkeley, CA: Nolo, 2012).

CHAPTER 5

INDUSTRY ANALYSIS

INTRODUCTION

An industry is a group of firms producing a similar product or service, such as airplanes, smartphones, fitness club memberships, or online education. Industries vary along many dimensions, including size, growth rate, structure, financial characteristics, and overall attractiveness. The trends affecting an industry also matter. For example, as the U.S. population ages, the growth of the fitness center industry is likely to depend increasingly on its ability to attract and retain people 50 years old and older. Fitness centers that are on top of this trend and adjust accordingly are likely to outperform those that aren't.

This chapter introduces and describes the industry analysis portion of the business plan. It's important that this section focus *strictly* on a firm's industry rather than its industry and its target market simultaneously. A firm's target market is the limited portion of an industry that it goes after or tries to appeal to at a certain point in time. Most firms do not try to service their entire industry. Instead, they focus on serving a specialized portion of the market well. Prime Adult Fitness's target market within the fitness industry are people 50 years old and older.

Separating the analysis of a firm's industry and its target market is important because it's premature for a new firm to select, or even talk about, a specific target market until an understanding of the broader industry is obtained. For example, if you were interested in starting a company to produce a new type of pesticide for orange trees, your target market would be orange growers. But before you make the decision to pursue that market, you should understand the pesticide industry in general. Is the industry large or small? Is it growing or shrinking? Is it dominated by large firms or small firms? Are firms in the industry making or losing money? What impact is organic farming or new environmental regulations having on pesticide sales? The answers to these and similar questions will determine whether the pesticide industry in general is an attractive industry to enter, and which segments within the industry offer the most promise. Your analysis will also give you a read on whether starting a firm to target orange growers is a good idea or whether other segments within the pesticide industry have greater potential.

The industry analysis should appear early in a business plan because it logically precedes the analysis of a firm's target market and marketing strategy. It also helps set up and support the remainder of the plan. The analysis normally includes, for example, an indication of the average growth in sales for the firms in an industry. This information helps a firm construct its own financial forecasts and justify its numbers. Similarly, the other major portions of a firm's plan, such as product selection, target market, and operations plan, are guided by the industry's characteristics and trends. For example, the increase in the number of home care businesses is tied directly to factors and trends in the broader health care market. Home care providers service patients who need periodic nursing care or treatments and can (and prefer) to receive this support in their homes rather than more expensive hospitals or skilled nursing facilities. The factors and trends spurring growth in the home care industry include the following:[1]

- The aging of the population, which is steadily increasing the number of people who need home care services

- The unfortunate prevalence of chronic disease, such as Alzheimer's, cancer, and diabetes, which in many cases requires consistent treatments

- Growing physician acceptance of home care as an alternative to placing patients in hospitals or skilled nursing facilities

- The affordability of home health care in comparison to other options, particularly inpatient hospital care

- Increasing preference among people who need consistent medical care to be treated in their homes rather than in a hospital or other facility

- Changes in family structures, which affects the availability of people to care for family members and subsequently impact the need for outside help

Together, these factors and trends point directly toward opportunities for additional startups to enter the home health care industry and provide differentiated services. For example, Florence Night and Day (www.florence-nightandday.com), which operates in Oklahoma, is not only a home care provider but also provides related services such as help with activities of daily living, medication reminders, safety monitoring, and transportation to doctor's appointments.

Now let's look at the first major section in an industry analysis and why it's important.

INDUSTRY DEFINITION

The first section of the industry analysis should briefly (no more than several sentences long) describe the firm's industry. The NAICS code should be provided. The older SIC system was replaced by the NAICS in 1997, although SIC codes are still used. The NAICS systems expanded the number of industry sections from 10 to 20 to reflect the broader number of industries that have come into existence. For the majority of business plans, it is sufficient to report the NAICS code. NAICS is a two- through six-digit hierarchical classification code system. Each digit in the code is part of a series of progressively narrower categories. The organization that supervises NAICS codes hosts a powerful search engine at www.naics.com, to help businesses identify their NAICS code. For example, if you type "fitness centers" into the search box you will find that the NAICS code for the fitness center industry is 713950.

Although it may seem like identifying a company's industry is a simple task, it's actually a tough call in many instances. A firm's industry can be defined narrowly or broadly. For instance, is Prime Adult Fitness in the fitness center industry or the recreation industry? Is JetBlue in the airline industry or the transportation industry? The distinction is important because it defines the scope of a company's industry analysis and helps identify its overall sphere of concern. The most practical approach for a business plan is to define a company's industry narrowly and include an analysis of the trends that influence broader industry categories if necessary. In the illustrations in this chapter, Prime Adult Fitness defines itself narrowly as part of the Fitness and Recreational Sports Center Industry (NAICS 713950). In a subsequent part of its industry analysis, it could have provided an analysis of trends of the broader industry—Arts, Entertainment, and Recreation (NAICS 71), but it wasn't necessary in this instance.

If your firm operates in two or more industries, you should identify all the industries that it participates in, and recognize that you will need to conduct an industry analysis for each of the industries. For example, if a company makes computer software for doctor's offices, it should state that it operates in the computer software industry and the health care industry and provide an industry analysis for both industries. Some discretion is allowed regarding the weight placed on the individual analyses. In some instances, when a firm operates in more than one industry, it may be appropriate to conduct a full analysis on the primary industry the firm operates in and an abbreviated analysis on the other.

The best Internet resources to assist in helping identify industries, and in completing all sections of the industry analysis, are IBISWorld, Bizminer, and Mintel. All three of these resources are available free through most university library Web sites. They are also highlighted in the Internet Resources Table in Appendix 2.2 at the end of Chapter 2. IBISWorld, in particular, provides a 20- to 40-page analysis for nearly every industry at the five-digit NAICS code level. Each analysis starts with a very distinct description of the respective industry, which may be helpful to you in completing this section of your business plan.

The Prime Adult Fitness industry definition is shown in Figure 5-1.

FIGURE 5-1 Industry Definition (Prime Adult Fitness Business Plan)

Prime Adult Fitness will compete in the "Fitness and Recreational Sports Centers in the US" industry (NAICS 71394 and SIC 7991). The industry comprises establishments engaged in fitness instruction and facilities management. Well-known companies in the industry include 24 Hour Fitness, Life Time Fitness, and Bally Total Fitness. The industry includes fitness centers and specialized facilities such as tennis centers, swimming pools, ice and roller rinks, and dance studios. The largest segment of the industry, fitness centers, represents 65 percent of industry revenues.

INDUSTRY SIZE, GROWTH RATE, AND SALES PROJECTIONS

This section of the industry analysis briefly discusses the size (in dollars), the growth rate (in percent), and future sales projections for the industry or industries your firms will be entering. It's important that this section consist of more than just numbers. Unless you are defining a relatively new industry, such as the smartphone app industry, the numbers are fairly easy to find. The key is to make sense of the numbers and present them in a way that builds the credibility of your business plan.

There are four general rules of thumb for completing this section. First, you should always display financial information, such as industry sales and growth rate, in a multiyear format, making it easy to spot trends. Reporting a single number, such as "the women's clothing store industry generated $42.1 billion in sales in 2012,"[2] is insufficient. In addition to that figure, your reader wants to know whether industrywide sales are growing or declining, and the rate of growth or decline. The best approach is to report three to five years of industrywide sales and industrywide growth rates. Always provide a citation for where your information came from.

The second rule of thumb is to display your information graphically if possible. Guy Kawasaki, the entrepreneur and investor introduced earlier in the book, has said that one of the most effective ways to make a business plan stand out is to include diagrams and graphics.[3] There is a risk in overdoing this, but supplementing the raw data for industrywide sales and sales growth with attractive graphs that visually depict the same data is an ideal opportunity.

The third rule of thumb is to provide information about your industry on a regional or local basis if appropriate. You don't need to go into detail—an analysis of your target market and competitors is provided in the next section of the plan, covered in Chapter 6. Still, in many industries, industrywide sales are not evenly distributed across the United States. In these instances, it might be of interest to your readers to know where the majority of the sales take place and where the largest increase or decrease in sales is expected.

The final rule of thumb is to avoid the temptation to report only positive or flattering information about your industry. This approach not only undermines the credibility of your plan, but it also is not intellectually honest. The numbers that are reported should also be viewed in their proper context. Just because an industry's numbers aren't glowing doesn't mean that good opportunities aren't available. Many average industries have product or service gaps that provide exciting opportunities for new businesses. If you believe that your company has the potential to outperform the average companies in its industry, state your industry's numbers fairly and honestly, regardless of how poor they look, and in the "trends" portion of the industry analysis, start laying the groundwork for why a company like yours might outperform the industry. You will have the opportunity in the next section of your business plan to describe your specific target market and the promise it offers.

The industry size, growth rate, and sales projection portion of the Prime Adult Fitness industry analysis is shown in Figure 5-2.

INDUSTRY SIZE

An industry's size is normally displayed in dollars over a three- to five-year period, as shown in the Prime Adult Fitness industry analysis in Figure 5-2. Some business plans also report the number of firms in their industry. The ideal size of an industry for a startup is large enough to allow different competitors to serve different segments profitably but small enough that it isn't attracting the immediate attention of larger potential competitors. There are no good rules of thumb or heuristics for what this size is—it's strictly a judgment call.

If your industry is broken down into easily identifiable segments, it may be appropriate to report the share (in percentage) of each segment. For example, the $42.1 billion women's clothing industry is broken down as shown in Table 5-1.[4]

IBISWorld provides this information on industries that are identified by NAICS codes. It's a judgment call as to whether this level of detail is appropriate for your plan.

Some plans also report the contribution that a specific industry makes to its larger industry sector. For example, for Prime Adult Fitness, the industry it will participate in, Fitness and Recreational Sports Centers (NAICS 71394), generated 13.7 percent of the sales of its larger industry sector, Arts, Entertainment, and Recreational Services (NAICS 71).

INDUSTRY GROWTH RATE

An industry's growth rate should be reported on a percentage basis, as shown in the Prime Adult Fitness industry analysis in Figure 5-2. You should provide an interpretation of what the numbers mean. There are many ways to do this. Some plans comment on how the industry growth rate compares to similar industries. Note that in its industry analysis, Prime Adult Fitness compares the growth rate

FIGURE 5-2   Industry Size, Growth Rate, and Sales Projections (Prime Adult Fitness Business Plan)

Industry Size

	2009	2010	2011	2012	2013
Industry Sales	$23.7 billion	$24.2 billion	$24.8 billion	$25.3 billion	$25.9 billion
Number of Establishments	32,864	32,820	33,068	33,385	33,527
Employment	536,231	527,086	548,375	561,536	573,328

Industry Growth Rates

	2009	2010	2011	2012	2013
Industry Sales	–1.8%	2.2%	2.3%	2.0%	2.5%
Number of Establishments	–1.8%	–0.1%	0.8%	1.0%	0.4%
Employment	–2.6%	–1.7%	4.0%	2.4%	2.1%

Industry Sales Projections

	2014	2015	2016
Industry Sales	$26.5 billion	$27.3 billion	$28.3 billion
Growth Rate	2.4%	3.1%	3.3%

Graphs

Source for all information: IBISWorld, May, 2013.

Summary
The industry is in the growth phase of its life cycle. Growth is being driven primarily by an increased awareness of the importance of fitness and exercise. The industry's biggest challenge is competing for the leisure time of its customers. Time-strapped customers are less likely to frequent a fitness club or other recreational sports centers.

The largest segment of the industry, fitness centers, is growing at a more rapid rate than the industry as a whole. According to IBISWorld (May 2013), fitness center memberships have risen from 46.4 million in 2003 to more than 52.6 million in 2013, a 13 percent increase. Although the industry is not recession proof, it has remained remarkably resilient through economic swings. As a result of both the psychological and health benefits that result from exercise, many people now view membership in a fitness center to be a necessity rather than a discretionary good.

The Fitness and Recreational Sports Centers industry is growing at a faster rate than three industries that compete for its customer's dollars—Sporting and Athletic Goods Manufacturing (which makes home fitness equipment), Golf Course and Country Clubs, and Marinas.

TABLE 5-1 Women's Clothing Store Industry Breakdown

Segment	Percent of Sales
Tops (including t-shirts, shirts, blouses, and sweaters)	32.0%
Pants, jeans, shorts, and skirts	24.0%
Dresses	18.0%
Coats, jackets, and suits	17.0%
Sports apparel (including swimwear, sweat tops, etc.)	6.0%
Other apparel	3.0%

of its industry, fitness centers, to three industries that compete for its industry's dollars—Athletic and Sporting Goods Manufacturing (which makes home fitness equipment), Golf Courses and Country Clubs, and Marinas. The fact that Prime Adult Fitness's industry is growing faster than these competing industries is a positive sign. Although you don't want to cherry-pick information that places your industry in a positive light relative to others, you do want your reader to share your enthusiasm for the industry you are about to enter. Prime Adult Fitness's favorable comparison of its industry to others is an appropriate way of doing that.

If you are defining an industry, such as smartphone apps, that isn't being actively tracked by a reliable source (e.g., IBISWorld), finding good sales data requires creativity and persistence. It normally involves searching for newspaper or magazine articles that report the industry's sales and sales growth or finding an industry trade association that tracks and reports the numbers. Mintel, one of the databases mentioned earlier, in an appendix to each of its industry analyses, provides the names, phone numbers, and Web site addresses of the major trade associations related to a particular industry. If you define a new industry you could search the industry analyses of related industries that Mintel follows to try to find a trade association that might track smartphone app sales as part of its larger mission. You could then call or e-mail the trade association to ask if it tracks smartphone app sales or to ask where to find the information.

A fuller list of suggestions for how to track down sales and sales–growth data for a newly defined industry, such as the smartphone apps industry, is provided in the Business Plan Insights box.

INDUSTRY SALES PROJECTIONS

This section should report future sales projections for your industry. If you are reporting on an established industry, IBISWorld and similar sources report their predictions. You can quote from these reports, but you should do so sparingly. Most of the readers of your plan are more interested in what you think than in what IBISWorld thinks. As indicated earlier in the book, a business plan not only lays out facts, but it also demonstrates to your reader how you think and interpret data.

╔══════════════════════╗
BUSINESS PLAN INSIGHTS
╚══════════════════════╝

Finding Industry Sales Data by Knocking On Doors

If you're defining a new industry, such as smartphone apps, one challenge you'll encounter is finding good sales data and sales–growth information. In these cases, finding the information becomes somewhat of a scavenger hunt. And like in a scavenger hunt, a willingness to knock on doors and dogged determination make a big difference.

Here are some suggestions of the doors you might metaphorically knock on to get sales data and sales–growth information for the smartphone app industry. Your industry might be much different from the smartphone app industry, but the types of resources included in this list represent a good place to start:

- Type "smartphone app industry" into the Google or Bing search bar to see if the information has already been compiled by a reliable source.

- Try to determine if there is a trade association or an annual trade show for smartphone apps, and contact the relevant organization to ask if industrywide sales data are available. You might narrow your search to see if there are trade shows or conferences that focus on specific types of apps, although the information you glean at these conferences may be more limiting. There may be trade shows based on the platform that the app is hosted on (i.e., iPhone, Android, RIM's Blackberry) or the type of app (i.e., productivity, games and entertainment, music).

- Search for newspaper and magazine articles on smartphone apps using public search engines such as Find Articles () and MagPortal (www.magportal.com) and more powerful search engines such as ProQuest and LexisNexis, which are normally available through a university library Web site.

- Search industry-specific trade magazines. For example, an obvious place to look for articles about smartphone apps is in *MacWorld,* a magazine dedicated to covering the entire Apple Inc. ecosystem. If you can't find an article, contact *MacWorld,* and ask if they have run an article on smartphone apps industry sales.

- Contact a company in the industry to ask for leads on finding industrywide sales data information. Don't be bashful. [x]cube Labs is a company that offers complete end-to-end services for mobile applications development across all major platforms, including Apple iPhone, RIM's Blackberry, Google's Android, as well as Microsoft's Windows Mobile. The company lists the phone number of its corporate headquarters on its Web site.

One thing you'll need to be careful about is discerning the credibility of your sources of information. Don't be afraid, however, to cite personal conversations if the information is credible. For instance, it's perfectly appropriate to cite a personal conversation with the director of a trade association if you feel reasonably confident the information you're being provided is credible.

You should include concrete numbers for what you think your industry's sales and sales growth rate will be for the next one to three years. If you project the numbers yourself, explain how you arrived at your estimates. A sensible approach, which works in most instances, is to simply extrapolate from the historic trend data you have available. In all cases, you should comment on what the predictions mean. If you are predicting a sharper increase in sales than would be expected by looking at historic trends, you should provide a rationale for your prediction. In most instances, you will point to improving industry trends as part of your justification for higher numbers. Briefly mention the key improving trends here, but do not elaborate. The third section of your industry analysis deals exclusively with industry trends.

INDUSTRY CHARACTERISTICS

This section talks about the structure of your industry and lays out its competitive landscape. The four key issues to deal with are industry structure, the nature of the participants in an industry, key ratios, and the industry's key success factors. Although you could comment on much more, it's simply impossible to include all the potential topics within the context of a 25- to 35-page business plan. Part of the art of writing a business plan is determining what to include and what to leave out. You will experience the frustration of having to leave out potentially important information as you write this section of your industry analysis.

The industry characteristics portion of the Prime Adult Fitness industry analysis is shown in Figure 5-3.

INDUSTRY STRUCTURE

This topic is particularly important. An industry's size and its growth rate, regardless of how positive they are, are basically moot points if an industry isn't structurally attractive for a startup. Industry structure, in the context of a business plan, refers to how concentrated or fragmented the industry is and whether the industry's competitive landscape is in general attractive or unattractive.

In regard to industry concentration, you should report how concentrated or fragmented your industry is. Concentrated industries are dominated by a few large firms, whereas fragmented industries include a large number of smaller companies. Normally, an industry is concentrated if large capital requirements are necessary to participate, or it has matured and a substantial amount of consolidation has taken place. An industry is typically fragmented if it's in the emergence stage of its life cycle and/or the cost of entry is relatively low. If you're launching into a fragmented industry, nothing more typically needs to be said—most startups launch into fragmented markets. If you're launching into a concentrated market, you'll need to provide a clear rationale in the next section of the plan (which focuses on your target market) of how you plan to compete. Some startups are able to launch into concentrated industries by finding target or niche markets that are less expensive to compete in or by lowering the overall capital requirements necessary to enter the industry through some innovative means. For example, many microbreweries have successfully entered the

FIGURE 5-3 Industry Characteristics (Prime Adult Fitness Business Plan)

Industry Structure

The industry is fragmented with no one company holding a market share of more than 5.0 percent. There are many small fitness centers, dance studios, gymnasiums, ice skating rinks, and similar facilities that decrease industry concentration. Barriers to entry are high at the high end of the market (full-service fitness centers) due to the high cost of real estate and equipment and low at the lower end of the market (smaller fitness clubs and dance studios) due to the plentiful nature of rental space available in strip malls.

Other structural characteristics of the industry include the following:

- *Growing Preference for Easily Accessible, Smaller Fitness Centers.* The market share of small fitness centers, such as 24 Hour Fitness, Snap Fitness, and Curves International, is increasing. These tightly focused centers serve a specific clientele and feature smaller facilities with fewer amenities in exchange for lower membership fees and the ability to locate near their customers.

- *The Aging of the Population.* Approximately 25 percent of fitness club members are 55 years old or older, as are 25 percent of all Americans. It is estimated that the present 55 year and older population will maintain a more active lifestyle and focus more on appearance and general well-being than previous generations. Older people also have more discretionary income, free time, and incentive to engage in preventative practices like fitness to avoid health problems than younger people. As a result of these factors, it is expected that the percentage of fitness club members who are 55 and over will continue to increase.

- *Competition.* Competition throughout the industry is strong. For-profit fitness and recreational centers must compete against centers that are nonprofit, such as the YMCA, and "substitute" fitness facilities such as those provided free or for a nominal fee by businesses for their employees and apartment buildings and condominium complexes for their tenants or owners. An increasing number of hotels and motels feature fitness centers that satisfy the needs of people who travel frequently.

- *Cost and Site Selection.* The best sites for full-service, high-end fitness centers are in densely populated suburban areas with an affluent population. This fact represents a challenge because these areas also have the highest real estate prices. Site selection is easier at the lower end of the market, where fitness centers such as 24 Hour Fitness and Curves International locate primarily in rented facilities in strip malls.

- *Increases in Premium Services.* The industry is benefiting from an increase in premium services, which are billed separately from a member's monthly membership fee. Examples of premium services include massage, acupuncture, access to a personal trainer, and childcare.

Nature of Participants

Firms in the Industry. The industry comprises a wide variety of participants, ranging from large, full-service fitness centers run by large chains to small, single-employee dance studios and ice skating rinks. No single firm captures more than 5 percent of industry sales. The largest firm in the industry is 24 Hour Fitness Worldwide (4.9 percent), followed by Life Time Fitness (4.1 percent), Bally Total Fitness (3.2), and Town Sports International (1.9 percent).

Segmentation. The most common way to segment the industry is by product/service as shown below.

FIGURE 5-3   (continued)

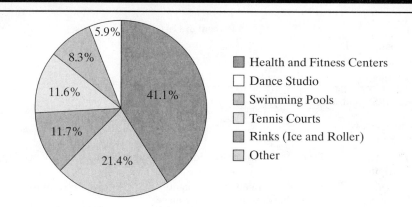

Health and Fitness Centers
Dance Studio
Swimming Pools
Tennis Courts
Rinks (Ice and Roller)
Other

Clientele. The clientele of the industry is segmented as follows.

Age	Share of Market
6–11 years old	4%
12–17 years old	8%
18–34 years old	35%
35–54 years old	33%
55 years and older	20%

Source: IBIS World, 2013

Key Ratios
To gain as vivid a picture of the industry as possible, the following ratios were obtained from the sources cited.

Operating and Financial Ratios

	2013	2014 (Projected)
IVA/Revenue	50.7%	$50.6
Revenue/Employee	$45,200	$45,500
Wages/Revenue	30.7%	31.3%
Employees/Establishment	17.1	17.1
Wages/Employee (many employees work part-time)	$13,886	$14,205

Industrial Value Added (IVA) The market value of goods and services produced by the industry minus the costs of goods and services used in production. IVA is also described as the industry's contribution to GDP, or profit plus wages and depreciation.

Source: IBIS World, May 2013

Cost Structure Ratios (For Major Cost Categories)

Item	Percent of Cost
Wages	30.7%
Purchases	20.0%

FIGURE 5-3 (continued)

Item	Percent of Cost
Depreciation and other costs	7.5%
Rent and utilities	12.0%
Advertising	10.0%

Source: IBISWorld, May 2013.

Key Success Factors
The key success factors for the industry are as follows:

- *Easy Access for Clients.* A convenient location with easy access and plenty of parking is helpful.
- *Effective Product Promotion.* An effective promotional strategy increases awareness and attracts greater membership and local patronage.
- *Employees with Good Technical Knowledge.* Skilled employees who can demonstrate the use of various types of equipment, assist participants, and answer exercise-related questions are important for maintaining good member relations.
- *Right Mix of Equipment, Classes, and Activities.* Because fitness and recreational centers must compete for their customer's time, and because an increasing number of fitness centers are targeting a specific clientele, it is important to carefully match the equipment, classes, and activities to the target clientele.
- *Member Retention.* The average attrition rate for fitness centers in the United States is approximately 37 percent. This means that 37 out of 100 people will cancel their memberships each year. The cost of recruiting new members is more than twice the cost of retaining an existing member. Fitness centers that are able to retain a higher percentage of their members have a competitive advantage.
- *Business Expertise of Operators.* The long-term success of a firm in the fitness industry ultimately depends on the skills of the operator in running the business profitably over time. This requires business-related skills along with traditional fitness-related skills and abilities.

highly concentrated brewery industry by brewing their beer locally and relying on a local niche market clientele. Although this approach limits the nationwide potential of the microbrewery, at least initially, it lowers the costs of branding and distribution. Similarly, some companies are able to lower the capital requirements of entering an industry on a broader scale through innovative approaches.

The second topic regarding industry structure is the general attractiveness (or lack of attractiveness) of an industry's competitive landscape. A structurally attractive industry, according to Harvard professor Michael Porter's "five forces" model, should have relatively high barriers of entry to keep competitors out, not enough rivalry to create cutthroat competition, no good substitutes for the basic product or service the industry sells, limited power of suppliers to negotiate input prices up, and limited power of buyers to force selling prices down.[5] You normally won't comment on each of these points in a brief industry analysis, but you should allude to the most salient ones.* For example, if you're entering an industry with high barriers to entry, that's good; high barriers to entry deter competitors, so you should highlight that aspect of your industry in this section of your industry analysis. Of course, if the entry barriers are high, you'll have to explain, not here but in the next section of the plan that deals with your target market, how you're able to enter.

NATURE OF PARTICIPANTS

The next section of this portion of your business plan deals with the nature of the participants in an industry. Your reader will already know whether the industry is consolidated or fragmented. In this brief description, you want to provide your reader with a "feel" for the nature and mixture of firms in your industry. Who are the major players in the industry? What percentage of market share do they control? Are the major competitors online firms or traditional firms? You also want your reader to visualize how your firm will fit in or see the gap that your firm will fill. Although the industry analysis does not talk about your firm per se, the reader knows what your company is by reading the previous sections of the plan. Draw a mental map for your reader that shows exactly where your firm will fit into the industry.

You should also discuss how the industry is segmented. This discussion can get fairly complex because industries can be segmented in different ways. For example, the computer industry can be segmented by product type (i.e., mainframes and workstations, servers, PCs, laptops, tablets, and handheld computers) or by customer segments served (i.e., individuals, businesses, schools, and government). Similarly, you can segment the smartphone app industry by target customers (i.e., parents, business travelers, fashion enthusiasts, music lovers, sports fans, news and magazine readers, casual gamers, social influencers, etc.) or by platform they run on (i.e., Apple iPhone, RIM's Blackberry, Google's Android, or Microsoft's Window's Mobile). The best approach is to segment your industry by your point of entry. So if you're starting a company to sell specially designed computers for elementary schools, it would make the most sense to segment the computer industry by customers served, as shown previously. As you discuss the different segments of your industry, if you know which segment is growing the fastest and/or is the most profitable, that's good information to convey. There are also industries that have clearly bifurcated, with the most successful companies serving either the top end of the market (in terms of quality of goods and price range) or the bottom end. This trend is seen in industries such as grocery stores, where most of the money is being made by high-end stores such as Whole-Food Markets and Trader Joe's and low-end providers such as Wal-Mart and Costco.[6] The worst place to be, in bifurcated industries, is right in the middle. Again, if

---

* If you're unfamiliar with Michael Porter's five-forces model, you should familiarize yourself with the model and what it means while writing this portion of your industry analysis. A description of the model is provided in any strategic management textbook.

you're able to identify the most promising areas of an industry, or the areas to avoid, that information should be reported.

Ratios

It's important to report an industry's key financial ratios and other ratios of interest. This information provides not only further insight into the structure and attractiveness of an industry but also a point of reference to compare a company's financial and nonfinancial projections against. For example, if a company reports in its industry analysis that the average firm in its industry earns a 6 percent net profit, and in later parts of the plan indicates that it will earn 12 percent for its first three years, the firm will need to explain how it plans to generate over twice the net income of the average firm. Similar comparisons can be made with the other numbers.

Key Success Factors

Key success factors in every industry define what an organization in the industry has to be good at to be successful. Most industries have 6 to 10 key factors. Most of the successful firms in an industry are competent in all of their industry's key success factors, and they try to differentiate themselves by excelling in two or three areas.

You should identify the key success factors for your industry and report them in the industry analysis. If they aren't readily apparent, reading through IBISWorld and Mintel industry profiles and looking at industry trade journals and magazines should reveal them. A technique that some people find helpful in identifying an industry's key success factors is to pose the rhetorical question, "For a company to be successful in this industry, it must be good at... (list 6 to 10 items)". The answer to this question is a good starting point in ascertaining the key success factors for an industry.

The key success factors vary widely by industry—they are not generic concepts. For example, the key success factors in the pet store industry are as follows:

- Attractive product presentation
- Staff with a clear knowledge of the pet industry
- High-traffic and high-visibility location
- Effective quality control (pet services must be up to standard for specific types of animals and breeds)
- Offer for sale a range of the most popular pets and pet supplies at different levels of price and quality

As you can see, this list is very specific to the pet store industry. A different industry would have a much different list.

Knowing the key success factors for an industry is important because any firm in an industry can be judged by the degree to which it covers its bases on each factor and excels (or has plans in place to excel) at one or more factors.

INDUSTRY TRENDS

The final portion of an industry analysis deals with industry trends. This is arguably the most important section of an industry analysis because it often lays the foundation for a new business idea in an industry (i.e., older people are becoming increasingly interested in fitness—thus, maybe a fitness club just for adults makes sense), and it typically provides the justification for claims made earlier in the industry analysis, such as why industrywide sales should be expected to continue to increase or decrease.

The two types of trends that are the most important to focus on are environmental trends and business trends. The best place to look for trend information is industry trade journals, industry-specific magazines, industry reports from resources such as IBISWorld and Bizminer, and through talking to industry participants. The Internet Resource Table in Appendix 2.2 at the end of Chapter 2 provides Web site addresses that are helpful in identifying the sources of this information. Many industries also have trade associations that keep their members abreast of current trends affecting their industry. For example, the International Health, Racquet and Sportsclub Association's Web site (www. ihrsa.org) has a feature called "This Week in the Fitness Industry." The feature provides fresh material each week about trends and innovations affecting the fitness industry.

The industry trends portion of the Prime Adult Fitness industry analysis is provided in Figure 5-4.

ENVIRONMENTAL TRENDS

As discussed in Chapter 2, environmental trends are very important. The strength of an industry often surges or wanes not so much because of the management skills of the firms in an industry, but because environmental trends shift in favor of or against the products or services sold by the firms in the industry.

The most important environmental trends are economic trends, social trends, technological advances, and political and regulatory changes. You should think through each area to determine if there are trends that are positively or negatively affecting your industry that should be commented on. For example, any industry that relies on the consumption of fossil fuels, such as the trucking industry and the airline industry, is being adversely affected by high fuel prices. In contrast, any industry that provides products or services to older people, such as health care and travel, stands to benefit by the aging of the population. Sometimes there are multiple environmental changes at work that set the stage for an industry's future. This point is illustrated in the following excerpt from IBISWorld's assessment of the future of the Musical Instruments and Supply Stores (industry) in the United States.

> Continued improvements in the economy will boost consumer spending, which will further encourage customers to increase their spending on discretionary goods, such as musical instruments. However, the industry will continue to face challenges from large, discount retailers

FIGURE 5-4 Industry Trends (Prime Adult Fitness Business Plan)

There are a number of environmental and business trends affecting the growth and attractiveness of the fitness and recreational sports center industry. They are as follows.

Trends That Favor the Industry

- Americans are increasingly aware of the need for exercise, weight control, good nutrition, and a healthy lifestyle among both adults and children.
- Nationwide economic conditions are stabilizing, which boosts consumer confidence and makes it easier for industry participants to raise money.
- An increased emphasis on wellness is evident across many sectors of society. In particular, positive press about the benefits of yoga, pilates, and similar activities cause people to seek out businesses to offer those services.
- The increasing costs of other sports and recreational activities, such as golf and boating, can result in people opting out of those activities in favor of joining a fitness club or other recreational sports center.
- Increasing health costs are motivating corporations to invest in corporate wellness programs. Many corporations now offer fitness club memberships as a benefit.
- A growing number of parents are purchasing fitness club memberships for their children. The increase is motivated by concerns surrounding childhood obesity and the reduction of physical education programs in schools.

Trends Working Against the Industry

- Leisure time is becoming less available. Time-strapped consumers find it harder to make time to frequent a fitness center.
- Increasing prices for gasoline and health care are lowering consumers' disposable income.
- Americans are becoming more obese, with 35.9 percent of people 20 years old or older considered overweight. Many of these individuals may not see themselves as fit enough to work out.
- An increasing number of "substitutes" for traditional fitness centers are becoming available, from businesses that feature fitness facilities on-site for their employees to apartment complexes that provide fitness facilities to their tenants as an amenity.
- Member attrition remains high at 37 percent per year on average. The cost of recruiting a new member is more than twice the cost of retaining an existing one.

and online. This external competition will remain a tough threat to overcome because these stores will continue to provide comparable goods at discounted prices. Furthermore, decreased leisure time availability and the increasing popularity of alternative activities will limit demand.[7]

This short statement illustrates the degree to which environmental change can affect one industry. Similar forces are at work in all industries, which should be discerned and reported in your industry analysis.

Some industries experience slow or no growth for years and then start to come back as savvy industry incumbents and new entrants realize that environmental change has turned in their favor. An example is the mattress industry.

During the 2007–2012 time period the industry declined in overall sales. During the next five years the industry is expected to steadily increase its sales. A number of significant environmental trends are now working in favor of the mattress industry:

- The recovering housing market is expected to encourage home sales over the next five years. As homeowners move into their new homes demand for mattresses will rise.

- Americans are expected to increase their travel resulting in hotel and motel expansion. New motel and hotel construction will spur mattress sales.

- An increased interest in wellness has created a market for mattresses that improve sleep quality and provide better back support.

- Increasing disposable income will boost demand for furniture and household items, including mattresses.

- An expansion in the number of assisted living centers, nursing homes, and skilled nursing facilities will spur demand for high-end mattresses with enhancements that allow them to be electronically adjusted.[8]

If you spend a few minutes browsing the Web sites of two of the largest mattress manufacturers, Sleep Number (www.sleepnumber.com) and Tempur-Pedic (www.temperpedic.com), you'll see that they're tapping into these exact trends. The types of trends depicted in the preceding bullet points are the types of trends that you'll want to discern for your industry. An awareness of these trends can help startups develop more impressive industry analyses and potentially more successful business plans.

BUSINESS TRENDS

Other trends impact industries that aren't environmental trends per se but are important to mention. For example, are profit margins in the industry increasing or falling? Is innovation accelerating or waning? Are input costs going up or down? Are new markets for the industry's staple products opening up, or are existing markets being shut down by competing industries? You can't cover every possible fact affecting an industry, but you should mention the major trends.

LONG-TERM PROSPECTS

The industry analysis should conclude with a brief statement of your beliefs regarding the long-term prospects for the industry. No new information should be provided at this point. Instead, draw from the preceding sections of the industry analysis to support your conclusions. Your conclusions should be precise and to the point. No more than several sentences are required.

When you read through reports on your industry, from IBISWorld, Mintel, and Bizminer, the reports will include their assessments of the future prospects of the industry. Resist simply repeating what others are saying. Your assessment

FIGURE 5-5 Long-Term Prospects (Prime Adult Fitness Business Plan)

The industry is likely to maintain its current trajectory. An increasing interest in fitness and the popularity of smaller, tightly focused fitness centers like 24 Hour Fitness and Snap Fitness is expected to continue to spur industry growth. The aging of the population is a long-term positive trend for the industry. Older people are becoming increasingly interested in fitness and have more money and spare time to devote to a fitness center. The nature of the industry is likely to change as a result of this development. Recreational centers that feature vigorous exercise, such as racquetball and tennis clubs, are likely to suffer, where fitness centers that offer specialized classes and equipment for older people are likely to benefit. Operating margins, which are generally between 7.0 percent and 10 percent, are likely to remain solid for well-managed centers. A bright spot for the industry moving forward is the growing prevalence of premium services. A number of fitness centers are now offering massage, acupuncture, nutritional counseling, access to personal trainers, and other personalized services. These services are billed separately from a member's normal membership dues, and have the potential to increase overall operating margins.

of the long-term prospects for your industry should reflect your thoughts and beliefs, and should be fully consistent with the information contained in the preceding sections of your industry analysis.

The Long-Term Prospects section for the Prime Adult Fitness industry analysis is shown in Figure 5-5.

HOW THE INDUSTRY ANALYSIS AFFECTS AND IS AFFECTED BY OTHER SECTIONS OF THE PLAN

Industry analysis is a foundational aspect of evaluating the merits of a prospective business venture. The industry that a company participates in, as a result of its structural characteristics, historical conditions, and current trends, basically defines the playing field that a firm will participate in. A careful analysis of a firm's industry also lays out what is realistically possible and what isn't realistically possible for a startup to achieve. There are some firms, like Dell in the computer industry and Starbucks in the specialty restaurant industry, which basically turned their industries upside down by introducing new business models and outperforming their industries on most if not all metrics. However, these firms are the rare exception rather than the rule. Most startups are constrained enough by their industries that their performance falls in line with what you would expect after reading their industry analysis.

The industry analysis affects the other sections of the business plan in that it provides a point of reference to work from. Savvy business plan writers find themselves referring back to their industry analysis frequently when writing other parts of their plan. The analysis is an anchor that describes how the average firms in an industry are doing and what the overall trends are, and most business plan writers benefit by constantly comparing their plan against this anchor. It also helps temper the enthusiasm of business plan writers and provides a useful reference for a plan's readers. For example, if a startup projected a growth in sales of 17 percent per year for its first five years, and its industry is only growing at 5 percent per year, an obvious incongruity exists. A savvy reader will think, "Isn't the industry only growing at 5 percent per year? How is 17 percent possible?" There may be an explanation, but the incongruity between the industry's sales and the startup's projected sales must be explained in the plan.

Chapter Summary

1. An industry is a group of firms producing a similar product or service, such as airplanes, music, electronic games, or fitness club memberships.
2. Separating the analysis of a firm's industry and its target market is important because it's premature for a new firm to select, or even talk about, a specific target market until an understanding of the broader industry is obtained.
3. It's important that the industry analysis appear early in a business plan because it logically precedes the analysis of a firm's target market and its marketing strategy. It also helps set up and support the remainder of the plan.
4. The major sections of an industry analysis include industry definition; industry size, growth, and sales projections; industry characteristics; industry trends; and long-term prospects.
5. If your firm operates in two or more industries, you should identify all the industries that it participates in and recognize that it will be necessary to conduct an industry analysis for each of the industries. Some discretion is allowed regarding the weight placed on the individual analyses. In some instances, when a firm operates in more than one industry, it may be appropriate to conduct a full analysis on the primary industry that firm operates in and an abbreviated analysis on the other.
6. The key to the industry size, growth, and sales projections portion of the analysis is to not just report the numbers. Make sense of the numbers and present them in a way that builds the credibility of your business plan.
7. The four key issues to deal with in the industry characteristics section of the analysis are industry structure, the nature of the participants in an industry, key ratios, and the industry's key success factors.
8. The topic of industry structure is particularly important. An industry's size and its growth rate, regardless of how positive they are, are basically moot points if an industry isn't structurally attractive for a startup.
9. The industry trends portion of an industry analysis is arguably the most important section because it often lays the foundation for a new business idea in an industry, and it typically provides the justification for claims made earlier in the industry analysis.
10. The industry analysis should conclude with a brief statement of your beliefs regarding the long-term prospects for the industry.

Review Questions

1. What is an industry? Why is it important to include an "industry analysis" in a business plan?
2. Why is it important that the industry analysis focus strictly on a firm's industry rather than its industry and its target market simultaneously?
3. Why is it important for an industry analysis to appear early in a business plan?
4. Why is identifying a company's industry a tough call in many instances?
5. What should you do if your firm operates in more than one industry?
6. What are the four general rules of thumb for completing the industry size, growth, and sales projections portion of the industry analysis?
7. What topic should be discussed in the "industry structure" portion of an industry analysis? Why are these topics important?
8. Why is it important to know how an industry is segmented?
9. Why is knowledge of the key success factors in an industry important? How can an industry's key success factors be identified?
10. Why is the industry trends portion of the industry analysis arguably the most important section of the analysis?

Application Questions

1. You just reviewed a business plan for a company that will make a fitness app that will allow its users track their exercise and monitor their fitness in an innovative way. One thing you noticed is that the plan didn't include an industry analysis. When you asked Caleb, the author of the plan, why the industry analysis was left out, he said, "Are you kidding? My industry is one of the hottest ones in America. I just read an article that said Health and Fitness apps are one of the top categories in both the Apple and the Android App Store. An industry analysis isn't necessary." Do you agree with Caleb? If he said to you, "Okay, persuade me that an industry analysis is necessary," what would you tell him?
2. Cybex International (www.cybex.com) is a company that makes premium exercise equipment for home and commercial use. What industry is Cybex in? (Provide an NAICS code.) Report the industry's past three years of sales and sales growth, and make a prediction for its sales and sales growth for the next year. Is the industry fragmented or concentrated? What are the environmental and business trends working for and against the industry's future growth? On a scale of 1–10 (10 is high), how attractive of an industry is the industry Cybex participates in for a startup to enter? Explain your answer.
3. Jennifer Carroll, a high school classmate of yours, is thinking about starting a company to compete with Crafty.com, the company that makes instructional videos for people who are interested in learning crafts such as knitting, quilting, crocheting, and cake decorating. Jennifer is writing a business plan

and is working on the industry analysis. Jennifer's having trouble nailing down the exact industry she will be competing in and is having trouble finding sources of information to help her discern the environmental trends that are impacting her industry. If Jennifer asked you for your help, how would you help her determine the industry her instructional video company will participate in, and what suggestions would you give her for finding information on the environmental trends that are impacting her industry?

4. Brooklyn Salsa (www.bksalsa.com) is a company that has launched an exciting new line of salsa dips and related products. Spend a few minutes looking at Brooklyn Salsa's Web site and studying its business concept. If the founders of Brooklyn Salsa had carefully studied the salsa segment of the broader food industry before coming up with their business idea, what factors about the salsa segment or the food industry might have led them to the idea for Brooklyn Salsa?

5. One industry mentioned in the chapter that is fairly "hot" is the mattress industry. Spend enough time studying the mattress industry to determine whether it is structurally attractive for new entrants. Report your conclusions.

Endnotes

1. A. Son, "IBISWorld Industry Report 62161 Home Care Providers in the US," *IBISWorld*, June 2013.
2. N. Panteva, "IBISWorld Industry Report 44812 Women's Clothing Stores in the US," *IBISWorld*, April, 2013.
3. G. Kawasaki, *The Art of the Start* (New York: Portfolio, 2004).
4. N. Panteva, "IBISWorld Industry Report 44812 Women's Clothing Stores in the US," *IBISWorld*, April, 2013.
5. M. Porter, *Competitive Strategy: Techniques for Analyzing Industries and Competitors* (New York: Free Press, 1980).
6. M. J. Silverstein, *Treasure Hunt* (New York: Portfolio, 2006).
7. N. Everett, "IBISWorld Industry Report 45114 Musical Instrument & Supplies Stores in the US," February 2013.
8. D. Kelly, "IBISWorld Industry Report 33791 Mattress Manufacturing in the US," January 2013.

MARKET ANALYSIS

INTRODUCTION

The industry analysis section of a business plan is normally followed by the market analysis. Whereas the industry analysis focuses on the broad business domain that a firm will participate in (i.e., airline industry, fitness and recreational sports industry, women's clothing industry), the market analysis breaks the industry into segments and zeroes in on the specific segment (or target market) that the firm will tackle. As mentioned in Chapter 5, most firms do not try to service their entire industry. Instead, they focus on servicing a specific market within the industry very well.

An important point to recognize at the outset of this chapter is that the market analysis section of a business plan is distinctly different from the marketing section. The market analysis section focuses on describing a firm's target market, customers, and competitors; how it will compete in the marketplace; and potential sales and market share. In contrast, the marketing section, which is covered in Chapter 7, focuses on the classic marketing functions that support a firm's product, including price, promotion, and distribution (product was covered earlier in the plan). Although some business plans commingle these two sections, it's much more effective to keep them separate.

The market analysis is an extremely important section of a business plan for two reasons. First, like the industry analysis, the market analysis helps define the nature of the business and the remainder of the plan. For example, the market analysis normally includes a forecast of a firm's sales, which directly impacts the size of its manufacturing operation, its marketing plan, the number of people it will need to hire, and the amount of money it will need. Similarly, the more a startup understands the needs of its target market, the more it can match its product attributes to those needs. For instance, in conducting market analysis,

GreatCall (www.jitterbug.com), a company that offers a smartphone service designed specifically for older people, found through a survey of smartphone users that the most important feature for users age 55 and older is just the ability to make or receive voice calls. As a result, GreatCall's phones are simple and easy to use and focus primarily on the ease of making and receiving calls.[1] In contrast, other smartphone manufacturers target the youth market. Consistent with the needs of their markets, they produce more stylish phones that offer advanced feature that are attractive to youths. For example, the Samsung Galaxy S4, which was a hot phone at the time this chapter was written (June 2013), offers a feature called Group Play. With Group Play, you can connect up to eight phones wirelessly to play games and share your favorite songs, photos, and documents. This functionality is exactly the type of feature that young people like, who are accustomed to interacting with small groups of friends at school and in their free time.

The second reason a market analysis is important, if done properly, is that it affirms that a company has a well-thought-out target market, understands its customers, and can generate sales in the face of competition. It also communicates the amount of potential that exists in a firm's target market. This latter point is particularly important because the potential of a firm's target market should be consistent with its overall goals and aspirations. If a firm wants to raise investment capital, for example, it must demonstrate that its target market has sufficient potential to enable it to rapidly increase sales and return to its investors an amount that is 5 to 20 times the original investment, which is what equity investors normally expect. In contrast, if the business plan is for more of a lifestyle firm, such as a high-end woman's clothing boutique, and the goal is to qualify for an SBA guaranteed loan, then the target market will still need to demonstrate potential but at a level more commensurate with the type of financing desired.

Because of the stakes involved, a well-developed market analysis usually takes considerable time and effort to complete and is scrutinized carefully by discerning readers. The authors of a business plan must have a complete understanding of their target market, customers, and competitors; how they will compete in the marketplace; and their potential sales and market share. Gaining this degree of insight and knowledge generally requires entrepreneurs to conduct both primary and secondary research as they work through the individual sections of the market analysis.

Now let's look at the first major section in a market analysis and why it's important.

MARKET SEGMENTATION AND TARGET MARKET SELECTION

To succeed, a firm must answer the basic question: "Who are our customers, and how will we appeal to them?" To determine the customers, you first segment the industry that the firm will participate in and then identify the specific target market it will tackle.

In some cases, a firm will have two markets, and you should describe the characteristics of both markets. For example, if you plan to sell your products through a retail store, you have two markets—the retail stores and the end user of your product. You can use your judgment regarding how much weight to apply to each market analysis.

The market segmentation and target market selection portion of the Prime Adult Fitness market analysis is shown in Figure 6-1.

FIGURE 6-1   Market Segmentation and Target Market Selection (Prime Adult Fitness Business Plan)

Market Segmentation

For the purpose of the Prime Adult Fitness business plan, the Gym, Health & Fitness Clubs in the U.S. industry is segmented by product type as follows:

Product/Service	Share of Industry Sales
Gyms and Fitness Clubs	65.0%
Other	10.0%
Dance Centers	7.0%
Swimming Pools	7.0%
Ice and Roller Rinks	6.0%
Tennis Centers	5.0%

Additional ways to segment the industry include by annual household income, by gender, and by sector (i.e., for-profit, not-for-profit, corporate).

Target Market Selection

Prime Adult Fitness will target the health and fitness club segment of the industry and people 50 years old and older. (Only people 50 years old or older will be granted membership.) The following factors led to the decision to select this market:

- *Industry analysis.* The industry analysis provides compelling evidence that older Americans are increasingly interested in fitness, have sufficient leisure time to engage in fitness activities, and have more disposable income than other age groups.

- *Additional evidence.* According to IBIS World's August 2013 report, the central characteristic of the gym, health and fitness clubs industry has been the growth of older people who are joining health clubs. Of the 52.6 million people in the United States who belong to health clubs, about 20 percent are older than 55. That percentage represents a 320 percent increase since the early 1990s.

- *Older people prefer to exercise with people their own age.* Substantial anecdotal evidence suggests that older people, in particular, prefer to exercise with people their own age. In fact, according to a study published in the April 2007 issue of the *Annals of Behavioral Medicine,* many older people would rather exercise alone than in a mixed group that includes younger people. This statistic causes us to believe there is tremendous upside potential in terms of the number of older people who would join a fitness center if there was a center just for them.

- *Current fitness centers are not meetings the needs of older people.* As illustrated in the "Buyer Behavior" section shown below, all-purpose fitness centers are not able to offer the environment, programs, or mix of classes that are optimal for older people.

FIGURE 6-1 (continued)

As shown by Curves International and others, a potentially profitable business model in the fitness industry is to target a single demographic very well by offering a tailored environment and mixtures of classes and facilities.

- *Insurance subsidies.* An increasing number of health insurers are providing subsidies to Medicare-eligible individuals to join fitness centers.

Target Market Size

Prime Adult Fitness plans to open a single location in Oviedo, Florida. Oviedo is a suburb of Orlando. The following steps were taken to estimate the size of Prime Adult Fitness's target market.

Step 1: Determine Prime Adult Fitness's trade area:

We feel that Seminole County, Florida, the county that Oviedo is located in, represents a reasonable approximation of Prime Adult Fitness's trade area. Most retail outlets obtain the majority of their business from a 5- to 10-mile radius of their location because people are not willing to drive farther if a similar service is available. Because Prime Adult Fitness will offer a unique service, it may draw from a larger area. The company's initial location will not be more than 16 miles from any address in Seminole County.

Step 2: Determine the number of people 50 years old and older in Prime Adult Fitness's trade area.

According to a report commissioned by Seminole County,[2] in 2014 there will be 61,643 people 55 years and older living in Seminole County. No breakdown is provided for the number of people 50 years old or older. We do know that there will be 67,341 people who are 45 to 54 years of age. If 40 percent of those people are between 50 and 54, that amounts to an additional 26,936 people. Combining the two numbers, we estimate there are 88,579 people 50 years old and older living in Seminole County.

Step 3: Determine the percentage of the people 50 years old and older in Seminole County who already belong to a fitness club.

According to the International Health, Racquet & Sportsclub Association (IHRSA), 16 percent of the American population currently belongs to a fitness club. According to Chron.com, 25 percent of that percentage is 55 years old and older. This number syncs with IBIS World's report that the 50+ age demographic is well represented in fitness centers. As a result, we can reasonably assume that 16 percent of Seminole County's 88,579 people 50 years or older, or 14,172 people, belong to a fitness center. To substantiate this number in its local market, Prime Adult Fitness distributed its concept statement and buying intentions survey to a random sample of 196 residents of Seminole County 50 years old or older. A total of 17.8 percent of the respondents indicated that they belong to a fitness center.

Step 4: Determine the total size (in dollars) of Prime Adult Fitness's target market for 2008.

Fitness clubs have three revenue drivers.

Revenue Driver No. 1: Monthly membership dues.

The average cost of belonging to a fitness center, of all varieties, in Seminole County is $60 per month. $60 per month × 14,172 people (the estimated number of people in Seminole County who are 50 years old or older and belong to a fitness center) × 12 months per year = $10,203,840.

Revenue Driver No. 2: One-time enrollment fees.

FIGURE 6-1   (continued)

The average one-time enrollment fee for joining a fitness center in Seminole County is $75 (all types of centers). Fitness centers, on average, turn over approximately 33 percent of their membership per year. As a result, if 33 percent of the total members are new, that would result in additional income of 4,676 new members per year (14,172 members × .33) paying the $75 fee, for a total additional income of $350,700.

Revenue Driver No. 3: Additional sources of income.

Fitness clubs have additional sources of income, which vary by center. Examples include massage services (which usually cost extra), tanning salons, coffee and smoothie bars, health maintenance and nutrition classes, and childcare. According to industry norms, the average fitness center's nondues revenue equals 20 percent of its sales. Based on conversations with owners and managers of Seminole County fitness centers, we've backed this number down to 15 percent. Thus, 15 percent on top of the income from revenue drivers No. 1 and No. 2, which totals $10,554,540, is $1,583,181.

Summary:

$ 10,203,840	Membership dues
$ 350,700	One-time membership fees
$ 1,583,181	Other income
$ 12,137,721	Total size of fitness club market for Prime Adult Fitness's trade area

Step 5: Determine the total size (in dollars) of Prime Adult Fitness's target market for 2014, 2015, and 2016.

According to our industry analysis, the Gym, Health and Fitness Clubs industry is expected to grow at a rate of 2.0 to 2.5 percent in the coming years. There is evidence that the fitness center portion of the industry will grow at a faster rate than the industry as a whole (as shown in Figure 6-1, the industry also includes segments such as dance centers and ice and roller rinks). A conservative 2.5 percent annual growth rate in people 50 years old and older who will belong to a fitness center in Seminole County, Florida, is used below.

2014: $12,137,721
2015: $12,441,164[*]
2016: $12,752,193
2017: $13,070,997

[*] Prime Adult Fitness plans to open on January 1, 2015.

MARKET SEGMENTATION

In many instances, a firm will already have shown how its industry is segmented in the industry analysis portion of the business plan. If this circumstance applies to your plan, simply recapping that analysis in this section may be appropriate. If you're starting from scratch, you should explain that market segmentation is the process of dividing a market into distinct subsets (or segments) that behave in the same way or have similar needs.[3] An important decision you'll need to make is how to segment your market. Markets can be segmented in many ways, such as by geography (city, state, country), demographic variables (age, gender, family size, income), psychographic variables (personality, lifestyle, values), behavioral variables (benefits sought, product usage rate, brand loyalty), and product type (varies by product). Sometimes a firm segments its market on more than one dimension to drill down to a specific market segment that the firm thinks it is uniquely capable of serving. For example, in its market analysis, GreatCall, the cell phone service provider for older people, probably segmented the cell phone market by age and by benefits sought. Samsung used this same segmentation strategy by targeting younger users and featuring a more sophisticated set of options.

To test whether you have segmented your market successfully, the requirements for successful market segmentation are as follows:

- Homogeneity of needs and wants appears within the segment.
- Heterogeneity of needs and wants exists between the segments.
- Differences within the segment should be small compared to differences across segments.
- The segment should be distinct enough so that its members can be easily identified.
- It should be possible to determine the size of the segment.
- The segment should be large enough to be profitable.

If you are satisfied that you have segmented your market in a way that meets the criteria shown in the preceding list and makes sense, given your business concept, you can stop here. As shown in Figure 6-1, Prime Adult Fitness segmented its market by product type and by age of buyer.

If you're unfamiliar with how to segment your market, both IBISWorld and Mintel provide suggestions for segmenting the industries that they follow. Another good choice is to consult industry trade journals and trade associations. You may also want to talk to some of the major participants in your industry, such as suppliers, distributors, and customers. One of the richest sources used to understand the segmentation of the fitness club industry, for the purpose of completing the Prime Adult Fitness business plan, was information obtained from the International Health, Racquet & Sportsclub Association (http://www.ihrsa. org), an industry trade association mentioned in Chapter 5 that represents more than 10,000 fitness clubs and recreational facilities in 70 countries.[4] Information from these types of sources should be sought out and used.

An exciting aspect of the entrepreneurial process is that it often results in the identification of new segments of an industry that weren't previously considered. For example, Curves International (www.curves.com), the fitness center for women, created a new segment in the fitness industry by segmenting the market by gender. Following the lead of Curves, firms are now segmenting the fitness industry in other innovative ways. An example is Baby Boot Camp (www. babybootcamp.com), a chain of fitness centers that has segmented its market by benefits sought. Each of Baby Boot Camp's 154 franchises focuses on helping new moms enhance prepregnancy fitness levels and meet the physical challenges of parenting by emphasizing strength training in a supportive environment.[5]

Selecting a Target Market

As alluded to previously, after a firm segments its market, it selects a segment within the market to target. If a firm does not have a preconceived notion about the market it plans to target, it will usually select the segment that represents the best prospects for entry. Even in these instances, the segment that represents the best prospects for entry (in terms of sales growth and profitability) might not be chosen because it isn't consistent with founders' passions and/or core competencies. In these cases, the founders normally select the target market that represents the best fit for them both professionally and personally.

The biggest mistake that people make when selecting a target market is to define their target market too broadly or to try to target more than one segment simultaneously. Startups are usually best served by segmenting their industry carefully and zeroing in on a specific market segment. An exception may be a firm that targets two or more extremely small but related segments. It's simply too difficult and expensive, in the vast majority of cases, to adopt a more aggressive strategy, at least initially. This sentiment is affirmed by Joel Kurtzman, the founder and chairman of Kurtzman Group, a small business-consulting firm, and author of the book *Startups That Work*. Commenting on this issue, Mr. Kurtzman wrote:

> A lucid and articulate business plan will identify specific market segments and individual customers, and offer a blueprint for attacking the marketplace. Our research shows that startups often go after too many market segments simultaneously, trying to be all things to all people and fail to satisfy anyone.[6]

For a new firm, focusing intently on a single market rather than several markets (or a larger market) makes sense because it allows a firm to become an expert in a specialized area, rather than trying to spread itself too thin, as alluded to by Mr. Kurtzman.

Before settling on a specific target market, a firm should assess the size of the market and study the trends that are affecting that market to make sure it is large enough and healthy enough to meet the firm's objectives. This subject is covered in the next section of the chapter.

Target Market Size and Trends

Estimating the size of a target market can be a tricky proposition. In many cases, you need to literally invent a methodology for making your estimate. The first rule of thumb is to not make frivolous predictions. Although there may be occasions when you have to make an educated guess or estimate, the key is to explain the path that led you to your conclusions. If the reader of your plan discerns that you are simply guessing, with no clear rationale for your guess, the credibility of your plan will be compromised.

If you are producing a product that is an enhanced version of something that is already available, such as a new type of toy or home health care service, the numbers will be fairly easy to get. IBISWorld, Bizminer, Mintel, and similar resources track the sizes of industries and segments within industry on a broad basis. You can also consult industry trade journals and trade associations as mentioned previously. Sometimes the size of a market segment isn't stated exactly in an industry report, but the number is easy to compute if you read through the report. For example, if you were thinking about developed a new line of camping equipment and wanted to know the size of the market for camping equipment in the United States that number is relatively easy to determine. IBISWorld reports that the Athletic and Sporting Goods Manufacturing in the U.S. industry (NAICS 33992), which camping equipment is part of, reported sales of $8.9 billion in 2012. The sales of camping equipment accounted for 9.5 percent of industry sales.[7] Thus, the market for camping equipment is roughly $845.5 million per year in the United States.

Estimating the size of a target market for a market that doesn't exist, or a market that is specific to a particular location or geographic area, is harder. You will probably need to do some marketing research. For example, to determine the size of its target market, Prime Adult Fitness, which will open a single location in Oviedo, Florida (a suburb of Orlando), used the approach carefully articulated in its business plan. Readers will normally judge a projection like this based on (1) the reasonableness of the assumptions made, (2) the degree to which the numbers are anchored in facts and sound analysis rather than guesses or speculation, and (3) the extent to which it appears that a good faith effort was made to make as accurate of a projection as possible, given normal time and budget constraints. All readers know that a projection is just that, a projection, and some latitude is normally provided. But there is no fooling a savvy reader if a projection is just a set of guesses that looks hastily prepared. Following that approach seriously undermines the credibility of a business plan.

A projection, like the one shown in Figure 6-1, must also be melded with common sense to arrive at a final judgment. For example, the numbers in Prime Adult Fitness's projection of its target market size are likely to be conservative because they estimate the dollar value of the *existing* fitness center market for people 50 years and older in its trade area. Prime Adult Fitness may be able to bring new people into the industry as the result of the unique nature of its offering (i.e., exclusively for 50+ aged adults), similar to how Curves brought new people into the fitness center industry by opening the first fitness centers exclusively for women. In the final section of the market analysis, which describes how a startup forecasts its initial sales, we'll show how much of its available target market, along with new people brought into the market, Prime Adult Fitness believes it can garner during the startup years.

A similar process is used to estimate the size of a new target market for a company that plans to produce a product and sell it nationwide. Again, the key is to follow a sensible process based on the best available data and conduct primary research if necessary. If you get stuck and can't find the information you need, the best recourse is to talk to a reference librarian to see if there are information sources that you are overlooking, and then talk to people in the industry you are interested in. The best place to start in regard to industry participants is to talk to the editors of industry-specific trade journals and the directors of industry trade associations. Industry participants, such as suppliers and distributors, are other good sources of information. Don't hesitate to reach out to people. Most people are flattered to be asked for their insights and opinions.

Along with reporting the approximate size of a firm's target market, this section of the market analysis should also comment on industry trends that have the potential to affect the target market positively or negatively, if the information has not already been sufficiently reported. The authors of Prime Adult Fitness's business plan, for example, did not include a section in its market analysis on target market trends because the information was already adequately covered. The same process for discerning trends discussed in Chapter 5, which covered industry analysis, can be applied here. An example of the type of trend that should be reported is a trend that is currently taking place in the online social networking industry. The industry is spreading beyond Facebook, Twitter, and other dominant players. An example is CafeMom (www.cafemom.com), a social networking site for mothers and mothers to be. Another example is Dogster (www.dogster.com), a social networking site for dog owners. Sites like CafeMom and Dogster can translate into successful businesses because they appeal to a specific clientele. Attracting a specific clientele to a signal site is attractive to advertisers who are trying to reach that clientele. A company that advertises on Dogster, for example, knows that a high percentage of the site's visitors are dog owners and that they purchase a steady supply of dog-related products.

The next section of the market analysis deals with buyer behavior within a company's target market. This section of the Prime Adult Fitness market analysis is shown in Figure 6-2.

FIGURE 6-2   Buyer Behavior (Prime Adult Fitness Business Plan)

The following are factors that affect the fitness club purchase decision for people in Prime Adult Fitness's target market:

- *Motivation.* Motivation remains the key to recruiting new members and keeping them engaged. According to a survey commissioned by Mintel, 67 percent of nonfitness club members said they would join a fitness club if they knew the activities would keep them motivated.

- *Income level.* People with incomes of $75,000 or more are most likely to join a fitness center, a statistic that works in favor of Prime Adult Fitness. A total of 44.2 percent of households in Seminole County, Florida, have incomes levels of $75,000 or more, which is well above the national average.

FIGURE 6-2 (continued)

- *Lifestyle.* It is estimated that the more mature market will maintain a more active life-style (than mature people in the past) and will continue to focus on physical appearance, maintaining proper weight, and general well-being. These trends suggest strong opportunities for fitness centers that will help mature people meet these objectives.
- *Environment.* Older people prefer to exercise in an environment that is tailored for their specific needs and stage in life, as noted in the target market section. To illustrate how deep these emotions run, the following is a sample of quotations taken from our survey of 196 people in Seminole County, Florida (all 50 years old and older), who were asked to comment on how they feel about fitness centers in general:

  "I enjoy my fitness center, but it caters primarily to people who are young and thin. To be honest with you, I've reached a point in my life where I want to be working out with people my own age." (Retired Homemaker, age 69)

  "I've tried several aerobics and exercise classes over the years, but the pace was always too quick. I enjoy water aerobics, but the classes don't meet at a convenient time for me. I think that because the people who run the place (the fitness center) are all in their 20s and 30s, they don't think too much about us older folks." (Insurance Agent, age 61)

  "My husband died when he was only 68. He was overweight and never exercised. That scares me. I'm 71 now, and I want to live long enough to see my grandchildren grow up. I should join a fitness center and start exercising, but the choices confuse me. I wish someone would take me by the hand and show me what to do." (Retired School Administrator, age 71)

- *Programs and facilities.* Older people prefer a different mixture of programs and different types of fitness machines than the population in general. As a result, older people who belong to all-purpose fitness centers are frustrated with exercise machines and programs that often don't suit their specific needs. To illustrate this point, the following is a comparison of the 10 most popular program offered by all-purpose fitness centers opposed to the 10 programs preferred by the 196 Seminole County residents 50 years old and older in our survey. The survey illustrates the potential benefit of tailoring a fitness center specifically to 50+ individuals.

Top 10 Programs Offered by All-Purpose Fitness Clubs (in order of popularity)	Top 10 Programs Preferred by a Sample of 196 People 50 Years Old and Older in Prime Adult Fitness's Trade Area
1. Free weights	1. Low-impact aerobics
2. Treadmills	2. Treadmills
3. Resistance machines	3. Yoga
4. Elliptical trainers	4. Fitness evaluation*
5. Stretching	5. Stretching
6. Abdominal machines	6. Nutrition and lifestyle classes*
7. Stationary cycling	7. Indoor walking track*
8. Low-impact aerobics	8. Elliptical machines
9. Yoga	9. Strength training*
10. Stair-climbing machines	10. Water aerobics*

*Not in list of top 10 programs offered by all-purpose fitness centers.

Source for Top 10 Programs Offered at Fitness Clubs: International Health, Racquet & Sportsclub Association's (IHRSA) 2012 Trends Report

---

FIGURE 6-2   (continued)

- *Location of exercise.* People who are 55 years old and older are more inclined to exercise indoors than any other age group. This statistic is particularly important when considering a Florida audience, which may be more inclined to exercise indoors as a result of the heat and humidity.

- *Health concerns.* According to a 2011 report by the Centers for Disease Control and Prevention, about 80 percent of older adults have one chronic health condition, and 50 percent have at least two.[8] Infectious diseases (such as the flu) and injuries also take a disproportionate toll on older adults. As a result, access to physical therapy and exercise regimes that address these problems is important to this age group.

- *Social interaction.* Older people often crave positive social interaction with their peer group. As a result, fitness centers that provide opportunities for social interaction and provide open spaces with tables and refreshments where people can gather and socialize have an advantage.

BUYER BEHAVIOR

It's important to include a section in the market analysis that deals directly with the behavior of the consumers in a firm's target market. As mentioned earlier, the more a startup knows about the consumers in its target market, the more it can gear products or services to accommodate their needs.

The brief discussion of buyer behavior in the Prime Adult Fitness market analysis, articulated as bullet points, is reflective of this. The company understands that the key to attracting people to its center is to provide an "environment" that motivates them to participate. As a result, in the marketing (Chapter 7) and operations (Chapter 9) sections of the plan, you'll see the specific steps that Prime Adult Fitness plans to take to tailor its center specifically for the needs of its clientele and make the center an uplifting and socially satisfying place to exercise. The Prime Adult Fitness plan highlights national statistics that show that people with annual incomes of $75,000 or more are the most likely to join a fitness center, a statistic that works in favor of Prime Adult Fitness. A total of 44.2 percent of households in Seminole County, Florida, the location of the first center, have income levels of $75,000 or more, which is well above the national average.

There is additional information that Prime Adult Fitness knows about the consumers it will be servicing, which is reflective of the type of information you should include in this section of your market analysis. Prime Adult Fitness knows the types of classes and programs its potential members want because it conducted a survey of a random sample of people 50 years and older in its trade area. As shown in Figure 6-2, the mixture of classes and programs desired by the target market differs from what is offered by generic fitness centers. The company also knows that older people today are more concerned about their physical appearance, maintaining proper weight, and their general well-being than older people in the past. A particularly important insight is that 80 percent of older adults have one chronic health condition, and 50 percent have at least two. This statistic prompted the founders of Prime Adult Fitness to include a physical therapy center within the fitness center. The company also knows that older people often crave positive social interaction. Again, in the marketing plan section and operations section of the business plan, you'll see how Prime Adult Fitness translates this insight into activities and business practices within the facility.

In this section of Prime Adult Fitness's business plan, the focus on the core needs of Prime Adult Fitness's target market, rather than the fitness industry in general, is particularly well done. A lot of information is available that explains why people, in general, join fitness centers and the types of activities they prefer. Some of this information applies equally to all age groups and should be included in Prime Adult Fitness's business plan. Prime Adult Fitness, however, is targeting the 50+ age group, not the population in general. So what's needed, mainly, is an understanding of what people 50 years and older want in a fitness center. Although this information is tougher to find, its inclusion is essential, even if you have to collect it yourself.

Many other issues pertaining to buyer behavior may be important to cover in this section, depending on the nature of your business. For example, in many business-to-business startups, it's important to discern specifically who the "decision makers" are in the businesses you'll be trying to sell to. Similarly, the length of the customer's buying process is often an important concern. Many startups find it hard to sell products to public schools, for example, because purchase decisions are often made by committees (which draws out the decision-making process), and the funding often has to go through several levels of teacher's committees and administrators to get approved. It's also important to know whether your product is a high-, medium-, or low-involvement purchase. A high-involvement purchase is one for which the buyer is prepared to spend a considerable amount of time and effort searching. In contrast, a low-involvement purchase is one that a buyer makes with minimum thought because it does not have much impact on his or her life. Prime Adult Fitness's product is clearly a high-involvement purchase—people normally want to know a lot about a fitness center before they commit to a $50 to $100 per month membership. As a result, it would be prudent for Prime Adult Fitness to have staff members available to provide facility tours, to answer questions, to introduce prospects to current members, to host open houses, and so forth. This is also the reason that many fitness centers offer free trial memberships because it's hard to get some prospects to commit unless they are able to actually spend time becoming familiar with the facility.

COMPETITOR ANALYSIS

A competitor analysis is a detailed analysis of a firm's competition. It helps a firm understand the positions of its major competitors and the opportunities that are available to gain a competitive advantage in one or more areas. The competitor analysis also communicates to the readers of your business plan that you have a complete understanding of your firm's competitive environment. One thing you should never say is that you don't have any competitors. Even though a company like Prime Adult Fitness may be the only fitness center in its area that caters strictly to older people, its potential clientele can still spend their money in a million other ways.

The first item included in a competitor analysis is an identification of a firm's direct, indirect, and future competitors. This item is followed by the presentation of the firm's competitive analysis grid, which is a tool for organizing the information a firm collects about its major competitors.

Prime Adult Fitness's Competitor Analysis is shown in Figure 6-3.

FIGURE 6-3 Competitor Analysis (Prime Adult Fitness Business Plan)

Direct Competitors

There are 44 fitness centers in Seminole county, Florida. They are broken down as follows:

- 7 all-purpose large centers, including two YMCAs, two Gold's Gyms, two LA Fitness Centers, and one Gold's Gym
- 37 smaller, more tightly focused centers, including four Planet Fitness and three Snap Fitness centers

There are no fitness centers in Seminole county that focus strictly on the 50+ demographic. The benefits of this demographic, however, are apparent to all centers, which are starting to offer more programs with older people in mind. In addition, many centers are attempting to become more "senior" friendly in a variety of ways. For example, LA Fitness, which has traditionally catered to a younger clientele, is now showing older people in its ads. Most YMCA's also participate in Silver Sneakers, the fitness program offered through health insurers to Medicare recipients. Still, for the most part, the larger fitness chains cater primarily to a young demographic. Many of the tightly focused centers, such as Planet Fitness and Snap Fitness, are not equipped to offer specialized services to an older clientele. Prime Adult Fitness is poised to establish a competitive advantage in Seminole county by focusing strictly on the 50+ demographic.

Indirect Competitors

Indirect competitors include companies that sell home fitness equipment. Seminole county is serviced by a number of sporting goods stores that sell treadmills, exercise bikes, rowing machines, and other home exercise equipment. Nationwide, according to IBISWorld, the Sporting Good Store industry has grown by an average of 2.4 percent over the past three years, about the same as the Gym, Health & Fitness Clubs industry. There are also a number of Web sites that sell exercise equipment, including eBay. According to Prime Adult Fitness's survey of 196 potential customers in Seminole county, 19 percent of the respondents indicated that they own home exercise equipment valued at $200 or more. An increase in the growth rate of the home exercise equipment market poses a threat to all fitness centers, Prime Adult Fitness included.

Future Competitors

The fitness industry should continue to grow, as indicated in the industry analysis earlier in this business plan. Seminole county will reflect this growth. Several nascent 50+ fitness chains exist, including Nifty After 50 and Club 50. Both of these companies are selling

FIGURE 6-3 (continued)

franchises and could move into the Seminole county market. Other startups may also follow suit. Prime Adult Fitness hopes to establish a strong brand and clientele before these
competitors move into the market.

Competitive Analysis Grid

Name	Prime Adult Fitness	Central Florida YMCA	LA Fitness	Gold's Gym
Geographic location	Even	Even	Even	Even
Staff	Advantage	Even	Even	Even
Fitness programs offered	Advantage	Advantage	Even	Even
Breadth and quality of equipment	Even	Even	Even	Even
Price	Disadvantage	Disadvantage	Even	Even
Social interaction	Advantage	Advantage	Even	Even
Tailored services	Advantage	Disadvantage	Disadvantage	Disadvantage
Breadth of clientele	Disadvantage	Advantage	Advantage	Advantage

Summary
The grid shows that Prime Adult Fitness will compete on par with its closest competitors
on geographic location and breadth and quality of equipment. It plans to achieve advantages in term of the quality of its staff, the fitness programs offered, social interaction,
and tailored services. Its primary disadvantage is price. Prime Adult Fitness Services feels
that establishing an absolute advantage in terms of tailored services is more than worth
the trade-off.

IDENTIFICATION OF DIRECT, INDIRECT, AND FUTURE COMPETITORS

The first step in a competitor analysis is determining who the competition is.
Depending on the nature of the business, this may be a more difficult task than
you might think. For example, take a company such as Blue Nile (www.bluenile.
com), the online jewelry store. Primarily, the company sells jewelry, but Blue Nile
is not only in the jewelry business. Because jewelry is often given for gifts, the
company is also in the gift business. If the company sees itself as in the gift business rather than just the jewelry business, it has a broader set of competitors—
and opportunities—to consider.

You should list your direct competitors, indirect competitors, and future
competitors; if you believe that your business will attract imitators, then future

competitors are inevitable. A brief description of each type of competitor follows:

- *Direct competitors.* These are businesses that offer a product that is very similar to yours. These competitors are the most important because they are going after the same customers that you are.

- *Indirect competitors.* These competitors offer close substitutes to the product you will be offering. These firms' products are important in that they target the same basic need that will be met by your product. For example, when people told Roberto Goizueta, the late CEO of Coca-Cola, that Coke's market share was at a maximum, he countered by saying that Coke accounted for less than 2 percent of the 64 ounces of fluid that the average person drinks each day. "The enemy is coffee, milk, tea [and] water," he once said.[9]

- *Future competitors.* These are companies that are not yet direct or indirect competitors but could move into one of these roles at any time.

Normally it's impossible to identify all of your direct and indirect competitors, let alone your future competitors. As a result, you should list a handful of competitors or classes of competitors in each category. You should provide a short assessment of the scope and intensity of your competition. You'll have the opportunity to talk about your competitive advantage after you present your competitive advantage grid.

The next section focuses on your competitive analysis grid, which is a comparison of your firm to your major competitors. To complete a meaningful competitive analysis grid, you must first understand the strategies and behaviors of your competitors. This requires you to engage in competitive intelligence, which is the process of gathering information about your competitors. Suggestions for how to approach this task are provided in the Business Plan Insights box.

COMPETITIVE ANALYSIS GRID

A competitive analysis grid is a tool for organizing and presenting the information you collect about your competitors. It can help you to see how you stack up against your competitors in key areas and illustrate your primary sources of competitive advantage. To be a viable company, a new venture must have at least one clear competitive advantage over its major competitors.

The Prime Adult Fitness competitive analysis grid is shown in Figure 6-3. The way to complete the grid is to show the key success factors for firms in your target market on the vertical axis of the grid and then show your firm along with your four or five major direct competitors on the horizontal axis. In each box, you rate yourself relative to your competitors on each of the key success factors. The purpose of this exercise is to see how you stack up against your major competitors on key success factors and to illustrate the areas in which you have an advantage (and have a disadvantage). For example, Prime Adult Fitness sees

---

┌───┐
│ **BUSINESS PLAN INSIGHTS** │
└───┘

Sources of Competitive Intelligence

To complete a meaningful competitive analysis grid, a startup must first understand the strategies and behaviors of its competitors. The information that is gathered by a firm to learn about its competitors is referred to as competitive intelligence. Obtaining sound competitive intelligence is not always an easy task. If a competitor is a publicly traded firm, a description of the firm's business and its financial information is available through annual reports filed with the Securities and Exchange Commission (SEC). These reports are public records and are available at the SEC's Web site (http://www.sec.gov).

More often than not, however, a new firm will compete primarily against other private companies. In these instances, the task is more difficult. Private companies are not required to divulge information to the public. As a result, when preparing your business plan, you have to find ways to ethically obtain information about your competitors. Here are some suggestions for doing that:

- Attend conferences and trade shows. Most industries have conferences and trade shows at which firms talk about the latest trends in the industry and display their products.

- Read industry-related trade publications, magazines, and Web sites, along with general business magazines, such as Inc. and Business Week.

- Read industry reports via online resources such as IBISWorld, Mintel, and Standard and Poor's. For example, for each of the industries that it covers, IBISWorld has a section in its report titled Major Competitors.

- Purchase competitor' products to understand their features, benefits, and shortcomings: The process of purchasing the product will also provide data about how the competitor treats its customers.

- Talk to customers about what motivated them to buy your product as opposed to your competitors' products. Customers can provide a wealth of information about the advantages and disadvantages of competing products.

- Study competitors' Web sites. Many companies put a lot of information on their Web sites, including their company's history, profiles of their management teams, product information, and the latest news about the company.

---

itself as superior to its competitors in terms of "tailoring its activities to its target market." The process of completing a competitive analysis grid also helps a firm fine-tune its offering. For example, if your business plan is for a retail store, and one of the key success factors in your industry is "hours of operation," in most cases, you would want to make sure you're equal to or have an advantage over your competitors in this area. Completing the competitive analysis grid may reveal that you're at a disadvantage in this area, which will help you make adjustments if appropriate.

Similar to all sections of the business plan, you should draw conclusions and help your reader interpret the information you are presenting. For example, as depicted in Figure 6-3, Prime Adult Fitness uses its competitive analysis grid to illustrate its sources of competitive advantage.

The next section focuses on how to estimate the annual sales and market share for a new firm. Prime Adult Fitness's estimates are shown in Figure 6-4.

FIGURE 6-4 Estimate of Annual Sales and Market Share (Prime Adult Fitness Business Plan)

Estimate of Annual Sales
The following steps were taken to estimate the size of Prime Adult Fitness's annual sales.

Step 1: Determine the number of members Prime Adult Fitness will have.
Prime Adult Fitness's target is 2,100 membership units within 12 months of opening its doors. A "unit" is a single member or a couple paying for a couple's membership.

Step 2: Based on 2,100 membership units, what will Prime Adult Fitness's annual sales be?
Prime Adult Fitness estimates it will take 12 months to reach 2,100 membership units. It is projecting 2,100 membership units at the end of 2014 (first year of operation), 2,226 in 2015, 2,360 in 2016, and 2,502 in 2017. It will generate income in the following three ways:

Membership Fees: The membership fees will be $70 per month for a single membership and $92.50 per month for a couple's membership. Based on discussions with industry experts, the founders estimate that 70 percent of its memberships will be single members and 30 percent will be couples.
For its first year, Prime Adult Fitness projects will obtain its 2,100 membership units in the following order (January, February, and March are the biggest months for fitness club's "new" memberships):

2014 Membership Unit Enrollment Projection

Number of New Members	Single Membership	Couples Membership	Total
January	180	80	260
February	180	80	260
March	175	75	250
April	175	75	250
May	150	60	210
June	150	60	210
July	100	35	135
August	80	35	115
September	70	35	105
October	70	35	105
November	70	35	105
December	70	25	95
Total	1,470	630	2,100

FIGURE 6-4 (continued)

Projected membership income:
2014: $1,251,275 (based on enrollment timing and projections)
2015: $2,050,146
2016: $2,173,560
2017: $2,304,342

One-Time Enrollment Fees: Prime Adult Fitness's one-time enrollment fee will be $150 for both singles and couples. An attrition rate of 25 percent per year is anticipated. These numbers translate into the following projected enrollment fee income.

2014: $315,000 (2,100 membership units × $150/unit)
2015: $110,100 (734 new membership units × $150/unit)
2016: $116,700 (778 new membership units × $150/unit)
2017: $123,750 (825 new membership units × $150/unit)

Additional Sources of Income: Prime Adult Fitness will collect license fee income from massage therapists, physical therapists, and mental health professionals who will provide services in its facilities on a fee basis. It will also operate a coffee and smoothie bar. Prime Adult Fitness anticipates that its additional income will be 12.5 percent of its membership fees.

2014: $124,123*
2015: $256,268
2016: $271,695
2017: $288,042

*This number is not 12.5 percent of 2014 membership income due to the timing of when people join the center.

Total Projected Sales from All Sources:

2014: $1,690,398
2015: $2,416,514
2016: $2,561,955
2017: $2,716,134

Estimate of Annual Market Share
Prime Adult Fitness, through focus groups and a study conducted by our Customer Advisory Board, believes that 50 percent of our membership will come from people who already belong to other fitness centers and 50 percent will be new members (to the fitness center industry). If 50 percent of revenues come from the existing market, Prime Adult Fitness will need to capture a 14.81 percent share of the 50+ market for people in Seminole County, Florida, who currently belong to a fitness center. We feel this number is achievable.

ESTIMATE OF ANNUAL SALES AND MARKET SHARE

The final section of the market analysis focuses on computing an estimate of your firm's initial annual sales and market share. In many business plans, this analysis is provided in the financial plan section, which is usually near the end of the business plan. As mentioned earlier in the chapter, the advantage of providing the estimate here is that it helps set up the remainder of the plan. For a company like Prime Adult Fitness, it must have a good handle on the type of membership and revenues to expect before the firm can plan its facility, project the number of employees it will need, plan its marketing budget, and so on.

There are four basic ways for a new firm to estimate its initial sales. All of the methods produce estimates—there is no way to precisely predict the sales of a new business. More than one method should be used if possible. The most important thing is to come up with an estimate that is based on sound assumptions and seems both realistic and attainable.

The first way to estimate the sales for a new business is to contact the premier trade associations in your industry and ask if they track the sales numbers for businesses that are similar to the business you plan to start. If the trade association doesn't track actual sales numbers for comparable businesses, ask if there are other rules of thumb or metrics that help new companies estimate sales. For example, many industries collect statistics such as "average sales per square foot" or "average sales per employee" for the firms in their industry. These numbers may be helpful to you in estimating your initial sales. To find the trade associations in your industry, conduct a general Google or Bing search or check the resource listed in the Internet Resources Table in Appendix 2.2 at the end of Chapter 2.

The second way to estimate a new firm's sales is to find a comparable firm, or a company that's selling a comparable product. Many financial experts feel that this is the most effective approach. For example, if you are planning to open a woman's clothing boutique, try to find a boutique that is similar to the one you are planning, and simply call the owner and ask for a chance to talk to him or her about the business. You should try to find a store out of your trade area so the owner doesn't see you as a potential competitor. As indicated in Chapter 3, even if the owner is only willing to talk in general terms (i.e., our annual sales are between $300,000 and $400,000 per year), that information is better than nothing. Of course, you'll need to use common sense to adjust the numbers based on whether your store will be smaller or larger than the comparable store, will be in a better location or a poorer location, and so on. You should report your assumptions so it's clear to the reader of your plan exactly how you arrived at your sales estimate. If you're planning to sell a product, such as a new type of smartphone accessory, the same approach applies. Try to find a company that won't be a direct competitor that is selling a similar product, and try to arrange a telephone appointment or engage in an e-mail exchange. In all instances, simply tell the person you're talking to that you're working on a business plan for your startup and you're trying to arrive at a sales estimate. Ask for help regarding what types of sales to expect for the first one to three years of your business based on their experiences. Many first-time entrepreneurs are surprised at how helpful businesspeople are in freely divulging this type of information.

The third way to try to estimate sales is to conduct Internet searches to try to find magazine and newspaper articles that focus on firms in your industry. On occasion, the articles will talk about the sales experiences of a similar early stage firm. If you know of a firm that's comparable to your firm, target that firm first in your search. To find articles, you should use general search engines such as Google and Bing and more powerful search directories such as LexisNexis Academic and ProQuest. The latter two directories are fee based but are normally free if accessed through a university library. Publicly traded companies report their sales number, and the numbers are available via Hoovers (www. hoovers.com) and through many other sources. These companies, however, are rarely good comparables because they are much larger than startups and are often multidivision firms.

The fourth way to estimate a startup's sales is to use a multiplication method to try to arrive at a reasonable number. Startups that plan to sell a product on a national basis normally use a top–down approach to arrive at this number. This typically involves trying to estimate the total number of users of the product, estimate the average price customers pay, and estimate how much of the market their business will garner. Startups that plan to sell locally, such as a restaurant or clothing boutique, normally use a more bottom–up approach. This approach involves trying to determine how many customers to expect and the average amount each customer will spend. The numbers are usually computed on a weekly, monthly, and yearly basis.

Sometimes the multiplication method gets fairly complicated, and you have to consider several industries and conduct primary research to get a good estimate. For example, if you had started Songkick, the online company that alerts people when their favorite bands are in their area, how would you have used the multiplication method to estimate your initial sales? One way to approach this task would be to gather data on the total number of people who attend concerts every year. The next step would be to locate data on the percentage of concert goers who buy their tickets online (once Songkick alerts someone that their favorite band is in their area, it offers tickets for the upcoming concert). Working with these numbers, you could then estimate the number of people who are concert goers who buy their tickets online. You would then have to conduct primary research to make an estimate of the percentage of the people in this group who might become Songkick members and buy their tickets via Songkick. The primary research activities might involve distributing your concept statement and buying intentions survey to a sample of your potential customers, talking to industry experts, and so forth. Don't be timid. Many successful startups talk face-to-face to over 100 potential customers, for example, before they get a good handle on their prospects. For a company like Songkick, there would also be a ramp-up period. For example, if Songkick determined that 20 percent of the people they talked to (who go to concerts and buy tickets online) are likely to become Songkick members, that doesn't mean that 20 percent of all people who go to concerts and buy tickets online will instantly become Songkick members. It will take time for Songkick to market its service and make people aware of its offerings. As a result, Songkick might estimate that 20 percent of its potential clientele will sign up in Year 1, another 20 percent in Year 2, and so forth.

To estimate its initial sales using the multiplication approach, Prime Adult Fitness used a variation of the bottom–up method as shown in its business plan in Figure 6-4.

The ideal scenario for startups is to use all four methods of estimating initial sales and then compare the estimates. The key is to arrive at your estimates by following a clear rationale and to present numbers that appear to be both realistic and obtainable.

Chapter Summary

1. The marketing analysis section of a business plan is distinctly different from the marketing section. The market analysis section focuses on describing a firm's target market, customers, and competitors; how it will compete in the marketplace; and potential sales and market share. In contrast, the marketing section focuses on the classic marketing functions, including product, price, promotion, and distribution.

2. The market analysis is an extremely important section of a business plan for two reasons. First, it helps define the nature of the business and the remainder of the plan. Second, it affirms that a company has a well-thought-out target market, understands its customers, and can generate sales in the face of competition.

3. Market segmentation is the process of dividing a market into distinct subsets (or segments) that behave in the same way or have similar needs. An exciting element of the entrepreneurial process is that it often results in the identification of new segments of an industry that weren't previously considered.

4. After a firm segments its market, it selects a segment within the market to target. The biggest mistake that people make when selecting a target market is to define their market too broadly or to try to target more than one segment simultaneously. Startups are usually best served by zeroing in on a specific target market.

5. Estimating the size of a target market can be a tricky proposition. The first rule of thumb is to not make frivolous predictions. The key is to explain the path that leads you to your conclusions. If you are producing a product that is an enhanced version of something that is already available, the numbers will be fairly easy to get. Estimating the size of a target market for a market that doesn't exist is harder.

6. It's important to include a section in the market analysis that deals directly with the behavior of the consumers in a firm's target market. The more a startup knows about the consumers in its target market, the more it can gear products or services to accommodate their needs.

7. A competitor analysis is a detailed analysis of a firm's competition. It helps a firm understand the positions of its major competitors and the opportunities that are available to gain a competitive advantage in one or more areas.

8. A firm's competitors include direct competitors, indirect competitors, and future competitors.
9. A competitive analysis grid is a tool for organizing and presenting the information you collect about your competitors.
10. There are four basic ways for a firm to estimate its initial sales: contacting trade associations, finding comparable firms, finding sales estimates for comparable firms in magazine and newspaper articles, and using the multiplication method.

Review Questions

1. Explain the purpose of the market analysis section of a business plan.
2. Describe the difference between the market analysis section and the marketing plan section of a business plan.
3. Explain the process of market segmentation and why it's important for a firm to select a specific target market.
4. Describe the requirements for successfully segmenting a market.
5. What is the biggest mistake that people make when selecting a target market?
6. Why is estimating the size of a target market referred to as a "tricky" proposition?
7. Describe why it's important to include a section on "buyer behavior" in a business plan.
8. Explain the purpose of a competitor analysis.
9. Explain why it's important to collect competitive intelligence, and describe some of the techniques that are used to collect it.
10. Briefly describe the four separate ways of estimating the annual sales and market share of a new business.

Application Questions

1. Recreate Prime Adult Fitness's estimate of the size of its target market, and substitute the county that your college of university is located in for Seminole County, Florida. How do your numbers compare with the numbers reported in Prime Adult Fitness's estimate?
2. Prepare a competitive analysis grid for Runkeeper (www.runkeeper.com), a company that makes an iPhone app that tracks workouts. Summarize what you learn about Runkeeper's competitive landscape and its points of differentiation through this exercise.
3. Put yourself in the place of an investor listening to Prime Adult Fitness present the market analysis portion of its business plan. Think of three penetrating questions that you would ask about the market analysis.
4. Imagine you're writing the business plan for a smoothie shop that you plan to launch near the campus of the college or university you attend. Make an estimate of your Year 1 sales using the bottom–up approach to the multiplication method.

5. Fitstar (www.fitstar) is a company that produces an app that turns an iPad into a personal trainer. When Fitstar first started (with a single app that offered personal training sessions via an iPad), how would you have estimated Fitstar's initial sales? Select one or more of the four ways of estimating a new firm's sales outlined in the textbook, and explain how you would have utilized each method.

Endnotes

1. Great Call Homepage, available at www.greatcall.com (accessed October 12, 2013).
2. Seminole County Florida, *Demographic Detail Summary Report*, available at http://www.seminolecountyfl.gov/ecodev/pdf/Demographic_Detail_Report.pdf, prepared February 2, 2010 (accessed October 6, 2013).
3. "Market Segmentation" (Wikipedia), available at http://en.wikipedia.org/wiki/Market_setmentation (accessed October 6, 2013).
4. International Health, Racquet and Sportsclub Association Homepage, ihras.org (accessed June 14, 2013).
5. Baby Boot Camp Homepage, available at www.babybootcamp.com (accessed October 4, 2013).
6. J. Kurtzman, *Startups That Work* (New York: Portfolio, 2005), 156.
7. D. Schmidt, "IBISWorld Industry Report 33992a Athletic & Sporting Goods Manufacturing in the US," *IBISWorld*, May, 2013.
8. "Helping People To Live Long and Productive Lives and Enjoy a Good Quality of Life," available at http://www.cde.gov/chronicdisease/resources/publications/aag/aging.htm (accessed October 10, 2013).
9. P. Kotler, *Marketing Insights From A to Z* (Hokoken, NJ: Wiley, 2003), 23.

MARKETING PLAN

INTRODUCTION

This chapter builds on Chapter 6, which discussed the market analysis. Whereas the market analysis focused on describing a firm's target market, customers, competitors, and potential sales, this chapter focuses on how the firm will actually find customers and close sales. It deals with the nuts and bolts of marketing in terms of price, promotions, distribution, and sales. For example, GreatCall (www.greatcall.com), the firm that makes the jitterbug cell phone for older users, may have a great product, a well-defined target market, a good understanding of its customers and competitors, and a sizeable market, but it still has to find customers and persuade them to buy its product. The marketing plan section communicates your specific plans for meeting these objectives.

The best way to describe a company's marketing plan is to start by articulating its marketing strategy, positioning, and points of differentiation, and then talk about how these overall aspects of the plan will be supported by price, promotional mix and sales process, and distribution strategy. If you haven't discussed your product yet, it should be talked about here. Most business plans provide a description of their product or service in an earlier section of the plan, however.

The marketing section must lay out specifically how you plan to make your target market aware of the existence of your product or service. Many business plans do a good job of describing the size of a company's target market and the merits of its product but do a poor job of dealing with the practicalities of how the product will be sold. Obviously, it's not possible to include a full-blown marketing plan in the four to five pages permitted in a business plan for the marketing section, but you need to provide your reader a sense of how you'll market and sell your product within the confines of a reasonable budget. It's also important to reinforce how your product provides its user unique value and differs from similar products in the marketplace.

There are two things to be mindful of as you write this section. First, all of the elements of a firm's marketing plan should be developed with the customer plainly in mind. This notion extends beyond producing a product or service that accommodates your customers' needs, to knowing the amount of disposable income they have, the periodicals they read, the media they watch, and so on, depending on the type of business you have. Knowledge of these, and similar factors, helps you to fine-tune your marketing strategy and lower expenses. An example of the potential benefits involved is provided by Ron Boire, the president of sales for Sony consumer electronics. In 2000, Sony (http://www.sony.com) ran an advertising campaign to try to resurrect the Sony Walkman, the original portable music player. The campaign, titled "The Walkman Has Landed," featured an alien mascot that looked like a cross between E.T. and Smurf. Sony ran its ads in print and media outlets that specifically catered to its target market—Generation Y consumers (13–30 years old). During the campaign, Boire was reminded of the value of restricting his ad dollars to media most likely to be seen by his target market:

> I think that our experience with the Walkman alien campaign that was started in 2000 best captures it. We were spending tens of millions of dollars on media and I had friends (over 30 years old) say, "You know, I've never seen the ads." It's like, "Good. That's a good thing that we've run hundreds and hundreds of slots and you've never seen one, because you're not the target. That means I'm targeting razor sharp."[1]

Although Sony is a large, multinational firm, the same logic applies to a startup. By knowing your customers and tailoring your marketing efforts specifically to them, you can deliver a sharper message and avoid the expenses associated with reaching people less likely to buy your product. The "Buyer Behavior" section in Chapter 6 contains information that, along with other insights you are able to accumulate, should inform all of your marketing-related decisions.

The second thing to be mindful of as you write this section is that you must detail exactly who will sell your product and how your sales process will work. Many business plans provide an overview of how their product will be priced and promoted but never zero in on how it will actually be sold. This is a critical issue that is often missing from business plans. You should describe your sales process and the methods that you'll use to sell your product, whether it is via a direct sales force, through distributors or wholesalers, through an alliance with companies that sell complementary products, or through some other means. If you plan to field a direct sales force, you should describe how you plan to recruit salespeople, how their jobs will be structured, and how they will be compensated. Knowing that you have thought through these issues will bolster the confidence your readers have in the plan.

This marketing chapter of the business plan contains four sections: overall marketing strategy, pricing strategy, sales process and promotions mix, and distribution and sales. The overall marketing strategy of the Prime Adult Fitness business plan is shown in Figure 7-1.

FIGURE 7-1 Overall Marketing Strategy (Prime Adult Fitness Business Plan)

Overall Marketing Strategy

The overall objective of Prime Adult Fitness's marketing strategy is to make people 50 years old and older aware of the benefits of exercise and to sell them on the idea that our fitness center is the best place for them to either start or continue exercising. We don't plan to accomplish this objective through splashy ads. Our overall approach will be to generate grassroots support and word-of-mouth referrals through a series of marketing tactics that will demonstrate how exercise and membership in Prime Adult Fitness enhances the lives of our members.

Our marketing strategy is also based on the notion that marketing is everyone's responsibility—our staff, our employees, our directors, our advisory board members, and even our members. Every program, every class, every piece of equipment we buy, and every interaction with our members will be based on the goal of fulfilling our mission, which is expressed through our tagline, "Meet Your Dreams." We so strongly believe that people 50 years old and older want to be fit and lead healthy lives that we've created a fitness center just for them. We want our target market to know how much we care. That sentiment will be reflected through our marketing strategy and tactics.

We are also keenly aware that we must reach our membership goals. The number 2,100 is our membership goal for 2014. That number will be a motivational tool and will be the central metric we use to hold ourselves accountable for translating our caring attitudes into business results. The slogan "Let's Care Enough to Reach 2,100" will appear on all our internal documents and will be a central part of our employee motivation program.

Positioning

Prime Adult Fitness's target market is the health and fitness club market for people 50 years old and older. Its position in the market is to offer a tailored offering (meaning its facilities and programs will be specifically geared to people 50 years old and older) at the high end of the market, in terms of amenities and price.

Points of Differentiation

- Only fitness center in our target market exclusively for people 50 years old and older
- Strong emphasis placed on the social aspect of belonging to a fitness center
- Well-trained staff that cares about the needs and lives of older people

Product Attribute Map

Prime Adult Fitness's positioning strategy and its primary point of differentiation are illustrated in the product attribute map shown below. As shown, Prime Adult Fitness will be the only fitness center in its trade area that ranks high on both (1) the degree to which it is tailored specifically to the needs of its clientele and (2) the extent to which it offers a high range of amenities for its members. It ranks slightly lower than generic fitness centers in terms of range of amenities. There are several aspects of general fitness centers, like large weight rooms (for free weights), that will be scaled down by Prime Adult Fitness, given our clientele.

FIGURE 7-1 (continued)

Prime Adult Fitness's second and third points of differentiation, a strong emphasis on socialization and a trained and caring staff, brings its positioning strategy and primary point of differentiation to life (and makes them sustainable). Its objective is to not only open and run a fitness center for 50+ individuals but also open and run a center that makes them feel safe, secure, welcome, and at home.

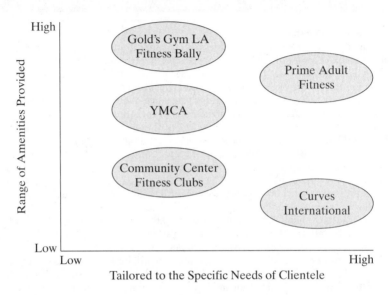

OVERALL MARKETING STRATEGY

Marketing strategy refers to a firm's approach to marketing its products and services stated in broad terms, which forms the basis of all of its marketing-related activities. It's a good idea to begin the marketing plan section of a business plan by articulating your marketing strategy because it sets the tone for the entire section. It also reassures your reader that your various marketing activities are part of an overall approach or plan. All firms have constraints regarding the resources they have to devote to their marketing and sales efforts. As a result, it's extremely important that a firm have an overall philosophy or approach to marketing that enables it to deploy resources in a purposeful and consistent manner.

Another important reason for having a marketing strategy and for articulating it in a business plan is to make sure that a firm's marketing efforts are consistent with its overall mission and understanding of the market. This desired congruence is clearly seen in Prime Adult Fitness's marketing strategy, which is shown in Figure 7-1. The company's marketing strategy is clearly a reflection of how the company feels about its target market (which is reflective of its mission) and what it learned in completing its industry analysis and market analysis.

There are two additional parts to this section: positioning strategy and points of differentiation.

POSITIONING STRATEGY

After selecting a target market, the next step is for a firm to select a "position" in the market. Position is concerned with how a firm is situated relative to its rivals (or potential rivals). In a sense, a position is the part of a specific target market that a firm is claiming for its own. To understand a firm's market position, you need to study the features of its goods or services. For example, BMW's position (luxury) in the automobile market differs from Chevrolet's position (functional). Clearly, these products differ from one another in substantial ways. Even within the luxury automobile market, BMW's position (more sports-driving oriented) differs from that of Lexus (more luxury-features oriented).

As shown earlier in Figure 7-1, Prime Adult Fitness has positioned itself at the top end of the fitness market, in terms of the range of amenities offered for its target market (people 50 years old and older). It will offer its members access to a premier selection of exercise equipment, fitness classes, and other programs in a modern comfortable 21,600 square foot facility. In exchange for these amenities, Prime Adult Fitness will charge a monthly membership fee that is also at the top end of the market. This is Prime Adult Fitness's position. There are other positions in its target market that it could have occupied. For instance, Prime Adult Fitness could offer a much more limited set of amenities to its members and charge a lower monthly fee, as 24 Hour Fitness and Curves have done in their target markets. Both positions may be viable and profitable. Determining which position to occupy and compete in is simply a judgment call on the part of a company based on its mission, its overall approach to the marketplace, and its competitive landscape.

POINTS OF DIFFERENTIATION

You should also clearly articulate your specific points of differentiation early in the marketing plan section of your business plan. These points were illustrated in your competitive analysis grid in Chapter 6. It's typically best to limit the points of differentiation that you talk about to two or three points, to make them memorable and distinct. Also, make sure that the value of these points is easy for your reader to see. For example, ZUCA (www.zuca.com), the backpack on rollers, has two distinct points of differentiation: It relieves back pain by putting the backpack on rollers, and it's sturdy enough for either a child or an adult to sit on. Laura Udall, ZUCA's founder, confirmed the meaningfulness of these points of differentiation through focus groups.[2] She even has a picture of her teenage son sitting on the ZUCA's seat, which anyone could imagine might be handy for kids waiting for the school bus. You should also make sure your points of differentiation aren't liabilities, if a discerning reader starts playing devil's advocate. For instance, if Udall said that the ZUCA will be offered in 20 different colors, on the face of it, that sounds good. But think about the ramifications of offering 20 different colors: complicated production process, limited channels through which the product is sold, and few retailers with enough shelf space to carry 20 different colors of a backpack. This type of disconnect or naivety undermines the credibility of a business plan.

There are many other potential sources of differentiation. The most compelling forms of differentiation are created through innovations that are difficult to imitate because they are created by competencies unique to a firm. Starbucks creates this type of differentiation through the ambiance of its restaurants. Apple does it through product design. Google does it through the speed and accuracy of its search results. Prime Adult Fitness hopes to create meaningful differentiation through its singular focus on servicing people who are 50 years old and older.

A useful way for a startup to visually depict its primary point of differentiation is through a product attribute map. A product attribute map is created by articulating two of a product's most important attributes, one on the x-axis of the map and the other on the y-axis. A firm then simply plots itself relative to its major competitors. Prime Adult Fitness's product attribute map is shown in Figure 7-1. The map clearly illustrate that Prime Adult Fitness is the only fitness center in its trade area that ranks high on both the degree to which it is tailored specifically to the needs of its clientele and the extent to which it offers a high range of amenities for its members. In the product attribute map assessment, the firm makes the further point that it plans to protect its primary source of differentiation (highly tailored service/ high level of amenities) through its two other sources of differentiation—a strong emphasis on socialization and a trained and caring staff.

PRICING STRATEGY

This section should explain how you plan to price your product or service. Price is an important issue because it determines how much money a company can earn. The price a company charges for its products also sends a clear message to its target customers. For example, Oakley (www.oakley.com) positions its sunglasses as innovative, state-of-the art products that are both high quality and visually appealing. This position in the market suggests the premium price that Oakley charges. If Oakley advertised innovative, state-of-the art products but charged a bargain basement price, it would send confusing signals to its customers. Its customers would wonder, "Are Oakley sunglasses high quality or aren't they?" In addition, the lower price wouldn't generate the sales revenue Oakley needs to continuously differentiate its sunglasses from competitors' products in ways that create value for its customers.

In this section, you should state how you plan to price your product or service and provide a brief rationale for your pricing philosophy. The Prime Adult Fitness business plan, shown in Figure 7-2, plainly states its pricing policy and then shows a comparison of the pricing structure to direct competitors and national averages. Although at first glance, price seems like a straightforward topic, it is actually quite complex. There are different methods for determining a product's price, and a variety of other issues are involved.

FIGURE 7-2   Pricing Strategy (Prime Adult Fitness Business Plan)

Pricing Strategy

Prime Adult Fitness will adopt a policy of value-based (opposed to cost-based) pricing and will price its initial enrollment fee and monthly membership fee on two criteria:

- Current prices charged by director competitors in its trade area
- The perceived value of its service by its target clientele

Prime Adult Fitness's Prices vs. Direct Competitors and National Averages

	Prime Adult Fitness	Direct Competitors in Trade Area	National Average
Initial (One Time)	Single: $150	Single: $145	Single: $150
Membership Fee	Couples: $150	Couples: $165	Couples: $199
	Family: n/a	Family: $165	Family: $199
Monthly	Single: $70	Single: $72.50	Single: $55
Membership Fee	Couples: $92.50	Couples: $87.50	Couples: $89
	Family: n/a	Family: $87.50	Family: $89

Sources: Direct Competitors, Prime Adult Fitness Survey

National Averages: International Health, Racquet & Sportsclub Association

Summary

The pricing schedule shown above demonstrates that Prime Adult Fitness's prices are on par with its direct competitors and national averages. The schedule was subjected to scrutiny in three focus groups, and no serious objections were raised.

This part of the marketing plan includes two sections: cost-based pricing versus value-based pricing and other pricing-related issues.

COST-BASED PRICING VERSUS VALUE-BASED PRICING

The two methods for determining the price of a product or service are cost-based pricing and value-based pricing. In cost-based pricing, the list price is determined by adding a markup percentage to a product's cost. The markup percentage may be standard for the industry or may be arbitrarily determined by you. The advantage of this method is that it's straightforward, and it's relatively easy to justify the price of a good or service. For this reason, many regulated utilities use cost-based pricing. The disadvantage is that it's not always easy to estimate what the costs of a product will be, particularly for a startup. After a price is set, raising the price is difficult, even if a company's costs increase. In addition, cost-based pricing is based on what a company thinks it should receive rather than what the market thinks a good or service is worth. Companies are finding it increasingly difficult to dictate prices to their customers, given customers' ability to comparison shop, even for industrial goods, on the Internet to find what they believe is the best price.[3]

In value-based pricing, the list price is determined by estimating what consumers are willing to pay for a product and then backing off a bit to provide a cushion. What a customer is willing to pay is determined by the perceived value of the product and by the number of choices available in the marketplace. Sometimes, to make this determination, a company has to conduct focus groups or try different pricing options in test markets. A firm influences its customers' perception of value through positioning, branding, promotions, and the other elements of its marketing plan.

Whether you choose cost-based pricing or value-based pricing is an important call. Most experts recommend value-based pricing because it hinges on the perceived value of a product or service rather than cost plus markup, which is a formula that ignores the customer. Value-based pricing also frequently produces a higher gross margin. A gross margin (a company's net sales minus its cost of goods sold) of 60 to 80 percent is not uncommon in high-tech industries. An Intel chip that sells for $300 may cost $50 to produce. This type of markup reflects the perceived value of the chip. If Intel had used a cost-based pricing method instead of a value-based approach, it would probably charge much less for its chip.

Of course, regardless of whether you choose cost-based or value-based pricing, your price must make sense given the realities of your market. Prime Adult Fitness included the table that compares its price to its direct competitors and national averages to reassure its readers that the target market will see the price as fair and reasonable given the alternatives.

OTHER PRICING-RELATED ISSUES

Most experts warn startups to resist the temptation to charge a low price for their products in the hopes of capturing market share. This approach can win a sale but generates little profit. In addition, most consumers make a price–quality attribution when looking at the price of a product. This means that consumers naturally assume that the high-priced product is also the better-quality product. If a firm charges a low price for its products, it sends a signal to customers that the product is low quality regardless of whether it really is.

A vivid example of the association between price and quality is provided by SmugMug (www.smugmug.com), an online photo-sharing site that charges a $40 per year base subscription fee. According to its Web site, the company has "Billions of Happy Photos" and "Millions of Happy Customers." What's interesting about the company is that most of its competitors, including Photobucket (www.photobucket.com), Flickr (www.flickr.com), and Picas Web Albums (https://picasweb.google.com) offer a similar service for free. Ostensibly, the reason SmugMug is able to charge a fee is that it offers higher levels of customer service and has a more user-friendly interface (in terms of how you view your photos online) than its competitors. But the owners of SmugMug feel that its ability to charge goes beyond these obvious points. Some of the free sites have closed abruptly, and their users have lost photos. SmugMug, because it charges, is seen as more reliable and dependable for the long term. (Who wants to lose their photos?) In addition, the owners believe that when people pay for something, they innately assign a higher value to it. As a result, SmugMug users tend to treat the site with respect, by posting attractive, high-quality photos that are in good taste. SmugMug's users appreciate this facet of the site, compared to the free sites, where unseemly photos often creep in.[4]

The overarching point of this example and the preceding discussion is that the price you're able to charge is largely a function of (1) the objective quality of your product or service and (2) the perception of value that you create in the minds of your customers relative to completing products in the marketplace. You should carefully assess each of these criteria as you set your prices and develop your pricing philosophy.

The next section focuses on a firm's sales process and its promotional mix. This section of Prime Adult Fitness's business plan is shown in Figure 7-3.

FIGURE 7-3   Sales Process and Promotional Mix (Prime Adult Fitness Business Plan)

Sales Process (or Cycle)

A foundational aspect of Prime Adult Fitness's sales and promotional strategy is its sales process. This is the process the company will use to recruit members and is the process that the in-house staff will follow when people walk into the center and inquire about membership. At times, the process will take weeks to unfold if Prime Adult Fitness personnel have multiple contacts with a prospect, and at times the process will unfold in a few minutes, as an employee provides a prospect a tour of the facility and answers questions.

The company has devised specific marketing tactics to support each step in the sales process. These tactics are a work in process and will invariably be enhanced and revised as Prime Adult Fitness learns more about the characteristics of its target market.

Stage in Process	Ways Prime Adult Fitness Will Support Each Phase of the Process
1. Prospecting (or sales lead)	• Referrals from current members • Direct mail (targeting households that meet Prime Adult Fitness's demographic profile) • Partnership with Central Florida Health Food[*] • Partnership with Oviedo Doctor's and Surgeon's Medical Practice[*] • Downloads from company Web site[*] • Responses from the company's radio and print advertisements
2. The initial contact	• All employees will be provided training in building rapport with prospects. • Prospects are provided an information packet about Prime Adult Fitness. • Radio and print ads will direct prospects to Prime Adult Fitness's Web site, which contains a short video and other promotional material.

FIGURE 7-3 (continued)

3. Qualifying the lead	• All employees will be trained to assess whether a prospect represents a qualified lead. Prospects that are qualified as good leads will be offered a tour of Prime Adult Fitness's facilities. • If a qualified lead does not join initially, he or she will be contacted by phone as a follow-up three days after the visit.
4. Sales presentation	• Qualified leads will be provided a facility tour. • Qualified leads will be shown a short film (nine minutes) featuring Prime Adult Fitness's facility and programs and the benefits of fitness for older people. • A packet of testimonials will be developed over time and provided to prospects as part of the sales presentation process.
5. Meeting objections and concerns	• Employees will be trained on how to meet the most common and obvious objections and concerns. • In regard to price objections, a brochure has been prepared that compares (1) Prime Adult Fitness's initial (one-time) enrollment fee and monthly membership fee to other fitness centers and (2) the cost of joining and belonging to a fitness center as opposed to other forms of recreation and entertainment (i.e., boating, golfing). • A similar brochure has been prepared to compare Prime Adult Fitness's amenities to the amenities of other fitness centers.
6. Closing the sale	• All employees will be trained to ask qualified prospects to join.
7. Follow-up	• Each new member will be contacted by phone 30 days after they join as a courtesy to see how things are going. After that, they will be contacted by phone once a year. Each phone call will also be used to ask for names of referrals. • Prime Adult Fitness will produce a monthly newsletter that will be mailed to each member. • Prime Adult Fitness's staff and employees will be trained to engage members and to thank them for their membership and solicit suggestions for improvement on a continual basis.

*Described under promotional activities.

Promotional Activities
Other promotional activities and tactics are planned as follows:

- *Partnership with Central Florida Health Food.* Prime Adult Fitness has entered into a cobranding relationship with Central Florida Health Food. Central Florida Health Food will periodically place coupons in its shopping bags that provide access to premiums for taking a tour of Prime Adult Fitness's facilities.

FIGURE 7-3   (continued)

- *Partnership with Oviedo Doctor's and Surgeon's Medical Practice.* Prime Adult Fitness has entered into a cobranding relationship with Oviedo Doctor's and Surgeon's medical practice, which will cover a range of activities. For example, the practice will periodically show a film that features Prime Adult Fitness and the benefits of exercise for older people in the waiting room of its facility.
- *Downloads from Web Site.* Prime Adult Fitness will place information on its Web site that can be downloaded. Some of the richest information will require a free registration prior to the download. The names and addresses taken from the registrations will be used as sales leads.
- *Radio Advertising.* Prime Adult Fitness will create radio ads that will be periodically run on WMFE, the public radio station that services Prime Adult Fitness's trade area.
- *Print Advertising.* Select print advertisements will be run.
- *Membership Drive.* Prime Adult Fitness will execute a membership drive in January and February of each year. January, February, and March are the three biggest months for new memberships in fitness clubs.

Annual Marketing Budget

Item	*Budget*
Promotional material (brochures, handouts)	$12,000
Radio advertising	$16,000
Print advertising	$12,000
Web site material, updating, and support (50% of cost of supporting site)	$6,000
Updating film portraying Prime Adult Fitness and the benefit of fitness for older people	$4,000
Other (including local sponsorships and community support)	$6,000
Total	$56,000

SALES PROCESS AND PROMOTIONS MIX

A firm's sales process (or cycle) depicts the steps it goes through to identify prospects and close sales. A firm's promotions mix refers to the specific tactics it uses, such as advertising and public relations, to support the sales process and enhance its overall brand. The entirety of this process is typically scrutinized carefully by discerning readers of a business plan. Sales and promotions is one area where hard work and ingenuity can make up for a lack of funds. It is also an area where money can be easily wasted if the sales process is not carefully thought through and executed, and promotional tactics, such as print and media advertising campaigns, are poorly conceived or badly implemented.

This section includes two subsections: sales process and promotions mix.

SALES PROCESS

A firm's sales process (or cycle) refers to the steps it goes through to establish relationships with customers and close sales. It doesn't matter whether a business is selling directly to customers or through an intermediary such as a distributor or a wholesaler; it still has a process through which it makes sales. The process varies by firm, but normally includes the following steps:

1. Prospect for (or gather) sales leads.
2. Make the initial contact.
3. Qualify the lead.
4. Make the sales presentation.
5. Meet objections and concerns.
6. Close the sale.
7. Follow up.

Ostensibly, following a structured process to generate and close sales benefits a company in four ways. First, it enables a firm to fine-tune its approach to sales and build uniformity into the process. Second, if the process is clear, selling becomes a set of clearly defined steps, rather than an awkward process where salespeople are always unsure about what to do next. Third, the process helps qualify leads, so the firm can spend its time and money pursuing the most likely buyers of the product or service. Finally, a fine-tuned sales process facilitates a company's growth. By having a repeatable process that works, a company can bring new salespeople on board who can get up to speed quickly and help ramp up overall sales. Most well-managed firms have a formal sales process, similar to the one shown previously, and train their employees accordingly.

Prime Adult Fitness articulates its sales process in its business plan (refer to Figure 7-3), which mirrors the process shown in the preceding list. The business plan also indicates Prime Adult Fitness's general plans for supporting each stage in the process. As indicated in the plan, the sales process is an early prototype of what it will most likely become because Prime Adult Fitness will invariably tweak the process as it gains experience in the marketplace. Still, the process shown in the business plan is an important starting point for developing a customized and effective sales process for the company.[5]

PROMOTIONS MIX

A firm's promotions mix includes the specific tactics that a firm uses to communicate with potential customers. The approaches to promotions discussed here include advertising, public relations, social media, and other promotion-related activities.

ADVERTISING

Advertising is making people aware of a product in hopes of persuading them to buy it. The major goals of advertising are to raise customer awareness of a product, explain a product's comparative features and benefits, and create an association between a product and a certain lifestyle (or a certain objective in a business-to-business context). These goals can be accomplished through a number of media, including direct mail, magazines, newspapers, radio, the Internet, television, and billboard advertising. The media used normally depends on a firm's target market. For example, a new piece of industrial equipment typically would be advertised through an industry trade magazine, whereas a consumer product would be advertised through the medium most likely to be viewed by the company's target audience.

Although selective forms of advertising may be appropriate for your business, there are many downsides to conventional forms of advertising, which steers most startups away from advertising on a broad basis. The major weaknesses include the following:

- Low credibility
- The possibility that a high percentage of the people who see the ad will not be interested
- Message clutter (meaning that after hearing or reading so many ads, people simply tune out)
- Relative costliness compared to other forms of promotions
- The perception that advertising is intrusive
- The possibility that a poorly crafted ad runs the risk of irritating the firm's target market

Because of these weaknesses, most startups do not advertise broadly. Instead, they tend to be very frugal and selective in their advertising efforts, such as limiting their print ads to industry trade journals or using highly focused pay-per-click advertising provided by Google or Bing or highly targeted ads on Facebook, Twitter, or other Web sites.

Despite the potential downsides, you shouldn't be reluctant to use advertising if it makes sense, given your target market, and you can clearly explain its rationale. For example, if you launched a Web site to sell plus-sized clothing for children, the only way to reach a specific audience and achieve the sales volume you desire may be via targeted pay-per-click advertising on the Internet. Many of the better pay-per-click programs, such as Google AdWords (www.google.com/adwords) and BingAds (bingads.microsoft.com), also helps businesses strictly control the amount of money they spend through their programs.

PUBLIC RELATIONS

Public relations refers to efforts to establish and maintain a company's image with the public. The major difference between public relations and advertising is that public relations isn't paid for. As a result, many startups emphasize public relations over advertising because it's free and helps build the firm's credibility. Many techniques fit the definition of public relations. Some of the more common techniques are as follows:

- Press release
- Event sponsorship
- Traditional media coverage (such as articles in newspapers and magazines)
- Articles in industry periodicals, such as trade journals
- Monthly newsletter
- Social media
- Blogging
- Civic, social, and community involvement

In most cases, firms believe that generating favorable public relations about their company is better than advertising because it is more grassroots and doesn't seem to be as self-serving. The key to getting public relations that's created by others, such as a newspaper or magazine article written about your company, is to create a human interest story that's associated with your firm. It also helps to be proactive in regard to speaking out on behalf of your industry and talking to trade groups and civic groups about your industry or area of expertise.

Lisa Druxman, the founder of FIT4MOM (http://fitformom.com), a franchise organization for new mothers, provides an example of how these efforts come together to create positive public relations for a firm. FIT4MOM (originally called Stroller Strides) is a concept that Druxman created to get herself back in shape after she had her first baby. It is an organized workout class where women push strollers, power walk, and exercise outdoors to meet their fitness goals and socialize with other new mothers. Prior to starting FIT4MOM, Druxman was the general manager of a health club. Druxman's story is a classic illustration of how public relations works and the potential payoffs are involved:

> When I (was) the general manager at the health club, I would regularly go on the news promoting new workouts. One day the TV station called me and asked, "Would you mind coming in with your baby and giving (some) tips on how to get back in shape?" So I did, and I promoted my class as if it were this big business—I gave out my home e-mail and personal cell phone number. By the time I got home from the station, I had 75 calls and e-mails from all over San Diego from people who were interested in taking my class. I had my grand opening class 3 weeks after that, with 40 people there and more news coverage.[6]

The key to Druxman's success, in this instance, was that she was able to tell her story through an unbiased third party, the TV program. Sometime you'll get lucky, like Lisa Druxman, and an opportunity to talk about your startup will fall in your lap. The more common way to garner the attention of a newspaper or magazine is via a press kit. A press kit is a prepackaged set of promotional material for a business that is distributed to the media. It includes information about a startup such as the story of where the business idea from the company came from, press releases highlighting the current accomplishments of the company, digital photos of the company's products, and so on. Media outlets, such as newspapers, magazines, blogs, radio programs, and television shows use press kits to formulate stories. The key to getting coverage is having an interesting story to tell, rather than simply extolling the value of your product or service. If you think your company has the potential to generate good public relations, you should make a press kit part of your promotions strategy.[7]

SOCIAL MEDIA

Social media consists primarily of blogging and establishing a presence and connecting with customers and others through social networking sites like Twitter, Facebook, and Google+.[8] The number one rule for determining whether to use social media is if the customers in a business's target market are active social media users. The largest group of social media users for men is in the 45–54-year age group and for women in the 25–34 years age group. Only 11 percent of men and 10 percent of women age 55 and older are active social media users.[9] Although Prime Adult Fitness may have some social media presence, these statistics suggest that putting substantial effort into a social media marketing campaign for Prime Adult Fitness is not a good choice. Most investors and others have a general notion of who the heaviest social media users are, and would not be surprised to see a lack of a social media strategy in Prime Adult Fitness's business plan. In fact, if Prime Adult Fitness proposed an aggressive social media strategy, it would send the wrong message. It would demonstrate that its founders were not looking closely at the data in regard to the demographic breakdown of social media users.

For startups that have discerned that customers in their target market are active social media users, social media can be a very effective. The idea behind blogs is that they familiarize people with a business and help build an emotional bond between a business and its customers. Similarly, businesses use social networking sites like Facebook, Twitter, and Google+ to build communities around their products and services. The benefits include brand building, engaging customers, lead generation, and online sales. An example of a company that makes effective use of blogging and social media is ModCloth (www.modcloth.com), an online retailer of vintage clothing for women. ModCloth's blog (http://blog.modcloth.com) not only draws attention to the company's products but also posts fun, entertaining, and informative articles and photos of interest to its target market. The blog also features contests that provide cash prizes and photos of customers wearing ModCloth products. The company is also active on social media, including Facebook and Twitter. Several times a day, ModCloth and its friends post fashion information, fun facts, and a variety of related information on its Facebook wall. This pace of activity makes people come back and creates a community of engaged customers. Extensive use of social media makes perfect sense for ModCloth. Its target market is 18–34-year-old women who are heavy social media users.

OTHER PROMOTION-RELATED ACTIVITIES

Many other activities can help a firm promote and sell its products. Some firms, for example, give away free sample or trial memberships as a way of exposing potential customers to their product or service. Many food companies distribute free samples in grocery stores and discount centers. Red Bull (www.redbull.com), the highly successful energy drink company, created interest in its product by initially offering free samples through sports clubs and other places in which athletes congregated. This type of initiative is often pursued to try to create "buzz" or word-of-mouth advertising for a product or service. Creating buzz means creating awareness and a sense of anticipation about a company and its offerings.[10] This process can start during feasibility analysis, when a company shows its concept statement or product prototype to prospective buyers or industry experts. Unless a company wants all activities kept secret (to preserve its proprietary technology or its first-mover advantage), the goal is to get people talking about the company and the exciting new product or service. You should investigate the many techniques for creating buzz or word-of-mouth marketing at a low cost.

One issue that is particularly important in executing a promotions plan is to focus on the benefits of a product or service rather than the features. The importance of this issue is explained in the Business Plan Insights box.

In most cases, putting together a specific budget for promotional activities is helpful. Prime Adult Fitness includes a promotional budget in its business plan as shown earlier in Figure 7-3.

The next section of this portion of the business plan focuses on distribution.

BUSINESS PLAN INSIGHT

Selling Benefits Rather Than Features

Many startups make the mistake of promoting the features rather than the benefits of their product or service. A promotional strategy that focuses on the features of a product, such as its technical merits, is usually much less effective than a campaign focusing on the merits of what the product can do. Consider an ad for Prime Adult Fitness that reads something like this, "Our fitness center, which is just for adults, has 16 exercises classes, a pool that is available for water aerobics and open swims, and a full spa and massage service." These are all features, and while features are nice, they typically don't entice someone to join a health club. A better way for Prime Adult Fitness to promote itself would be to say, "Our fitness center, which is just for adults, will feature classes and exercise equipment that help adults maintain their fitness, avoid the onset of certain alignment, and lead healthier lives." This statement focuses on benefits by telling prospects how joining Prime Adult Fitness will enhance their lives.

As a general rule of thumb, it's more effective to tote the benefits of a product or service rather than the features.

DISTRIBUTION AND SALES

Distribution encompasses all the activities that move a firm's product from its place of origin to the consumer. For a company like Prime Adult Fitness, distribution is not a major issue because it's a service business that provides for its own sales functions. As a result, the company relies on working through the sales process and on promotional activities to gain memberships to its fitness center—so there is no separate distribution and sales section in this business plan. The landscape is much different for other companies. When Laura Udall first invented the ZUCA (backpack on wheels), she had to decide how the product would be distributed and sold. There were many choices. ZUCA could hire and field its own sales force, or work through intermediaries, such as wholesalers, distributors, or manufacturing representatives, as will be explained in more detail later in this chapter.

This section of your business plan should clearly identify your distribution and sales plan, in terms of who will make the sales. To assist you with thinking through these issues, this part of the chapter includes two sections: distribution and sales alternatives, and sales strategy and related issues.

DISTRIBUTION AND SALES ALTERNATIVES

The first step in determining a distribution and sales strategy, for a firm that is more complex than Prime Adult Fitness on this dimension, is to sort through the choices. For example, imagine you are starting a company that produces electronics products for consumers. You could opt to field a sales force that approaches companies such as Best Buy and Walmart to persuade them to carry your product. You could also sell direct to consumers without the need for salespeople, through catalogue or Internet sales. Another option is to sell through an intermediary, such as a distributor, a wholesaler, or a manufacturer's representative. If you decided to go this route, your intermediary would call on Best Buy and Walmart to try to persuade them to carry your product on your behalf.

A similar set of choices would apply if you were selling a service rather than an electronics product. Hotels, for example, sell their services (typically rooms) directly through their Web sites and telephone reservation services, and also through intermediaries, such as travel agents, tour operators, airlines, and so forth. For example, if you were planning a trip to Walt Disney World in Orlando, Florida, you could book your flight, rental car, and hotel through Orbitz (http://www.orbitz.com), Travelocity (http://www.travelocity.com), or many other similar services. In this instance, Orbitz and the others are acting as intermediaries for the service providers.

There are also blended approaches, regardless of whether you are selling a product or service. Many firms sell direct plus through intermediaries. For example, many businesses sell their product via their Web site (direct) and also through distributors (intermediaries) who help them secure shelf space in retail stores. If handled awkwardly, this approach can cause what's called "channel conflict." Channel conflict occurs when a business sells online (capturing all the profits itself) and also wants retailers to sell its products through their stores. The retailers may be less motivated to carry or push the business's product thinking that customers might see the product in their store and then go online to buy it. Despite this potential complication, many businesses sell both online and through distributors and manage the potential conflict effectively.

The key to making the right choices among these alternatives is to think carefully first about where people in your target market shop, and then about the most effective and economical ways to get your products some shelf space in those outlets. You also need to think about the operational ramifications of your choices. Although it might sound good to get your product placed in Best Buy or Walmart from the outset, few startups are prepared to ramp up production fast enough to satisfy these types of retailers. In addition, you need to carefully weigh the choice of retail outlets and other resellers (such as Orbitz and Travelocity) with your brand and the image you want to convey to your target market.

SALES STRATEGY AND RELATED ISSUES

The description of your distribution and sales plan should make it clear whether you plan to field your own sales force. If you do decide to employ sales personnel, you should describe how many salespeople you will initially need, how their numbers will be ramped up as your company grows, and how they will be compensated. You will probably need to talk to industry experts and study industry trade journals and reports to make these calls. You'll also rely heavily on the sales projections for your firm created in Chapter 6 to assess your needs.

If you plan to see direct, through Internet or catalog sales, you should report whether you plan to inventory your product and fulfill orders yourself or whether you plan to use a fulfillment service like Shipwire or Amazon Fulfillment. Traditionally, businesses that have produced physical goods have managed the fulfillment and shipping of orders themselves. There are now other options. For example, a company that sells medical products can contract with a fulfillment service such as Shipwire (www.shipwire.com) to receive, warehouse, and ship its products. The sale would still be made through the medical products company's Web site, but the site would be electronically monitored by the fulfillment service, and when an order came in, the fulfillment service would process and ship the order. The order could even be shipped in a box with the medical products company's logo on it. Of course, there is a fee for this service, but an increasingly number of small businesses are opting in favor of this option rather than managing the fulfillment and shipping of orders themselves.

If you plan to distribute your products through intermediaries, you should briefly explain how the intermediaries will be chosen, and the ways in which the intermediaries will interface with the sales outlets in your industry. In most cases, you will have to support your distributors and other intermediaries with training, technical support, shipping, point-of-sale advertising material, and other forms of sales support. If any out-of-the ordinary levels of support apply in your case, they should be identified.

An exciting element of distribution and sales strategy for new firms is that the conventional forms of distribution and sales don't always have to be followed. One way a new firm can innovate and provide unique value in the marketplace is via distribution and sales. For example, Dell (www.dell.com) revolutionized the computer industry by deciding to sell directly to the consumer, first over the phone and later via the Internet, rather than through retail stores, which was the conventional method for selling computers in 1984 when Dell was founded. Similarly, IKEA (www.ikea.com), the Swedish furniture company, introduced a new concept in the furniture industry by opening retail outlets that are essentially display stores, and after an item is selected, the purchaser is directed to a loading dock where a boxed and unassembled version of the item is provided. Both of these companies have succeeded, in part, because their approach to distribution and sales were novel and fit their respective target markets. Dell's target market is the business customer who doesn't need help from a salesperson in a retail store to buy a computer and who are glad to avoid a trip to the store. IKEA's target market is singles and young families who don't mind trading off some home assembly work for a lower price.

Again, if any of these special circumstances apply in regard to your distribution and sales strategy, they should be discussed in this portion of your business plan.

Chapter Summary

1. The best way to describe a company's marketing plan is to start by articulating a marketing strategy, positioning, and points of differentiation, and then talk about how these overall aspects of the plan will be supported by price, promotional mix and sales process, and distribution strategy. If you haven't discussed your product yet, it should be talked about here.
2. There are two things to be particularly mindful of as you write the marketing section of your business plan. First, all the elements of a firm's marketing plan should be developed with the customer plainly in mind. Second, you must detail exactly who will sell your product or service.
3. This marketing section of the business plan contains four subsections: overall marketing strategy, pricing strategy, sales process and promotions mix, and distribution and sales.
4. A firm's marketing strategy is its approach to marketing products or services stated in broad terms, which forms the basis of all of its marketing-related activities.
5. After selecting a target market, the next step is for a firm to select a "position" in the market. Position is concerned with how a firm is situated relative to its rivals. In a sense, a position is a part of the market or a specific target market that a firm is claiming for its own.

6. Price is an important issue because it determines how much money a company can earn. The price a company charges for its products also sends a clear message to its target customers.

7. The two methods for determining the price of a product or service are cost-based pricing and value-based pricing. In cost-based pricing, the list price is determined by adding a markup percentage to a product's cost. In value-based pricing, the list price is determined by estimating what consumers are willing to pay for a product and then backing off a bit to provide a cushion. Most experts recommend value-based pricing because it hinges on the perceived value of a product or service rather than cost plus markup, which is a formula that ignores the customer.

8. A firm's sales process (or cycle) refers to the steps it goes through to establish relationships with customers and to close sales.

9. Advertising is making people aware of a product in hopes of persuading them to buy it. The major difference between public relations and advertising is that public relations isn't paid for. As a result, many startups emphasize public relations over advertising because it's free and helps build the firm's credibility.

10. One issue that is particularly important in executing a promotions plan is to focus on the benefits of a product or service rather than the features.

11. Distribution encompasses all the activities that move a firm's product from its place of origin to the consumer.

Review Questions

1. Describe the difference between the market analysis section of a business plan and the marketing section.
2. Why is it important for the marketing plan to be developed with the customer plainly in mind?
3. What is a company's marketing strategy, and why is it important?
4. What is meant by a company's "positioning" strategy?
5. What is the purpose of a product attribute map?
6. Describe the difference between cost-based pricing and value-based pricing.
7. What is the price–quality attribution?
8. Describe the differences between advertising and public relations? Which of the two alternatives do startups tend to prefer?
9. Provide several examples of public relations strategies.
10. Describe how firms should approach the topic of distribution and sales.

Application Questions

1. Spend some time looking at jitterbug's Website (www.greatcall.com/jitterbug). Comment on each element of jitterbug's marketing plan (product, price, promotion, and distribution and sales). On a scale of 1 to 10 (10 is high), rate the strength of jitterbug's overall marketing plan. Justify your rating.

2. Spend some time studying the Web site of ModCloth (www.modcloth.com), an online company that makes apparel products for women. Describe ModCloth's position strategy and its points of differentiation from its competitors.

3. Study the Web site of Game Truck (www.gametruckparty.com), a franchise organization that will bring a video game party in especially equipped trucks directly to your home or business. Make a list of the types of public relations activities that the owners of Game Truck and their franchisees could engage in to promote the company.

4. Brainstorm a business idea of your own. Write an elevator speech for your business idea following the guidelines for preparing an elevator speech provided in Chapter 1. Next, develop a sales process for your business following the outline provided in Figure 7-3.

5. Think of a company, other than Netflix, Dell, or IKEA, which has innovated in a very meaningful way in regard to how it distributes and sells its product or service. Write a short critique of how this innovative distribution or sales strategy has contributed to the company's success.

Endnotes

1. N. Capon, *The Marketing Mavens* (New York: Crown Business, 2007), 131.
2. "Laura Udall" (Mom Inventor's Inc.), http://www.mominventors.com, Posted June 25, 2007 (accessed September 17, 2013).
3. M. J. Silverstein, *Treasure Hunt* (New York: Portfolio, 2006).
4. Don MacAskill, CEO of SmugMug (nPost), Posted January 16, 2007 (accessed September 17, 2013).
5. Sara Williams, *Business Start Up 2010* (Harlow, England: Pearson, 2010).
6. Ladies Who Launch homepage, http://www.ladieswholaunch.com (June 27, 2007).
7. B. Barringer, *Launching a Business: The First 100 Days* (New York: Business Expert Press, LLC).
8. B. Barringer and R. Duane Ireland, *Entrepreneurship Successfully Launching New Ventures* (Upper Saddle River, NJ: Pearson, 2012).
9. "Who Likes Social Media," *KISSMetrics* (http://blog.kissmetrics.com/social-media-by-demographic), Posted February 2, 2011 (accessed September 15, 2013).
10. M. Schindehutte, M. Morris, and L. Pitt, *Rethinking Marketing* (Upper Saddle River, NJ: Pearson, 2009).

CHAPTER 8

MANAGEMENT TEAM AND COMPANY STRUCTURE

INTRODUCTION

This pivotal chapter describes a startup's management team and company structure. Many investors and others who read business plans look first at the executive summary, and then go directly to the management team section to assess the strength of the people starting the firm. This practice stems from the prevalent belief that unless a proposed new venture has a strong management team, little else matters. Affirming this sentiment, Joel Kurtzman, the author and business consultant introduced in Chapter 6, said:

> In my own view, business is about people first and everything else second. Strategies, processes, structures, and systems are only as good as the people implementing them. Good ideas never succeed on their own.[1]

This view, which is widespread in startup circles, illustrates the importance of carefully constructing the management team section of the business plan, particularly for startups that are seeking funding. Investors read more business plans with interesting ideas and exciting markets than they are able to finance. As a result, it's often not the idea or market that wins funding among competing plans, but the perception that one management team is better prepared to execute their idea than the others.

TABLE 8-1 Combinations of Ideas and Management Teams		
	Untested *Management Team*	*Tested* *Management Team*
Untested Idea	1	2
Tested Idea	3	4

Key:

1. Untested idea, untested management team. Untested ideas are exciting, though risky. In this case, the management team will need to build a convincing case that it's up to the challenge of bringing an untested idea to market.
2. Untested idea, tested management team. This is the strongest combination. Untested ideas, which typically have the largest upside potential, are best launched by a tested management team.
3. Tested idea, untested management team. This is potentially the weakest combination. Tested ideas normally compete in crowded fields with stiff combination. This is a high-risk environment for an untested management team.
4. Tested idea, tested management team. This is an okay combination, but typically will not produce impressive returns. Tested ideas tend to compete in crowded markets with stiff competition. In this environment, even a tested team may produce only average returns.

In their evaluation of management teams, investors and others tend to evaluate management teams in the context of the type of business they're proposing and the type of funding or financing they're seeking. The 2 × 2 matrix shown in Table 8-1 illustrates this point. The matrix shows four types of new ventures, defined by whether the initial management team is untested or tested and by whether the business idea is tested or untested. As shown, the best candidates for investment reside in Box 2—untested idea and tested management team. In this instance, the tested management team must prove that it is tested (in this portion of the business plan) to have the best chance of attracting investment dollars. Untested ideas typically have more upside potential because they do not reside in crowded markets. Firms that occupy the other boxes are less likely to obtain funding, at least initially, but it depends on the investor or the lender. Many bankers, for example, confine their startup investments to tested ideas and tested management teams to minimize the risk in their loans.

This part of the business plan is divided into five sections: Management Team, Board of Directors, Board of Advisors, Other Professionals, and Company Structure. The sections should be crisp and to the point, and weighty material, such as the resumes of the key employees, should be placed in an appendix to the entire plan. There are two issues that you should be particularly sensitive to as you write these sections of the plan.

First, the way your management team is assembled provides an indication of the extent to which you're open to advice and you're able to generate enthusiasm for your firm. For example, along with a description of the management team, Prime Adult Fitness's business plan shows that it already has a 5-member board of directors, a 4-member general advisory board, and a 10-member customer advisory board. Prime Adult Fitness also reports that it has received advice from several unpaid consultants. These types of efforts are impressive. They show that the people behind Prime Adult Fitness are open to advice, are willing to share power, and are able to garner support for their business idea. The initiatives may also cause a reader of their business plan to think, "If these people are able to fill three volunteer boards in a short period of time, I bet they'll have no trouble selling their business concept to paying customers."

The second thing to be sensitive to as you write the management team section of your business plan is to clearly describe how the team will evolve. Almost all new ventures have gaps in their management teams at the business plan stage. That's normal. What's important is to describe where the gaps are and how they'll be filled. In addition, you want to avoid the impression that you're naive or are unsure about the order in which to fill the gaps. For example, during the various stages of product development, a company such as ZUCA (the backpack on rollers), needs expertise in marketing and sales to make sure the product it's developing is saleable after it's produced. In the context of this example, for a startup to say that a marketing and sales person will be hired after the product is developed shows a lack of understanding of the proper upfront role of marketing input. If the startup can't afford to hire a marketing person during its product development stage, that's understandable, but evidence should then be provided that shows where the firm is getting access to marketing expertise. Similarly, if a company is proposing a product that it will manufacture but has no manufacturing expertise on its management team, that's a serious concern. Leaving issues like these unaddressed or unresolved gives the impression that the founders of the firm don't really know what they're doing and erodes the credibility of a business plan.

Along with these two issues, you should be aware that if the business will be launched by two or more cofounders, the reader of the plan will try to gain a sense of whether the composition of the cofounding team makes sense. The attributes of an effective cofounding team is explored in the Business Plan Insight Box Feature.

BUSINESS PLAN INSIGHTS

Attributes of an Effective Cofounding Team

Many businesses are launched by two or more people. There are four key criteria to consider in putting together an effective cofounding team. You want to get this right because an effective cofounding team can provide a business a significant advantage in terms of bandwidth and the capacity of the cofounders to provide each other emotional

(Continued)

support. In contrast, an ineffective cofounding team can lead to conflict, heartache, and multiple business challenges.

1. Complementary rather than redundant skills. The founding team should have complementary rather than redundant skills. For example, if one cofounder is a computer programmer, the other cofounder or cofounders should be people with different skills, such as marketing, operations, or finance.

2. Priorities and work habits should be in sync. While the cofounders don't need to be clones of one another, they do need to have similar priorities and work habits. For example, if one cofounder is willing to work 16 hours a day to get a project done on time, and the other cofounder or cofounders would rather quit after eight hours a day and try to renegotiate the contract due date for the project, that difference in work style will invariably cause conflict. Similarly, if one cofounder believes that wearing a coat and tie when meeting with clients should be the norm and other cofounder or cofounders insist on wearing blue jeans and t-shirts, obvious disagreement could arise.

3. Common goals and aspirations. It's critical that the cofounders have common goals and aspirations for the business. For example, if it's the goal of one co-founder to build a billion dollar business, and the other cofounder or cofounders would be perfectly satisfied growing the business to $10 million in sales and then selling out, problems could ensue.

4. Have a Founder's Agreement. A founders' (or shareholders') agreement is a written agreement that deals with issues such as the relative split of the equity among the founders of the firm, how individual founders will be compensated for the cash or "sweat" equity they put into the firm, and how long the founders have to remain with the firm for their shares to fully vest. The time to work these issues out is before, not after, a business launches. The agreement should be prepared by an attorney who is experienced in dealing with startups. A copy of the agreement should be placed in the appendix of the business plan.

Now, let's look at each individual section of the management team and company structure of a business plan.

MANAGEMENT TEAM

The management team of a new firm typically consists of the founder or founders and a handful of key management personnel. Early stage firms may have only the founder or founders and plans to add additional personnel. The description of a firm's management team should be largely factual but should be presented in a way that makes it easy to visualize where the firm is today and where it plans to be in the foreseeable future in regard to key management team personnel.

The introduction to this section should cover the basics. Indicate the name or names of the founders, how many employees the company has, where the major gaps are, and how quickly the company will be adding personnel. Keep the introduction brief—you'll have chances to fill in the details later.

FIGURE 8-1 Management Team and Company Structure (Prime Adult Fitness Business Plan)

Introduction

Prime Adult Fitness's management philosophy focuses on integrity, teamwork, enthusiasm, and providing a stimulating environment for both the company's employees and its members. Employees will be selected based on their qualifications for the job and their commitment to serving the physical and mental health needs of our 50+-year-old members.

Management Team

Jeremy Ryan, Cofounder and CEO, Age 46

Responsible for strategy formulation and the overall success of the company. Jeremy started a successful fitness franchise in South Florida and grew it to 38 units in 3 years before selling to a larger company. Prior to that, he spent 11 years as VP of operations and 3 years as VP of sales for a privately held Miami fitness center that grew to 5,500 members. Jeremy has an MBA from Miami University and has published more than 30 articles in fitness trade journals and national magazines regarding the fitness needs of older people. Jeremy's passion for fitness is drawn largely from his father who, after surviving a heart attack at age 49, pledged to improve his quality of life by joining a fitness center and exercising regularly. Today, Jeremy's father is an active 73-year-old retiree.

Elizabeth Sims, Cofounder and CFO, Age 49

Responsible for raising capital and for the financial management of the company. Elizabeth served as the CFO of Jeremy Ryan's fitness franchise in South Florida and left the company when it was sold. Prior to that, Elizabeth, who is a CPA, spent 9 years with a Big 5 accounting company, and 10 years as a cost accountant for a Fortune 500 company. While with the Big 5 accounting company, she supervised the accounting practices of 3 publicly traded fitness franchises and 11 privately owned fitness chains.

Sarah Peterson, COO, Age 51

Responsible for the day-to-day operations of the company, the maintenance of the company's facilities, and the acquisition and installation of new equipment. Sarah has 9 years of experience as the COO of a 250-bed nursing home and 17 years as a public school teacher and principal. Sarah is the cofounder of a nonprofit organization named *Healthy After 50*, which disseminates information to aged 50+ individuals about nutrition, physical fitness, and mental health. Sarah has a master's degree in education from the University of Virginia.

Jill Campbell, Program Manager, Age 52

Responsible for all the fitness and related classes that will be offered by the company. Jill is an exercise physiologist and has spent the past 12 years practicing in a private wellness/exercise center in Jacksonville, Florida. Prior to that, she was a registered nurse, assigned to the trauma center of an urban hospital. Jill has a master's degree in exercise physiology from the University of Missouri and a nursing degree from Creighton University in Omaha, Nebraska.

Alex Jackson, Marketing and Sales, Age 57

Responsible for marketing, sales, and membership growth of the company. Alex has 11 years' experience as a senior marketing executive for a major fitness machine manufacturer, where he won several "salesperson of the year" awards. Prior to that, he spent 25 years in the U.S. Marine Corps (11 years as a recruiter). Alex is a world-class triathlete for his age group.

Skill Profile and Gaps in Management Team

The following skill profile depicts the most important skills required at the top management team level of the company and where the gaps exist.

FIGURE 8-1 (continued)

	Executive Leadership	Finance	Operations	Marketing & Sales	HR/Recruiting	Member Care & Relations	Program Management	Information Systems	Accounting
Jeremy Ryan	X								
Elizabeth Sims		X							X
Sarah Peterson			X					X	
Jill Campbell							X		
Alex Jackson				X					
Gap 1					O				
Gap 2						O			

X = position filled, O = position vacant

Summary: Two significant gaps exist in the management team: the director of HR/Recruiting and the director of Member Care and Relations. Both positions will be recruited and filled within six months. Currently, the HR/Recruiting position is being filled on a volunteer basis by Timothy Kemp, a Prime Adult Fitness board member and angel investor. The Member Care and Relations position is not currently open. It will become a functioning position when Prime Adult Fitness begins actively recruiting members.

Ownership and Compensation

Name	Position/Affiliation	Base Compensation	Percent Ownership in Company	Personal Investment in Company
Jeremy Ryan	Cofounder and CEO	$68,500	20.0%	$100,000
Elizabeth Sims	Cofounder and CFO	$62,000	20.0%	$100,000
Sarah Peterson	Chief Operations Officer	$60,000	10.0%	$50,000
Jill Campbell	Program Manager	$60,000	7.5%	$37,500
Alex Jackson	Marketing and Sales	$58,500	7.5%	$37,500
Timothy Kemp	Board Member and Angel Investor	N/A	15.0%	$175,000
Options Pool			20.0%	
Total		$309,000	100.0%	$500,000

The three major parts to this section are management team personnel, management team ownership and compensation, and common mistakes to avoid. This section of Prime Adult Fitness's business plan is shown in Figure 8-1.

MANAGEMENT TEAM PERSONNEL

A brief profile of each member of the management team should be provided, starting with the founder or founders of the firm. Each profile should include the following information:

- Title of the position.
- Duties and responsibility of the position. This item should explain specifically what the individual will do and how the individual's work will contribute to the development of the firm.
- Previous industry and related experience. This item should explain who the individual has worked for and how the individual's past experiences relate to the new firm.
- Previous successes. This item should highlight the individual's past successes and accomplishments, particularly as they relate to the challenges of helping launch a new firm. For example, has the individual been involved in previous startups, launched divisions within larger firms, spearheaded successful teams and projects, and so forth.
- Education background.

Although they should be kept brief, the profiles should illustrate why each individual is qualified and will uniquely contribute to the success of the firm. Certain attributes of a management team should also be highlighted if they apply in your case. Investors and others tend to prefer team members who've worked together before. The thinking here is that if people have worked together before and have decided to partner to start a new firm, it usually means that they get along personally and trust one another.[2] This scenario helps relieve a persistent worry—that the initial managers of a firm won't get along with one another. In Prime Adult Fitness's business plan, Elizabeth Sims' short bio indicates that she worked with Jeremy Ryan, Prime Adult Fitness's CEO, in his previous venture. In addition, the skills and ability of the members of the team should complement one another rather than reinforce a single skill or competency. Many companies initially develop around a single competency, such as writing software code, producing music, managing logistics, and so on. This factor often defines the nature of the initial management team, and the management team gets stacked with people from the same discipline. A startup that resists this tendency and develops a more well-rounded management team from the beginning has a leg up on others. It's also appropriate to include personal information about the members of the management team, if it's pertinent. For example, Jeremy Ryan's bio indicates that his passion for fitness is drawn largely from his father who, after suffering a heart attack at the age of 49, pledged to improve his quality of life by joining a fitness center and exercising regularly.

The next step in describing the management team is to identify the gaps that exist. A good way to do this, and simultaneously depict the skills that exist in the initial team, is to develop a management team skill profile. This is what Prime Adult Fitness did, as depicted in its business plan shown earlier in Figure 8-1. A management team skill profile is a grid that lists the major skills needed in a firm on the horizontal axis (marketing, finance, manufacturing, IT, etc.) and the current members of the management team on the vertical axis. The grid is completed by indicating which skills are satisfied by each management team member. The skills with no coverage represent gaps in the management team. The best way to draw attention to the gaps is to list under the current management team member's names Gap 1, Gap 2, Gap 3, and so forth, depending on the number of gaps that exist. This procedure illustrated the skills or competencies that currently have no coverage and roughly the number of people who need to be hired. You can then briefly discuss the nature of the gaps and your plans for rectifying them. Some of the gaps may currently be filled through access to expertise other than a full-time employee. For example, a particular gap may be filled by an advisory team member, a part-time management employee, or an outsource provider. Simply explain how you are dealing with each of these individual situations. In Prime Adult Fitness's case, its gap in HR/Recruiting is currently being filled by Timothy Kemp, one of its board members and investors, as shown in Figure 8-1.

MANAGEMENT TEAM OWNERSHIP AND COMPENSATION

You must also fully disclose the ownership structure of the new venture and the compensation of the members of the management team. This should be done in a table format because it's easier to quickly assess the information. The owners of the firm may include management team members and outside investors. Prime Adult Fitness, as shown in Figure 8-1, listed each owners, their percent ownership in the company, and their base compensation, if they are employed by the firm. The ownership percentages may not always add up to 100 percent, if the firm has established an options pool for future hires, as in the case with Prime Adult Fitness. An options pool is an inventory of company stock, usually in the neighborhood of 15 to 20 percent of the total stock, which is set aside for future employees. Having an options pool is particularly important if a firm is looking for investors. Attracting high-quality people to a startup often necessitates the granting of stock options as an incentive form of compensation. Investors know this and will be reassured if the owners of the firm also realize this and have made provisions to make stock options available to future key hires.

Finally, it should be clear, in the table or in another part of this section, how the money for the firm has been raised so far. As explained earlier in this book, most investors like to see that the founders, at a minimum, have "skin in the game," meaning they have invested their own money. If the founders don't have enough confidence in the venture to invest their own money, why should anyone else invest?

COMMON MISTAKES TO AVOID

There is a common set of mistakes to avoid when putting together your initial management team and writing this section of the business plan. These mistakes raise red flags and undermine the credibility of your plan. The most common mistakes are as follows:

- Placing unqualified friends or family members in key management positions
- Assuming that previous success in other industries automatically translates to your industry
- Presenting a "one-man team" philosophy—meaning that one person (or a small group of people) is wearing all hats with no plans to bolster the team
- Hiring top managers without sharing ownership in the firm
- Not disclosing management team skill or competency gaps
- Vague or unclear plans for filling the skill or competency gaps that are disclosed or clearly exist

If any of these items are present in your management team and your business plan, you should review them to contemplate if they should be revised or corrected.

The next section of the plan focuses on the role of a new firm's board of directors in regard to its management team. This section of Prime Adult Fitness's business plan is shown in Figure 8-2.

BOARD OF DIRECTORS

The importance of this section varies by plan. If a new venture organizes as a corporation, it is legally required to have a board of directors. A board of directors is a panel of individuals elected by a corporation's shareholders to oversee the management of the firm. In a very early stage firm, or a small firm, the board may be restricted to the principles running the firm. In these instances, the board serves little more than a legal function. In other instances, however, the board plays an active role in the management and oversight of the firm.

If your firm has a board of directors, and it plays an active role in the management of your firm, it should be included as part of your management team. Technically, a board of directors has three responsibilities: (1) appoint the firm's officers, (2) declare dividends, and (3) oversee the affairs of the corporation.[3] The optimal size of a board of directors for a startup is three to five people. A board is typically made up of both inside and outside members. An inside director is a person who is also an officer of the firm. An outside director is someone who is not employed by the firm. A three-member board of directors normally consists of one inside director and two outside directors, and a five-member board has two inside directors and three outside directors. A list of the most

FIGURE 8-2   Board of Directors (Prime Adult Fitness Business Plan)

Prime Adult Fitness's board of directors was formed when the company was incorporated. All board members serve on a volunteer basis. There are three outside directors and two inside directors. There are no plans to compensate board members. All of the board members live in Central Florida. The board meets monthly. Individual board members interact with Prime Adult Fitness's top management team frequently.

Outside Directors

Dr. Kenneth Jamison, Family Practice Physician, Age 62

Dr. Jamison practices medicine in Oviedo, Florida, the home of Prime Adult Fitness, and is an outspoken advocate of fitness and preventive health care for people 50 years old and older. Dr. Jamison received his MD from Duke University and is board certified in family practice medicine. Dr. Jamison writes a widely read column for a local paper on health-related issues.

Martha Ford, Attorney, Age 52

Ms. Ford is a partner in the law company Campbell, Campbell & Ford. She specializes in providing legal advice to startups and small businesses. Ms. Ford received her law degree from the University of Iowa.

Timothy Kemp, Retired Entrepreneur, Angel Investor, Age 64

Mr. Kemp is a retired entrepreneur, having started and sold five successful companies. He has won several "entrepreneur of the year" awards. Mr. Kemp's last startup, K9 Medical Services, was purchased by a large pharmaceutical company and is still in business under its original name.

Inside Directors

Jeremy Ryan, Cofounder and CEO, Prime Adult Fitness

Elizabeth Sims, Cofounder and CFO, Prime Adult Fitness

desirable qualities in a board of directors and the most desirable qualities in individual board members is provided in Table 8-2.

If you include this section in your plan, you should list your board members and provide a very brief bio for each member. You don't need to provide a separate bio for the inside directors (i.e., members of the management team) who were discussed earlier. An active board of directors provides guidance and lends legitimacy to a firm. These attributes are discussed next.

PROVIDE GUIDANCE

Although a board of directors has formal oversight responsibilities, its most useful role is to provide guidance and support to the managers of the firm. Many well-intended entrepreneurs and management teams simply "don't know what they don't know," which often results in missteps early in the life of a startup. Experienced board members often see these potential missteps before they occur and help management teams avoid them. Many CEOs interact with their board members frequently and obtain important input. The key to making this happen is to select board members with needed skills and useful experiences who

TABLE 8-2   Attributes of an Effective Board of Directors

- Strong communication with the CEO
- Customer-focused point of view
- Complementary mix of talents
- Decisiveness
- Mutual respect and regard for each other and the top managers of the firm
- Ability and willingness to stand up to the CEO and the top managers of the firm
- Ability to focus
- Strong ethics

Attributes of Strong Board Members

- Strong personal and professional networks
- Willingness to make personal introductions on behalf of the firm
- Emotional stability
- Strong interpersonal communication skills
- Pattern recognition skills
- Ability to partner
- Investment and operating experience
- Ability and willingness to mentor the CEO and top managers of the firm

Source: Adapted from D. Jaffe and P. Levensohn, "After the Term Sheet: How Venture Boards Influence the Success or Failure of Technology Companies," White paper, Levensohn Venture Partners (http://www.levp.com), November, 2003.

are willing to give advice and ask insightful and probing questions. The extent to which an effective board can help shape a firm and provide it a competitive advantage in the marketplace is expressed by Ram Charan, an expert on the role of boards of directors in corporations:

> They (effective boards) listen, probe, debate, and become engaged in the company's most pressing issues. Directors share their expertise and wisdom as a matter of course. As they do, management and the board learn together, a collective wisdom emerges, and managerial judgment improves. The on-site coaching and consulting expand the mental capacity of the CEO and the top management team and give the company a competitive edge out there in the marketplace.[4]

Boards can also help fill competency gaps at the time a company is started and on an ongoing basis. It's not uncommon for a company to shift the emphasis of its board to match its stage of development. For example, startups that are focused primarily on product development at the outset may include several product development experts on their board and replace these individuals with marketing specialists when their product comes to market. If a firm gets investment capital, the investor will normally occupy a seat on its board of directors. Investors do this to not only protect their investment but also assume a formal role in lending advice and assistance to the firm.

LEND LEGITIMACY

Providing legitimacy for a firm is another important function of a board of directors. Well-known and respected board members bring instant credibility to the firm. For example, just imagine the positive buzz a firm could generate if it could say that Mark Cuban, owner of the Dallas Mavericks, Landmark Theatres, Magnolia Pictures, and Chairman of the HDTV cable network AXS TV, joined its board. This phenomenon is referred to as signaling. Presumably, a high-quality individual would be reluctant to serve on the board of a low-quality firm because that would put his or her reputation at risk. So when a high-quality individual does agree to serve on a board of a new firm, the individual is in essence "signaling" that the company has the potential to be successful.[5]

Achieving legitimacy through high-quality board members can result in other positive outcomes. Investors and others like to see management teams, including the board of directors, that have people with enough clout to get their foot in the door with potential suppliers and customers. Board members are also often instrumental in helping young firms arrange financing or funding.

These guidance and legitimacy issues should be woven into the short descriptions of the board members provided in the business plan, as appropriate. A final point is that the majority of firms will have an active board of directors at some point if they grow to any appreciable size. As a result, if a company currently doesn't have a board of directors, it may be prudent for the business plan to indicate that it anticipates having a board of directors at some point in the future and will make the board part of its overall management team.

The next section focuses on the board of advisors, a source of counsel and advice that all firms, regardless of size, can take advantage of. This section of Prime Adult Fitness's business plan is shown in Figure 8-3.

FIGURE 8-3   Board of Advisors (Prime Adult Fitness Business Plan)

Prime Adult Fitness has two active boards of advisors. The general advisory board consists of 4 members, and the customer advisory board consists of 10 members.

General Advisory Board

Dr. Jason Steele, Sports Medicine Specialist, Age 37

Dr. Steele is a sports medicine specialist practicing at a local clinic. He has a passion for the care of older people and attracts many active older adults to his practice. Dr. Steel's passion for the care of older adults stems partially from personal experience. He and his wife are the primary caregivers to his maternal grandfather and his wife's paternal grandmother.

Primary role: To provide medical advice on the selection of exercise equipment and classes, and to provide training to Prime Adult Fitness's instructors regarding how to help older people (particularly those who have not been exercising) establish an appropriate and safe exercise regime.

FIGURE 8-3   (continued)

Cynthia Rains, Public School Teacher, Age 66

Ms. Rains is a lifelong resident of Central Florida and has taught at Oviedo High School for 26 years. She is active and has belonged to fitness clubs for many years.

Primary role: To provide a layperson's advice on the selection of exercise equipment and classes, and to provide tours, on a volunteer basis, of Prime Adult Fitness's facility.

Rosa Torres, Clinical Psychologist, Age 46

Ms. Torres is a clinical psychologist, having spent the last 10 years of her career working in the wellness field for older adults. Her particular specialty is neurobics, which is a relatively new field that focuses on mental exercise. Prime Adult Fitness will have several classes focused on neurobics and will feature a neurobics center in its facility.

Primary role: To help shape Prime Adult Fitness's approach to neurobics.

Bradley Manning, Retired Fund-raiser, Age 66

Mr. Manning spent the majority of his professional life in various fund-raising roles, primarily for nonprofit organizations.

Primary role: To provide advice for building membership.

Customer Advisory Board

Prime Adult Fitness maintains a 10-member customer advisory board. The board members participate in focus groups, serve on committees that are helping shape the activities of the company, and participate in related activities. Board members serve on a volunteer basis for a one-year term.

BOARD OF ADVISORS

A board of advisors is a panel of experts asked by a firm's managers to provide counsel and advice on an ongoing basis. Listening to advice from experienced individuals can be extremely helpful, particularly in areas where the founders of a firm lack experience.[6] Unlike a board of directors, a board of advisors possesses no legal responsibility for the firm and gives nonbinding advice.[7] As a result, many people are more willing to serve on a company's board of advisors than on its board of directors because it requires less time and no legal liability is involved. A board of advisors can be established for general purposes or can be set up to address a specific issue or need. For example, some startups set up customer advisory boards shortly after they are founded to help them fine-tune their initial offerings. Prime Adult Fitness, as noted earlier, has a 10-member customer advisory board to help select exercise equipment and decide on the schedule of fitness classes and activities. Similar to a board of directors, the main purposes of a board of advisors is to provide guidance and lend legitimacy to a firm. Both of these attributes are seen in the advisory board set up by Laura Udall, the entrepreneur who started ZUCA backpack on rollers company (http://www.zuca.com). When asked about the types of advice and support she gets from people outside her immediate management team, Udall said:

> The company has a board of directors, but I also have created a wonderful board of volunteer advisors that has been very helpful with tactical and strategic decisions. The advisory board has evolved over the years as a result of my network. I asked each of the members to join as a result of their specific expertise. It now includes a CFO/COO of a prominent corporation, an executive in the luggage industry, a mom inventor who has founded several successful companies, a product designer, and a manufacturing expert.[8]

Imagine the type of advice and support Udall gleans from this group of advisors. Most boards of advisors have between 5 and 15 members and interact with each other and with a firm's managers in several ways. Some advisory boards meet three or four times a year at the company's offices or in another location. Other advisory boards meet in an online environment. In some cases, a firm's board of advisors will be scattered across the country, making it more cost-effective for a firm's managers to interact with the members of the board on the telephone, through video conferencing or via e-mail rather than bringing them together physically. In these situations, board members don't interact with each other at all on a face-to-face basis, yet they still provide high levels of counsel and advice. The fact that a startup has a board of directors does not preclude it from establishing one or more advisory boards. For example, Coolibar (www.coolibar.com), a maker of sun protective clothing, has a board of directors and a medical advisory board. According to Coolibar, its medical advisory board "provides advice to the company regarding UV radiation, sunburn, and the science of detecting, preventing, and treating skin cancer and other UV-related medical disorders, such as lupus."[9] The board currently consists of nine medical doctors, all with impressive credentials. Similarly, Intouch Technologies (www.intouchhealth.com), a medical robotics company, has a board of directors along with a business and strategy advisory board, an applications and clinical advisory board, and a scientific and technical advisory board.[10]

Although having a board of advisors is widely recommended in startup circles, most startups do not have one. As a result, one way you can make your startup stand out is to have one or more boards of advisors. In terms of your business plan, you should identify your boards of advisors and provide a brief bio for each member. A description of Prime Adult Fitness's general advisory board and its customer advisory board is provided in its business plan as shown previously in Figure 8-3.

The next section of this part of the business plan focuses on the role of "other professionals" in rounding out a company's management team. This portion of Prime Adult Fitness's business plan is shown in Figure 8-4.

FIGURE 8-4   Other Professionals (Prime Adult Fitness Business Plan)

Prime Adult Fitness relies on the advice, counsel, and encouragement of professionals in our community on an as-needed basis. None of our professional advisors are paid a regular retainer.

Other Professionals
Attorney, Cameron Campbell, partner in the law firm of Campbell, Campbell & Ford. Mr. Campbell is a well-known Orlando, Florida, attorney with 23 years of experience. Mr. Campbell is the partner of Prime Adult Fitness board member Martha Ford.
CPA, Katherine Chen, Private Practice. Ms. Chen has 19 years of auditing and general accounting experience.
SBDC, SCORE, and the Central Florida Technology Incubator. Prime Adult Fitness has sought the advice from counselors associated with each of these agencies.

OTHER PROFESSIONALS

At times, other professionals assume important roles in a new venture's success. If this applies in your case, a separate heading should be included in the management team section of your business plan to make note of these individuals or their firms. The other professionals that are often mentioned include attorneys, bankers, investors, college professors, and business consultants.

Briefly identify the professionals, including attorneys and accountants, that apply in your case and provide a short bio if appropriate. The objective is to not only disclose who you're working with but also assure the readers of your plan that you're getting good quality advice. Similarly, if you have a relationship with a banker or investor, that should be disclosed. Other potentially key relationships, such as a relationship with a college professor who is helping you develop your product and/or is mentoring you through the business startup process, should be mentioned. Often, the substance of a particular relationship isn't as important to the reader of your plan as the fact that the relationship exists. There is an oft-repeated story about the early days of eBay that illustrates this point. During its beginning stages, eBay's partners, Pierre Omidyar and Jeff Skoll, decided to recruit a CEO. They wanted someone who was not only experienced but also had the types of credentials that Wall Street investors' value. They soon discovered that every experienced manager they tried to recruit asked if they had venture capital backing, which at the time they did not. For a firm trying to recruit a seasoned executive, at least at that time, venture capital backing was a sort of seal of legitimacy. To get this valuable seal, Omidyar and Skoll obtained funding from Benchmark Venture Capital, even though eBay didn't really need the money. Writer Randall Stross recalls this event as follows:

> eBay was an anomaly: a profitable company that was able to self-fund its growth and that turned to venture capital solely for contacts and counsel. No larger lesson can be drawn. When Benchmark wired the

first millions to eBay's bank account, the figurative check was tossed into the vault—and there it would sit, unneeded and undisturbed.[11]

This strategy worked for eBay. Soon after affiliating with Benchmark, Bob Kagle, one of Benchmark's general partners, led eBay to Meg Whitman, an executive who had experience working for several top firms, including Procter & Gamble, Disney, and Hasbro. Whitman served as eBay's CEO from 1998 to 2007.

Consultants make up another important source of advice for many startup firms. A consultant is an individual who gives professional or expert advice. Consultants fall into two categories: paid consultants and unpaid consultants. Unpaid consultants include organizations such as the Small Business Development Center (www.sba.gov/sbdc) and SCORE (www.score.org). These sources often prove to be very useful. Startups generally use paid consultants sparingly because of the costs involved. An exception might be a startup that needs help in a specialized area, such as building a product prototype or providing independent certification of the technical merits or safety of a particular product. In addition, some startups use services of consulting companies such as Bain & Company (http://www.bain.com) and Accenture (http://www.accenture.com) but usually on a limited basis. In all cases, sources of advice should be noted in the business plan if they are substantive and worth mention. Again, the impression you want to give is that you are actively engaged and are seeking advice regarding your business venture.

The next section of this part of the business plan focuses on company structure. This section of Prime Adult Fitness's business plan is shown in Figure 8-5.

COMPANY STRUCTURE

This section focuses on how your company will be structured. Even if you are a small firm, you should outline how the company is currently structured and how it will be structured as it grows. It's important that the internal structure of a company makes sense and that the lines of communication and accountability are clear. Including a description of your company's structure also reassures the people who read the plan that you know how to translate your business idea into a functioning firm. Company structure is a "nuts-and-bolts" type of issue that deals within the interworkings of a firm. It's exactly this type of issue, however, that entrepreneurs must take seriously to develop smoothly functioning firms.

The most effective way to illustrate how a company will be structured and the lines of authority and accountability that will be in place is to include an organizational chart in the plan. An organizational chart is a graphic representation of how authority and responsibility are distributed within a company.[12] The organizational chart should be presented in a graphical format, similar to the manner in which Prime Adult Fitness's organizational chart is shown in its business plan in Figure 8-5. If you're unable to display your organizational chart in a graphical format, a narrative discussion of the key reporting relationships in your

FIGURE 8-5   Organizational Chart (Prime Adult Fitness Business Plan)

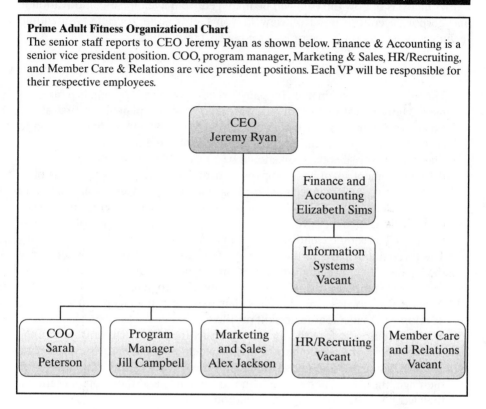

Prime Adult Fitness Organizational Chart
The senior staff reports to CEO Jeremy Ryan as shown below. Finance & Accounting is a senior vice president position. COO, program manager, Marketing & Sales, HR/Recruiting, and Member Care & Relations are vice president positions. Each VP will be responsible for their respective employees.

firm should be provided. Companies are generally organized along functional, product, or geographical lines. If you're not familiar with these distinctions, you should consult an organizational behavior or a principles of management textbook, so your organizational chart conforms to the norms your readers expect. The organization chart needs to show what the business looks like today and what it intends to become in the short-term or intermediate-term future. As a result, there may be some unfilled boxes on the organizational chart, consistent with the "gaps" in management personnel shown in the skill profile discussed earlier. In all cases, you should provide a brief interpretation of the organizational chart and discuss the most signification relationships that are displayed.

If your firm has more than one founder, you should comment on the specific role that each founder will take on as the firm moves forward. A frequent source of tension in new ventures, particularly if two or more founders start out as "equals," is a failure to delineate the specific roles they will fill. The organization chart is an effective tool for showing that the founders have worked out which of the "boxes" each will fill. Knowing that this issue has been resolved will be reassuring to the readers of your plan.

Some business plans complement their discussion of company structure with a brief analysis of how the firm will be managed from a leadership, motivational, and corporate culture point of view. If you feel it is appropriate, you should include a short section in your plan that covers these topics.

Chapter Summary

1. The management team and company structure section is pivotal in a business plan. Many investors and others who read business plans look first at the executive summary and then go directly to the management team section to assess the strengths of the people who will be starting the firm.
2. There are two issues that you should be particularly sensitive to as you write the management team and company structure section of your business plan. First, the way your management team is assembled provides an indication of the extent to which you're open to advice and are able to generate enthusiasm for your firm. Second, as you write the management team section of your business plan, you should clearly describe how the management team will evolve.
3. The three major parts to the "management team" portion of this section of the business plan are management team personnel, management team ownership and compensation, and common mistakes to avoid.
4. A good way to describe the gaps that exist in a management team is to develop a management team skill profile.
5. You must fully disclose the ownership structure of the new venture and the compensation of the members of the management team in the business plan. A table that shows the names of each of the owners of the firm, along with their age, their percent ownership in the company, and their compensation if they work for the firm is the best method.
6. There are a set of common mistakes to avoid when putting together your initial management team and writing your business plan. These common mistakes include placing unqualified friends or family members in key management positions, assuming that previous success in other industries automatically translates to your industry, presenting a "one-man team" philosophy, hiring top managers without sharing ownership in the firm, not disclosing management team skill or competency gaps, and having vague or unclear plans for filling the skill or competency gaps that are disclosed or clearly exist.
7. A board of directors is a panel of individuals elected by a corporation's shareholders to oversee the management of the firm. Many firms have active boards of directors that provide guidance and lend legitimacy to the firm.
8. An advisory board is a panel of experts asked by a firm's managers to provide counsel and advice on an ongoing basis.
9. At times, professional, such as attorneys, bankers, investors, and consultants, assume important roles in a new venture's success. These individuals and firms should be identified and included as part of a firm's overall management team in its business plan.

10. The most effective way to illustrate how a company will be structured and the lines of authority and accountability that will be in place is to include an organizational chart in the business plan.

Review Questions

1. Why is the "management team and company structure" section referred to as pivotal in a business plan?
2. To what degree does the way a firm assembles its management team provide an indication of the extent to which the managers of the firm are open to advice and are able to generate enthusiasm for their firm?
3. Why is it important to show how a company will evolve in regard to the composition of its management team?
4. Why do investors tend to prefer management teams members who have worked together before?
5. Describe what a management team skill profile is and how it is set up.
6. Why is it important to fully disclose the ownership structure of a new venture and the compensation of the members of its management team in the business plan?
7. What are some of the common mistakes to avoid in putting together an initial management team?
8. What role does a company's board of directors play in its overall management team?
9. What is a board of advisors? What role does a board of advisors play in the management of a firm?
10. Describe the purpose of an organizational chart.

Application Questions

1. Steve Perkins developed and launched a successful smartphone app that helps people manage their finances. He just received funding and plans to develop several additional smartphone apps that deal with personal finances, investing, and planning for retirement. Steve will need to hire several employees to ramp up his company and is concerned about making smart hiring decisions. Up to this point, he's been his company's only employee. Steve's question to you is, "What are the factors I should be thinking about in terms of building my management team and roster of employees?"
2. Melanie Ford has read several books on how to write a business plan. All of the books explained the importance of the management team section, stressing the number one thing that investors focus on is the strength of a new venture's management team. Melanie can't figure out why this is true. Recently, she wrote a letter to the editor of *Inc.* magazine and asked, "Why do investors put so much stock in the portion of a business plan that deals with the strength of the management team? If a startup's product doesn't do well in the marketplace, what's the value of having a top notch management team?" If you were the editor of *Inc.* how would you reply to Melanie's letter?

3. If you were one of the founders of Prime Adult Fitness, make a list of the activities that your 4-member general advisory board and your 10-member customer advisory board could help you with.

4. Imagine you are starting a firm with a partner, and you are both college seniors with limited work experience. You don't have impressive credentials to include in the management team section of your business plan. How can you construct this section of the plan, and the company itself, in a way that reassures the readers of the plan that you know what you are doing and will get the advice you need to launch a successful business?

5. Kim Smith, David Whitten, and Shelly Andersen are proposing to launch a company that will help college students streamline the process of applying for student loans and other forms of financial aid. They submitted their business plan to an investor, who just sent them a text that read, "I'm going through the Management Team section of your business plan, and don't see an organization chart. Can you submit it to me?" They replied to the text by saying, "We haven't fleshed out a formal organization chart yet. Once we launch the firm, we'll sort out what our specific roles will be and develop the organization chart." To what degree do you think this reply will satisfy the investor? Why is it important to have a formal organization chart agreed upon and in place prior to the launch of a business?

Endnotes

1. J. Kurtzman, *Startups That Work* (New York: Portfolio, 2005), 6.
2. K. Eisenhardt and C. Schoonhoven, "Organizational Growth: Linking Founding Team Strategy, Environment, and Growth among U.S. Semiconductor Ventures, 1978–1988," *Administrative Science Quarterly* 35 (1990): 504–529.
3. B. Barringer, *The Truth About Starting a Business* (Upper Saddle River, NJ: FT Press, 2009).
4. R. Charan, *Boards at Work* (San Francisco: Jossey-Bass Publishers, 1998), 3.
5. L. W. Busenitz, J. O. Fiet, and D. D. Mosel, "Signaling in Venture Capitalist-New Venture Team Funding Decisions: Does It Indicate Long-Term Venture Outcomes?" *Entrepreneurship Theory and Practice* 29 (2005): 1–12.
6. S. Blank and Bob Dorf, *The Startup Owner's Manual* (Pescadero, CA: K&S Ranch, Inc., 2012).
7. A. Sherman, *Fast-Track Business Growth* (Washington, DC: Kiplinger Books, 2001).
8. "Featured Mom Inventors: Laura Udall," *Mom Inventors*, Posted March 5, 2009 (accessed August 25, 2013).
9. Coolibar homepage, www.coolibar.com (September 1, 2013).
10. Intouch Health homepage, http://www.intouchhealth.com (September 1, 2013).
11. R. Stross, *eBoys* (New York: Crown Books, 2000), 29.
12. Investorwords.com homepage, http://www.investorwords.com (August 24, 2013).

OPERATIONS PLAN AND PRODUCT (OR SERVICE) DEVELOPMENT PLAN

INTRODUCTION

This chapter is divided into two parts. The first part of the chapter describes the operations section of a business plan, which focuses on how you will produce your product or service and run your business. This is an important section that should appear in every business plan. The second half of this chapter focuses on a topic that is singled out in some business plans and is not in others—the status of the development of a product or service. If you are developing a nonexistent product, such as Laura Udall did when she developed the ZUCA (backpack on rollers for kids), you'll need to include a chapter that describes the design and development of the product. If you're opening a more traditional business, such as a restaurant or a woman's clothing boutique, then you don't normally need a chapter on product design and development. In these instances, you can include product-relevant information in the operations section. For purposes of illustration, we'll show both the operations plan and the product design and development plan for Prime Adult Fitness.

Both of the topics discussed in this chapter require you to strike a careful balance between adequately describing the topic and not going into too much detail. Your readers will want an overall sense of how the business will be run and how your product will be developed, but they generally will not be looking for detailed explanations. It is best to keep each section short and crisp. If you provide too much information, the reader may believe that you are too immersed in the details of running your business to see the bigger picture.

The most important rule of thumb for writing the operations section and the product design and development section of your business plan is to focus on the aspects of each of these areas that are either essential to the success of your business or that set you apart from your competitors. Routine topics should be dealt with lightly and quickly. For example, anyone reading the operations section of Laura Udall's business plan for the ZUCA (www.zuca.com) would have wanted to know, in particular, how her product (backpack on rollers) was going to be manufactured, how they would be stored, how long they would be held in inventory before they were sold, and how the products would be shipped to distributors, retailers, or consumers if they were sold through ZUCA's Web site. These issues, due to their importance to ZUCA's success, should have been discussed in sufficient detail. Less critical issues, such as the physical location of ZUCA's office and warehouse and the type of insurance its needs, could have been dealt with more briefly and quickly. Obviously, the critical issues will vary from plan to plan. The important thing is to identify the critical operational and product development issues facing your business and devote the majority of your available space to discussing these issues.

Now, let's look at the operations plan section of a business plan.

OPERATIONS PLAN

The operations plan section of the business plan outlines how your business will be run and how your product or service will be produced.[1] The topics that are generally included are operating model and procedures, business location, facilities and equipment, and operations strategy and plans. Other topics may be included depending on the nature of the business.

The degree of importance that the reader of your plan will place on the operations plan varies dramatically by plan. For example, if you plan to open a sporting goods store and have a substantial amount of retail experience on your management team, your reader probably wouldn't delve deeply into this part of your plan. The most important operational issues may be store location and layout, and your reader, because of the amount of retail experience on your team, may trust you to figure out the rest. In contrast, if you're taking on the challenge of producing an entirely new product, the operations section may be pivotal, even if you have experienced product development people on your team. There is a vast difference between thinking up a new product idea and actually designing a business to manufacture, market, and sell it. Savvy readers know this and will be looking for convincing evidence that the product can actually be built and that the founders have a handle on the operational aspects of the business.

The first section of the operations plan focuses on the operating model and procedures. This section of Prime Adult Fitness's business plan is shown in Figure 9-1.

FIGURE 9-1 Operations Model and Procedures (Prime Adult Fitness Business Plan)

Introduction

Prime Adult Fitness will operate a full-service fitness center for people 50 years old or older. The operating model and procedures for the center are explained in the following sections.

General Approach to Operations

Operating a fitness center for people 50 years and older is a unique situation. It requires a careful balance of not drawing undue attention to the age of the members while at the same time tailoring all the activities of the center for an older clientele. It also requires an extreme sensitivity to the needs of older members. Fitness centers that cater to older people have found that the upper end of the age range is normally well represented. As a result, our operation plans and procedures must fully anticipate providing services to members in their 70s, 80s, and even 90s.

The biggest challenge in operating a fitness center is to motivate people to join and make exercise a part of their daily or weekly routine. People will find many reasons to not exercise. As a result, the operations of the center will be geared to (1) providing an uplifting environment for the members, (2) providing high-quality classes and equipment, (3) encouraging people to socialize and make Prime Adult Fitness one of the centerpieces of their life, and (4) establishing a rapport between Prime Adult Fitness staff and employees and our members. Both backstage (behind the scenes) and front-stage (what the members see and experience) operational issues are critical.

Backstage (Behind-the-Scene Operations Activities)

- *Staff Selection.* The staff and employees will be carefully selected. Along with the skills they need to perform their job, staff members must be able to relate to older adults, their families, and guests in a professional, thoughtful, and caring manner.
- *Operations Manual.* An operations manual has been prepared to document and articulate the day-to-day operational procedures of the center.
- *Exercise Classes and Programs.* The exercise classes and programs will be the backbone of the center's offerings. All the classes will have special names, such as "Sunrisers," "Water Dynamics," or "Bones in Motion." This tactic helps members identify the classes and teachers.
- *Exercise Machines.* The exercise machines will be modern and up-to-date. Specific employees will be trained to maintain the machines.
- *Member Motivation.* One of the most important ingredients to our success will be to make our members feel safe, secure, and successful. Older exercises need to feel that the staff cares and will respond if they need assistance. Staff at all levels will be trained to offer this type of service and attention. In addition, gentle follow-up and encouragement is needed to keep people coming to a fitness center. The staff will be encouraged to remember the names of the participants in their classes and devise a system for letting people know they are missed when they miss a class or quit coming for a while. It is often the personal connection to teachers, classmates, and staff that keeps people motivated to come back to exercise.
- *Employee Orientation.* All employees will go through a three-hour orientation before they begin work, where they will become acquainted with the operations manual and the philosophy of the center.
- *Employee Education.* Staff members and teachers will routinely attend workshops and conferences to understand current trends in fitness, obtain certifications, and tap into other resources.

FIGURE 9-1   (continued)

- *Emergency Plans.* Emergency action plans, policies, procedures, and rules have been established and are documented in the operations manual. All employees will be trained in the procedures. There will be no ambiguity or indecision when an emergency occurs. If a member is injured or needs medical attention, all employees will know the procedure to follow.
- *Waivers.* After a member finishes orientation (which is required for all new members), he or she will be asked to sign a waiver. The waiver acknowledges that the individual has gone through the orientation, understands the risks of exercise, has checked with a doctor about starting an exercise regime, and holds Prime Adult Fitness harmless if any type of medical problem occurs.

Front Stage (What the Members See and Experience)

- *Member Tours.* A prospective member will be provided a tour of the facility, and offered a free 10-day trial period to try the facilities and classes. (Facilities that use this approach normally experience an 80 to 85 percent conversion rate.)
- *Orientation.* After an individual decides to join, he or she will go through a 30-minute orientation before being allowed to start using the facility.
- *Operating Hours.* The center will be open from 6:30 AM. until 9:00 PM. Monday through Saturday and will be closed on Sundays.
- *Staff Assistance.* Fitness center staff will be available to teach members how to use the equipment and help them track their efforts.
- *Fitness Classes and Programs.* The fitness classes and programs will be offered at various times during the day. Most classes will run for either 30 or 60 minutes. Nontraditional classes will also be offered, such as outdoor "walking" classes where members will walk in groups through neighborhoods near the center.
- *Workshops.* Along with fitness classes, workshops on nutrition, increasing the quality of sleep, dance movements, and neurobics (brain exercises) will be provided.
- *Family Swims.* There will be two scheduled "family swims" per week where members can invite their families as guests to use the larger pool. Guests will not be permitted at other times during the week. Other fitness centers have found that establishing a "guest policy" alleviates potential conflicts regarding the use of facilities.
- *Multipurpose Room Rental.* The multipurpose rooms will be available for rent, by members only, for special occasions such as birthday parties and anniversary parties. Part of the reason for doing this is to make the center a central place in our member's lives.
- *Game Room.* A well-stocked game room will be available for members to pay mind-stimulating games, such as Sudoku, and socially stimulating games, such as bridge.
- *Monthly Newsletter.* Members will receive a monthly newsletter.

Inventory
Because of the nature of its operations, Prime Adult Fitness will not be required to carry a significant amount of inventory.

Schedule of Classes and Management of Peak Times
To make maximum use of our proposed facility, the classes and programs will be scheduled throughout the day, to relieve congestion in the center at obvious peak times of the day, which are before and after work. Prime Adult Fitness anticipates that 50 percent of its clientele will be retirees. As a result, Prime Adult Fitness should not experience the early-morning and late-afternoon bottlenecks experienced by most fitness centers.

OPERATIONS MODEL AND PROCEDURE

The primary objective of this section is to show that you have a firm grasp on the operational details of launching and running your business. It is usually not necessary to include a step-by-step description of how the business will be run, but major items should be covered. As mentioned previously, in many instances the operations section of a business plan will not be carefully dissected, but in some instances, the information that's included represents make-or-break issues for a firm. For example, a company such as InstyMeds (www.instymeds.com), which features vending machines that provide patients access to prescription medications instantly after they're prescribed by a doctor in a hospital emergency room or an urgent care center, will ultimately be judged by whether its system works. If the machines are difficult to understand or operate, frequently run out of the most commonly prescribed medications, or have trouble processing insurance information (i.e., if you have insurance, the machine will ask for your insurance information and will only charge you your co-pay amount), the company will have no chance of being successful.

A useful way to illustrate how your business will be run is to first articulate your general approach to operations in terms of what's most important and what the make-or-break issues are. You can then frame the discussion in terms of "backstage," or behind-the-scene activities, and "front stage," or what the customer sees and experiences. As an alternative, some business plans frame the discussion of their operations in the context of a "day in the life of a business." The Prime Adult Fitness business plan, as shown in Figure 9-1, is framed using the backstage/front-stage metaphor.

Another useful way to illustrate how a product or service is produced is to include an operations flow diagram in your business plan. An operations flow diagram shows the key steps in the production of a product or the delivery of a service. Many manufacturing startups, in particular, include an operations flow diagram to illustrate the participants in their value chain. Often, the operations flow diagram also depicts how the company intends to improve the flow of activities in its operations compared to industry norms; for example, IKEA (http://www.ikea.com) is the Swedish furniture company known for its brightly colored furniture and its approach of requiring customers to assemble their furniture (in exchange for a lower price). Figure 9-2 demonstrates IKEA's operations flow. Traditional furniture manufacturers tend to complete more of the activities themselves, whereas IKEA has opted to outsource the manufacturer of its parts to contract manufacturers and outsource the assembly and delivery of its furniture to its customers. In IKEA's case, its operations flow diagram paints a fairly clear picture of how the company operates.

Although the approaches explained previously help describe how a company's operations work, issues usually need to be singled out and discussed in more detail in this section. Examples of issues that fall into this category include the following:

- An explanation of whether you'll handle your own order fulfillment and shipping or outsource that function to a fulfillment and shipping specialist like Shipwire or Amazon Fulfillment

FIGURE 9-2 IKEA's Operations Flow Diagram (IKEA only Performs Design, Ship and Warehouse, and Sale)

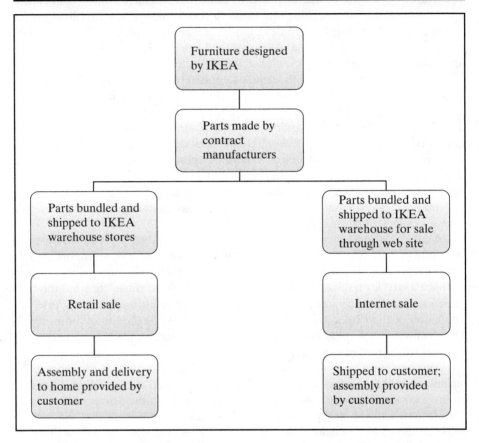

- An explanation of how inventory will be stored and how frequently it will be turned over, if applicable
- A description of the length and nature of your product or service's production cycle (when do you pay for inputs?; how long does it take to produce the product?; when does the customer buy the product?; when do you get paid?)
- An explanation of where bottlenecks are likely to occur in your manufacturing process or service delivery and how these will be handled
- An explanation of how seasonal production loads will be handled without service disruption (normally accomplished by building up inventory and using part-time help during peak periods)
- An explanation of how your quality control will be managed
- An explanation of how your after-sale service, if applicable, will be handled

An example of how these issues come into play is provided by Oopsy Daisy (www.oopsydaisy.com), a company that makes murals and other high-quality artwork for children's bedrooms and playrooms, schools, and hospitals. The company contracts with 140 independent artists for original designs and converts the designs into murals and similar artwork in its manufacturing facilities. Its artwork is then sold through channels set up and maintained by others including Amazon.com, The Land of Nod catalog, Target stores, and a host of individually owned stores and boutiques.[2] Although Oopsy Daisy's operations flow is well designed and easy to envision, it doesn't tell the whole story. There are additional issues, represented in the bullet point shown previously, that are equally critical to its operations and its ultimate success, and should be explained, either through one of the general discussion formats described earlier or under a separate heading. For example, how long does it take to produce a mural or similar piece of art? Is each product hand made, or is the process automated? How long is the average piece of art held in inventory before it is sold? If an Oopsy Daisy product doesn't sell in a store or boutique, can it be returned? If so, who pays for the shipping and what happens to the product then? How long does it take, on average, between when a product is shipped to a store or boutique and when Oopsy Daisy is paid? What happens if Oopsy Daisy increases its inventory for Christmas or another peak period, and its products don't sell well? These are the types of operations-oriented questions that would immediately occur to a discerning reader of Oopsy Daisy's business plan.

The next section of the operations plan deals with a business's location. This portion of the Prime Adult Fitness business plan is shown in Figure 9-3.

FIGURE 9-3   Business Location (Prime Adult Fitness Business Plan)

Prime Adult Fitness is proposing to operate a single facility at 201 Oak Drive in Oviedo, Florida. This location is considered to be ideal for Prime Adult Fitness for the following reasons:

Advantages of Location

- *Ideal Community.* Oviedo has a higher percentage of older people and people with a higher income than national averages. Both of these metrics are important to support a full-service fitness center for people 50 years old and older.
- *Suburb of Orlando.* Oviedo is a suburb of Orlando. Although Oviedo's population is only 35,000, it is part of a densely populated suburban area adjacent to a city. Prime Adult Fitness's trade area, Seminole County, Florida (the county in which Oviedo is located), has approximately 88,500 people 50 years old or older. Oviedo, and its surrounding area, continues to grow, with new neighborhoods and more multifamily complexes, such as apartment building and townhouses, being built on a continual basis.
- *Visibility and Parking.* The Prime Adult Fitness location will be on a busy thoroughfare, with two lanes in each direction divided by a grassy medium. The road was widened in 2005, so no new road construction is anticipated in the immediate future. This fact was confirmed by the Oviedo City Engineer. Adequate access is provided into and out of the facility's parking from Oak Street or from Blackstone Blvd. Blackstone Blvd. runs adjacent to the Prime Adult Fitness parking lot to the east.
- *Proximity to Suppliers.* Locating in an urban area provides the company easy access to suppliers.
- *Proximity to University.* Prime Adult Fitness will be 12 miles from the University of Central Florida, which is a large university. The proximity to the university provides the company access to a labor pool of young people who enjoy working in a fitness environment and have a passion for working with older people. Prime Adult Fitness plans to work with the university to arrange work-study internships for students.

BUSINESS LOCATION

This section of your plan describes the geographic location of your business. In some instances, location is an extremely important issue, and in other instances, it isn't. For example, one of the reasons Jeff Bezos located Amazon.com in Seattle is that Seattle is a major distribution hub for several large book publishers. By locating near these distribution facilities, Amazon.com has enjoyed a cost advantage that it wouldn't have had otherwise.

There are several specific instances in which a business's location is a critical factor in its capability to operate efficiently and effectively:

- Proximity to a qualified labor force
- Closeness to suppliers
- Access to transportation, such as a major airport or an interstate highway
- Access to international shipping alternatives, such as a major airport, a rail hub, and/or a seaport
- Proximity to customers with a profile conducive to a firm's business, such as a high-income neighborhood for an upscale clothing boutique or a certain ethnic population for an ethic restaurant
- Access to favorable state and local tax rates
- Access to economic incentives for locating in a certain area, such as tax abatements and/or low-priced land or labor
- Proximity to a high-quality community, in terms of public education, recreational opportunities, health care, and the arts, to attract a high-quality workforce

On a more fine-grained level, for restaurants and retail businesses, the specific location within a mall or shopping center, or a certain side of a busy street, may make a dramatic difference. For example, restaurants that feature breakfast food, such as a doughnut shop or a coffee shop, typically want to be on the side of a street that has the heaviest amount of traffic in the mornings. A miscue in a strategic area like this could cost a firm a substantial amount of business.

You should describe the rationale for your location in this portion of your business plan. For example, as shown previously in its business plan in Figure 9-3, Prime Adult Fitness decided to locate in Oviedo, Florida (a suburb of Orlando) because it is an upper-income community in an area with a relative heavy concentration of people 50 years old and older—its target market. It would have made much less sense for Prime Adult Fitness to locate in an area with opposite demographic characteristics.

The next section of a startup's operations plan focuses on its facilities and equipment. This section of Prime Adult's business plan is shown in Figure 9-4.

FIGURE 9-4   Facilities and Equipment (Prime Adult Fitness Business Plan)

How the Equipment and Programs Are Being Chosen

An overarching objective of Prime Adult Fitness is to manage a fitness facility that has programs, classes, and equipment specifically tailored for our target audience—people 50 years old and older. To accomplish that goal, the following steps have been completed and are currently under way to guide our selection of facilities, programs, and equipment.

- *Visits to Other Fitness Centers.* Although there is not another facility exactly like the one Prime Adult Fitness envisions, there are a number of fitness facilities (sponsored primarily by retirement communities and health care organizations) that have been built and equipped specifically with an older clientele in mind. A committee comprising two members of the Prime Adult Fitness management team, two general advisory board members, and two customer advisory board members visited six facilities to collect information and meet with their staffs. The committee also visited two all-purpose fitness facilities in the Orlando area and two in Jacksonville, Florida, which were gracious enough to provide tours and talk about their efforts to accommodate older patrons.
- *Focus Groups.* Prime Adult Fitness has conducted three focus groups with prospective members in Seminole county to solicit their input regarding facilities and equipment. Two more focus groups are scheduled.
- *Attendance at Industry Trade Shows.* The Prime Adult Fitness initial management team has attended three industry trade shows that display fitness equipment and program material.
- *Advisory Boards.* Both the Prime Adult Fitness General Advisory Board and the Customer Advisory Board have been actively involved in providing input on important topics.

Building and Future Growth

Prime Adult Fitness has identified a 21,600 square foot, two-story facility (201 Oak Drive, Oviedo, Florida) that is available for lease. The company has signed an option to lease the property for seven years, pending funding, with an option to buy the property at the end of the seven-year lease. The facility was built by a real estate investment trust in 1998 and was leased to a major fitness chain, which occupied the facility and used it as a fitness center until the chain retrenched and closed all of its fitness centers in the Southeast United States. For purpose of comparison, the average Bally Total Fitness or Gold's Gym is in the 30,000 square foot range.

Prime Adult Fitness is projecting 2,100 membership units by the end of 2014 (first year of operation), 2,226 by the end of 2015, 2,360 by the end of 2016, and 2,502 by the end of 2017. A membership unit is a single or a couple's account. We believe that approximately 70% of our membership units will be single members and 30% will own a couples membership. As a result, 2,502 membership units translates into approximately 3,250 people using the facility. The building's capacity is 3,500. Once the total number of people using the building approaches 3,500, a new facility will be opened to tap a new trade area. The building will take some retrofitting to suite Prime Adult Fitness's needs. The process to complete this work and the costs involved are discussed in a later part of the plan. The building, after the retrofitting is complete, will feature the following:

- A four-lane fitness pool (83 degrees)
- A therapy pool (93 degrees)
- A general exercise room that includes the fitness equipment
- Four rooms for exercise classes and programs

FIGURE 9-4   (continued)

- One multipurpose room
- A game room
- Men's and women's locker rooms
- A reception area designed to encourage people to gather and linger
- A suite specially equipped for massage and physical therapy
- A kitchen
- A coffee and juice bar
- A small movie theater
- Office space for the staff
- Three small janitorial rooms
- A mechanical service area (i.e., water heater, furnace, etc.)
- Guest restrooms

Equipment

Prime Adult Fitness is in the process of selecting fitness equipment that will facilitate the specific needs of our clientele. Generally, lower-intensity equipment will be chosen than that offered by a traditional fitness center, and weights and resistance equipment specifically designed for older people will be obtained. The selection of the specific equipment is a work in progress. A committee comprising Sarah Peterson (COO), Jim Campbell (program manager), Dr. Kenneth Jamison (director and family practice physician), and Dr. Jason Steele (advisory board member and sports medicine specialist) is in the process of researching options and will make a formal recommendation to the Prime Adult Fitness management team and board.

Government Codes and Regulations

A committee comprising Elizabeth Sims (CFO), Sarah Peterson (COO), and Martha Ford (advisory board member) has investigated and determined the government codes and regulations that Prime Adult Fitness must comply with if it occupies the Oak Drive facility. The committee has also been in regular contact with the city of Oviedo and Seminole county, Florida, to anticipate all zoning, parking, and neighbored impact issues that will be associated with opening the center. There are no issues that are anticipated to be of concern.

FACILITIES AND EQUIPMENT

This section describes a firm's facilities and equipment. You should list your most important facilities and equipment and briefly describe how they will be (or have been) acquired, in terms of whether they will be purchased, leased, or acquired through some other means. If you will be producing your own product, you should describe the production facility that you have or are looking for. This is a particularly important consideration for a business-to-business startup, especially if you are an original equipment manufacturer (OEM). An OEM is a company that sells parts to other companies that use the parts in products they sell. Most manufacturers are very discerning about the OEMs they do business with and regularly visit and inspect their facilities. As a result, if you are an OEM and plan to maintain your own production facilities, you will need to convince the reader of your plan that your facility (or the one you hope to acquire) will pass muster with discerning customers.

If you will be producing a product and will contract or outsource your production, you should comment on the facilities of your business partners. If the contracting or outsourcing will be done in a foreign country, you should explain how you located your contracting or outsource partner and how you know that its facilities are suitable for your purposes. You may also want to comment on the degree to which you will hold your foreign partners accountable for the working conditions in their factories and for their environmental standards.

If your facilities are nondescript, such as generic workspace for computer programmers, a lot of explanation is not required. If your business plan is for a restaurant or retail store, and you already have a facility, it may be helpful to include a floor plan and interior and exterior photos. If you're still in the process of locating a facility, or plan to build, a tentative floor plan and an artist's or architect's rendition of the facility you want to have is appropriate. If your facility is subject to any distinct zoning or OSHA regulations, or you will need special permits to operate, those should be disclosed. In terms of equipment, you should comment on any especially critical or expensive equipment you will require.

If your business is projecting fairly rapid growth, you should comment on how you'll be able to grow within your existing facilities or how you plan to transition from your existing facility to a larger one. You don't necessarily have to have all the answers at this point. It's important, however, to show your reader that you're aware of this issue and that it's part of your ongoing planning process.

The next section of your operations plan focuses on operations strategy and plans. This section of Prime Adult's business plan is shown in Figure 9-5.

FIGURE 9-5   Operations Strategy and Plans (Prime Adult Fitness Business Plan)

Relationship between Business Strategy and Operations Strategy
The Prime Adult Fitness business strategy and competitive advantage hinge on two things:

(1) meeting the needs of our 50+-year-old clientele in a manner that is specifically tailored to them and (2) reaching our annual membership goals through new members and member retention. Our operations strategy, described previously, is specifically geared to meeting these objectives, and will be updated on an ongoing basis. Our overarching objective is to fully understand the needs of our clientele and to serve them in an efficient and caring manner.

In-House vs. Contract Activities
To maintain consistency for our members, full-time and part-time employees will conduct the vast majority of our operations. Contract employees will be used occasionally to teach specialized classes. There are two exceptions to this general rule:

- *Massage Service.* A massage service will be offered in our facility on a fee basis. The service will be offered by a local massage company, which is fully certified and has been carefully selected. Prime Adult Fitness will receive lead generation income representing a percentage of the fees collected.
- *Physical Therapy.* A physical therapy service will also be offered and will be staffed by personnel from an Orlando area hospital. Prime Adult Fitness will receive a lead generation income representing a percentage of the fees collected.

Operations Strategy and Plans

This section deals with strategic and longer-term issues pertaining to your operations strategy. An important issue that is normally covered is the portion of your production process (or service delivery process) that you'll perform in-house as opposed to the activities that will be done by others. You may want to refer to your operations flow diagram to explain the choices you've made or plan to make. The model that many firms use in constructing their operations flow (or supply chain) is to perform the activities in-house that they are particularly good at and find partners to do the rest. Although this approach sounds simple, the task of actually finding reliable partners and managing the operations flow can be complex. As a result, if you will rely heavily on partners to help you produce your product or deliver your service, you should provide an explanation of how the entire process will work.

An example of how complex and managerially taxing selecting partners and managing an operations flow or supply chain can be is provided in the Business Plan Insights box. The feature focuses on Patagonia (http://www.patagonia.com), a company that sells rugged clothing and gear to mountain climbers, skiers, and other extreme-sport enthusiasts.

BUSINESS PLAN INSIGHT

Outsourcing the Manufacturing of a Product: A Practice That Requires More Work Than You Might Think

Many startups that plan to produce a product indicate in their business plan that the actual production of the product will be "outsourced" or produced by a contract manufacturer. Although this approach sounds good and is often successfully implemented, it requires more work and explaining than you might think. Often, companies are not able to find a partner that can build its entire product. In these instances, several outsource partners or contract manufacturers must be located, and the company must coordinate the work among its partners. In addition, in most cases, the production of a company's product isn't simply handed over to another company with no further work involved. A company must constantly monitor the quality of goods it is receiving from its outside partners and must interact with its partners on a continual basis.

An illustration of the amount of work that's involved with managing two or more contract manufacturers is provided by Patagonia (http://www.patagonia.com), a company that sells clothing to extreme sports enthusiasts. Patagonia has never owned a fabric mill or a sewing shop. Instead, to make a ski jacket, for example, it buys fabric from a mill, buys zippers and facings from other manufacturers, and then hires a sewing shop to complete the garment. To meet its own environmental standards and ensure product quality, it works closely with each partner to make sure the jacket meets its rigid standards.

As a result of these standards, Patagonia does as much business as it can with as few partners as possible and chooses its relationships carefully. Once a relationship is established, Patagonia doesn't leave adherence to its principles to chance. Its production department monitors its partners on a consistent basis. Although Patagonia avoids the work of actually producing its products, a substantial amount of work is involved in managing those that do.

Another operational issue with strategic implications is the extent to which a firm's operations are clearly supportive of its business strategy. For example, if you plan to sell a high-quality product, then your approach to operations should reflect that in everything you do (i.e., partner selection, manufacturing process, customer service, quality control). It may be helpful to include a sentence or two in this part of your plan that clearly makes the link between your business strategy and your operations strategy. For example, Silpada Designs (http://www.silpada.com), a company that sells high-end jewelry through in-home parties, emphasizes quality in the products it sells. Its products are crafted by skilled artisans and made from the finest .925 percent Sterling Silver and semiprecious composites and human-made materials available. Most of its designs are proprietary or exclusive to Silpada Designs. The company offers its clients a 60-day exchange and refund policy and a lifetime guarantee to protect against manufacturer defect. This level of diligence and commitment to customer satisfaction is an example of how a company backs up its business strategy (i.e., high quality) with an appropriate operational response (i.e., skilled artisans, high-quality materials, and a lifetime guarantee).[3]

PRODUCT (OR SERVICE) DEVELOPMENT PLAN

As indicated at the outset of this chapter, if you are developing a completely new product or service, you need to include a section in your business plan that focuses on the status of your development efforts. Many seemingly promising startups never get off the ground because their product development efforts stall or the actual development of a product or service turns out to be more difficult than anticipated. In addition, in many cases, building a working prototype of a product is not enough. A startup must also have a credible plan for ramping up the production of a product to satisfy the sales estimates in its financial projections.

This section of your business plan has four parts: development status and tasks, challenges and risks, costs, and intellectual property. The portion of the Prime Adult Fitness business plan that focuses on development status and tasks is shown in Figure 9-6.

DEVELOPMENT STATUS AND TASKS

The purpose of this section is to describe the present state of the development of your product or service. Most products follow a logical path of development that

---

FIGURE 9-6 **Development Status and Tasks (Prime Adult Fitness Business Plan)**

Timeline

If funding is obtained, Prime Adult Fitness will open at 201 Oak Drive in Oviedo, Florida, on January 1, 2014. The following milestones have been completed and remain to be completed to open the center.

Completed Milestones

November—December, 2012	• Completed feasibility analysis
January, 2013	• Incorporated business
	• Selected board of directors and advisory boards
	• Applied for trademarks and copyrights
February—March, 2013	• Signed seven-year lease on building (subject to funding)
	• Hired architect to plan building retrofitting
	• Hired, by two founders, three other members of initial management team
	• Conducted a series of focus groups, visits to other fitness centers, and special meetings of the advisory boards to plan the retrofitting of the building, begin selecting fitness equipment, and start planning the initial classes for the center

Milestones to Be Completed

April—June, 2013	• Obtain commitment for funding
	• Begin retrofitting of building when funding is obtained
July—October, 2013	• Supervise retrofitting of building
	• Make final decisions on fitness equipment, complete planning of initial classes and programs
November—December, 2013	• Begin hiring and training staff and employees to open business
	• Ramp up marketing and public relations initiatives
	• Begin offering "pilot" exercise classes to solicit feedback
	• Host three open houses
January 1, 2014*	• Have grand opening and begin operations

Retrofitting of Building

The 21,600 square foot building Prime Adult Fitness will occupy will require approximately $1 million of retrofitting to make suitable for the company's purposes. Prime Adult Fitness will pay for 75 percent of the retrofitting, and the building owners will pay 25 percent. An architectural firm, experienced in designing facilities for older people, will provide plans for the retrofitting. The following special issues have been considered in drawing up plans to retrofit the facility:

FIGURE 9-6 (continued)

- Maximum use of natural light through installing additional skylights and windows
- Reduction in noise throughout the facility through the installation of special noise reduction material
- An improvement of the ventilation system throughout the building so that the locker rooms can be warmer than the exercise areas
- Resurfacing of the areas adjacent to the swimming pools with special material to alleviate concerns about slipping on the surface
- Installation of ramps for entering and exiting both pools (to accommodate people who have trouble navigating stairs to walk into the pool on an even surface)
- Installation of special assistance locker room space in both the men's and women's locker rooms to accommodate physical therapy patients (who may need assistance dressing before and after pool treatments)
- Installation of additional grab bars throughout the facility
- Updating the color schemes and general décor of the facility
- Installation of updated information systems

includes product conception, prototyping, initial production, and full production. Depending on the sophistication of your product development or service development process, products and services typically pass tests that probe their performance and technical merits as they pass from one step in the development process to the next. You should explain the process you'll follow to move your product from one stage to the next.

You should describe specifically the point that your product or service is at and provide a timeline that describes the remaining steps. Prime Adult Fitness, as shown in Figure 9-6, framed its timeline in the context of milestones. You should also describe how the process of completing the development of your product or service will unfold, in terms of the steps that need to be completed and the people who will be involved. Many startups, for example, involve prospective customers in testing early versions of their products and services to obtain feedback. If these types of tests have already been conducted, you should briefly comment on the process you've used and your results to date.

If you are a very early-stage firm and only have an idea, you should carefully explain how a prototype of your product will be made. A prototype is the first physical depiction of a new product. For a new product, such as ZUCA's backpack on rollers or InstyMeds's prescription dispensing vending machines, a prototype is needed to test the merits of the product and get substantive feedback from others.[4] For example, regardless of how good InstyMeds's concept looked on paper, the only way for the founders of the company to ensure themselves and others that the system worked was to build one or more prototypes of the vending machines and test them under various conditions. It's one thing for a company such as InstyMeds to say that its vending machines will authenticate prescriptions, verify insurance information, accept payment, and reliably dispense prescription medication. It's another thing to show convincing evidence that patients have used prototypes of the machines without a single failure in terms of the functionality of the machines and their ability to keep the most commonly prescribed medications in stock.

For a company like Prime Adult Fitness, which will not produce a physical product, a prototype can take the form of a "sample daily schedule" of the fitness center's activities and a booklet that provides illustrations of what the exterior and interior of the center will look like. Short descriptions of the classes that will be offered and the programs that will be available, along with short bios of some of the instructors, are also helpful. If this information can be put together in a tight, attractive package, it can serve the role of a prototype and can be distributed to people for feedback.

There are many ways to get a product prototype made if the process requires specialized equipment or expertise. For example, ThomasNet (www.thomasnet.com), a directory of U.S. manufacturers, has a listing of rapid prototyping services. Similarly, freelance job sites like Odesk (www.odesk.com) and Guru (www.guru.com) can help you locate independent contractors that are specialists in building prototypes utilizing 3-D printers and other means. In some instances, a virtual prototype, which is less expensive than a physical prototype, is sufficient. A virtual prototype is a computer-generated 3D image of an idea. It displays an invention as a 3D model that can be viewed from all sides and rotated 360 degrees.

If your product or service is beyond the prototype stage, explain the stage of development of your product. After a company has a working prototype of its product, usability testing often takes place. Usability testing is a form of product/service feasibility analysis, which measures a product's ease of use and the user's perception of the experience. Usability tests are sometimes called user tests, beta tests, or field trials, depending on the circumstances involved. Usability testing is particularly important for software and Web site design. Resources for conducting usability tests were provided in Chapter 3. Web sites like Odesk and Guru can also be used to identify freelancers who can assist you in setting up appropriate usability tests for your product or service.

As you write this section of your overall product or service development plan, be aware that there is typically a direct correlation between how far away you are from having an actual product or service that can be sold in quantity to how risky the reader of your plan will perceive your business to be. A helpful illustration of this point is made by Stanley Rich and David Gumpert, the authors of *Business Plans That Win*.[5] Rich and Gumpert place companies into four distinct categories, in terms of how ready their products or services are to being sold:

- *Level 4: Going Concern.* In these companies, the product or service has not only been developed, but it is being produced and sold to customers who are satisfied.

- *Level 3: Ready to Go.* Companies at this stage have completed development and engineering of their product or service (the product actually exists). It is ready to be introduced to the market and ready for aggressive marketing and sales efforts.

- *Level 2: Almost There.* Companies at this stage have built a prototype, which works but isn't ready for marketing and production because it still needs additional evaluation and engineering. It also needs additional input from prospective customers to verify user benefits.
- *Level 1: A Great Idea, But . ...* Companies have an idea for a product or service but haven't moved beyond the idea stage. No prototype of the product exists.

According to Rich and Gumpert it's tough for Level 1 companies to get funding, unless they have an exceptionally highly qualified management team (that can be depended on to develop the product) or a product or service idea that is an obvious winner. Because most startups do not meet either of these criteria, Rich and Gumpert urge companies to move beyond Level 1 and put some development work into their products or services before they present their business plans to investors or others. If they don't, according to Rich and Gumpert's logic, in most cases, the business will be seen as too risky to merit funding. This stipulation requires a startup to basically self-fund or bootstrap its early product development efforts. If your company fits this description, you should briefly mention how you have funded your product development efforts to date.

One nice touch that dresses up a business plan is to provide a picture of your product if it exists or an artist's rendition of what the product (or service setting) will look like after it's developed. It's normally easier for readers to relate to a product (or service setting) that they have a good visual image of it.

The next section of your product or service design and development plan deals with the challenges and risks involved. The portion of the Prime Adult Fitness business plan is shown in Figure 9-7.

FIGURE 9-7 Challenges and Risks (Prime Adult Fitness Business Plan)

The following challenges and risks are associated with the design, maintenance, and use of Prime Adult Fitness's facilities:

- *Completion of Retrofitting.* Any delay in completing the retrofitting of the building, according to the "milestones to be completed" schedule would severely impact the scheduled opening of the facility on January 1, 2014.
- *Purchase and Installation of Fitness Equipment.* The final decisions for purchasing and leasing fitness equipment are currently under way and will ramp up once funding is obtained. Any delays in the proper shipping and installation of equipment would severely impact the scheduled opening date.
- *Exceeding Costs of Budgeted Items.* The initial opening and staffing of the facility has been carefully budgeted, as shown in the financial section of this plan. Exceeding the budget would be problematic for the firm financially.
- *Final Clearances from the City of Oviedo and Seminole County, Florida.* Final clearances regarding city and county regulations pertaining to the opening of our facility cannot be completed until the building retrofitting initiative is complete.

Prime Adult Fitness is confident that the risks inherent in these four items have been minimized.

CHALLENGES AND RISKS

This section should disclose any major anticipated design and development challenges (and risks) that will be involved in bringing your product or service to market. You should be very candid and transparent in identifying these issues for two reasons. First, your reader will anticipate that challenges and risks exist and will want to know what they are. Second, your reader will want to see evidence that you are aware of the risks and challenges that exist. The last thing you want to do is paint an overly rosy picture of how quickly and effortlessly your design and development process will unfold. Experienced readers know that product and service development is an inherently bumpy and challenging process and will want insight into the challenges and risks you anticipate with your particular offering. If you omit this section, gloss over it, or provide an overly optimistic outlook, the credibility of your business plan will be undermined.

You should discuss the possible effects the challenges and risks you disclose could have on the development of your product or service, the costs involved, and your timeline for bringing the product or service to market. You should also discuss how you plan to avoid or deal with the challenges and risks involved if they occur.

The next section of your product or service design and development plan deals with the costs involved. The corresponding section of the Prime Adult Fitness business plan is shown in Figure 9-8.

FIGURE 9-8 Costs (Prime Adult Fitness Business Plan)

Design and Development Budget
The budget associated with the building and facilities, to bring Prime Adult Fitness to its opening date, is as follows:

Item	Cost
Retrofitting Building	$ 750,000
Exercise Equipment *	$ 150,000
Office and Computer Equipment	$ 60,000
Furniture	$ 30,000
Sales and Marketing Materials	$ 40,000
Other	$ 15,000
Total	$ 1,045,000

*Special Note—Exercise Equipment

A total of $150,000 of exercise equipment will be obtained as follows:

Method Used to Obtain Equipment

Purchase	$ 50,000
Lease	$ 50,000
Financed by Vendors	$ 50,000

Costs

This section should provide a budget for the remaining design and development work that needs to be done to bring your product or service to market. The budget should include the costs of labor, material, consulting fees, prototyping, usability testing, and so on. You will probably need to talk to experienced people in your industry to arrive at accurate estimates, particularly if you're not far along in your design and development efforts.

In most cases, exceeding your design and development budget will be one of the risks disclosed in the challenges and risks section shown previously. You should discuss the impact that exceeding your budget could have on your startup's overall cash flow and financial stability.

The last section of the product (or service) design and development portion of your business plan focuses on intellectual property. This portion of the Prime Adult Fitness business plan is shown in Figure 9-9.

Intellectual Property

This section should describe any patents, trademarks, copyrights, or trade secrets that you have secured or plan to secure relative to the products or services you are developing. If your startup is still an early-stage company, and you have not taken action on intellectual property issues yet, you should get legal advice so you can at a minimum discuss your plans in this area.

The four forms of intellectual property that should be discussed in this section are patents, trademarks, copyrights, and trade secrets. Intellectual property is any product of human intellect that is intangible but has value in the marketplace. It is called "intellectual" property because it is the product of human imagination, creativity, and inventiveness. Traditionally, businesses have thought of their physical assets, such as land, buildings, and equipment, as their most important assets. Increasingly, however, a company's intellectual assets

FIGURE 9-9 Intellectual Property (Prime Adult Fitness Business Plan)

Patents	Due to the nature of its operations, Prime Adult Fitness does not anticipate filing for any patents.
Trademarks	All of Prime Adult Fitness's distinctive marks, including its name, its logo, and its tagline, have been trademarked. Its Internet domain name (http://www.primeadultfitness.com) has been obtained.
Copyrights	The company will routinely copyright appropriate material.
Trade Secrets	Prime Adult Fitness considers the following material to be trade secrets: operating manuals, employee orientation material, membership lists, prospects lists, business plan, results of membership surveys, and financial records. This material is not allowed to leave Prime Adult Fitness's premises, nor is it allowed to be copied without the permission of an officer of the firm.

are the most valuable. Prime Adult Fitness's intellectual assets and the forms of intellectual property protection used to secure them, are shown in its business plan in Figure 9-9.

Prime Adult Fitness has moved quickly to protect its intellectual assets, particularly its trademarks. It has also established a firm policy to protect its trade secrets. A trade secret is any formula, pattern, physical device, idea, process, or other information that provides the owners of the information with a competitive advantage in the marketplace. Trade secrets include customer lists, marketing plans, product formulas, financial forecasts, employee rosters, logs of sales calls, laboratory notebooks, operations manuals, and similar material. Unlike patents, trademarks, and copyrights, no single government agency regulates trade secret laws. Instead, trade secrets are governed by a patchwork of state laws. The federal Economic Espionage Act, passed in 1996, does criminalize the theft of trade secrets.

The key to protecting trade secrets is to keep them confidential and reveal them only on a need-to-know basis to employees within the firm. In general, information that is known to the public or that competitors can discover through legal means (like looking at a company's Web site or picking up a brochure at a trade show) doesn't qualify for trade secret protection. It is also prudent to safeguard information that you deem as a trade secret through simple commonsense means. For example, a company's customer or membership list should be available only through a password-protected computer file and only to employees who have a legitimate reason to use it.[6]

The primary rule of thumb for deciding if intellectual property should be protected is to determine whether it's related to a firm's competitive advantage. If it is, then legal protection should be pursued. Trademarks and copyrights can be obtained fairly inexpensively. Patents are expensive to obtain, which poses a challenge for many startups. The total cost of applying for a patent ranges from $5,000 to $50,000, depending on the nature of the patent. In addition, a patent must be applied for within one year of when a product or process is first offered for sale, put into public use, or is described in any printed publication (such as a concept statement) or the right to file a patent application for the product or process is forfeited. Thus, the decision regarding whether to spend the money to apply for a patent on a product or process must be made soon in the life of a new firm. One provision of the patent law that is particularly important for entrepreneurs is that the U.S. Patent and Trademark Office allows inventors to file a provisional application for a patent, pending the preparation and filing of a complete application. This part of the law grants "provisional rights" to an inventor for up to one year, pending the filing of a complete and final application. This provision of the law allows a startup to stake a claim to a particular invention for up to a year while it's deciding whether to move forward with a complete patent application. As of October 2013, the fee for filing a provisional application for a patent was $65 to $260 depending on the size of the business. You usually need to employ an attorney, however, to help prepare the application.

One sticky point in business plans is to decide how much to reveal about a company's potential intellectual property, knowing that the plan will be read by people who ultimately won't be involved with the venture. Although a company wants the readers of its business plan to fully grasp its potential, the fear is that by revealing too much, a startup risks losing the confidential nature of its plans, particularly as it relates to products that may be patented and trade names that will eventually be legally protected. There is no good answer to this conundrum, so you must make a judgment call. The vast majority of business ideas are not unique enough that this issue becomes a problem, but that isn't always the case. To resolve this dilemma, some startups provide just enough information in their business plans to entice their readers to want to know more and then reveal more information to interested parties on a case-by-case basis.

A full discussion on intellectual property and its importance is beyond the scope of this book. If you feel that patents, trademarks, copyrights, and trade secrets will be important to your startup, you should locate a credible publication to further acquaint yourself with the pluses and minuses of paying for intellectual property protection before you complete this portion of your business plan.

Chapter Summary

1. This chapter is divided into two parts. The first part of the chapter describes the operations section of a business plan, which focuses on how you will produce your product or service and run your business. This is an important section that should appear in every business plan. The second half of the chapter focuses on a topic that is singled out in some business plans and is not in others—the status of the development of a product or service.

2. The most important rule of thumb for writing the operations section and the product design and development section of your business plan is to focus on the aspects of each of these areas that are either essential to the success of your business or that sets you apart from your competitors. Routine topics should be dealt with lightly and quickly.

3. The operations plan section of the business plan outlines how your business will be run and how your product or service will be produced. The topics generally included are operating model and procedures, business location, facilities and equipment, and operations strategy and plans. Other topics may be included depending on the nature of the business.

4. A useful way to illustrate how a product or service will be produced is to include an operations flow diagram in your business plan. An operations flow diagram shows the key steps in the production of a product or the delivery of a service.

5. Although the operations flow diagram explains how a product or service is produced, there are other issues that are relevant for this section. These issues include an explanation of how your inventory will be stored and how frequently it will be turned over, a description of the length and nature of your product or service's production cycle, an explanation of where bottlenecks

are likely to occur in your manufacturing process or service delivery and how these will be handled, an explanation of how seasonal production loads will be handled without service disruption, an explanation of how your quality control will be managed, and an explanation of how your after-sale service, if applicable, will be handled.

6. This product design and development section of your business plan has four parts: development status and tasks, difficulties and risks, costs, and intellectual property. Many seemingly promising startups never get off the ground because their product development efforts stall or the actual development of a product or service turned out to be more difficult than anticipated.

7. Most products follow a logical path of development that includes product conception, prototyping, initial production, and full production. Depending on the sophistication of your product development or service development process, products and services typically pass tests that probe their performance and technical merits as they pass from one step in the development process to the next. You should explain the process you followed to move your product from one stage to the next.

8. If you are a very early-stage firm and only have an idea, you should carefully explain how a prototype of your product will be made. A prototype is the first physical depiction of a new product.

9. One sticky point in business plans is to decide how much to reveal about a company's potential intellectual property, knowing that the plan will be read by people who ultimately won't be involved with the venture. Although a company wants the readers of its business plan to fully grasp its potential, the fear is that by revealing too much, a startup risks losing the confidential nature of its plans, particularly as it relates to products that may be patented and trade names that will eventually be legally protected. The vast majority of business ideas are not unique enough that this issue becomes a problem, but that isn't always the case.

Review Questions

1. Why is it important to include an operations plan in a business plan?
2. When writing the operations plan and the product (and service) design and development plan sections of a business plan, why is it important to strike a careful balance between adequately describing the topics and not going into too much detail?
3. What is the most important rule of thumb for writing the operations and the product design and development sections of your business plan?
4. According to the chapter, there is a vast difference between thinking up a new product idea and actually designing and manufacturing the product. Explain the nature and importance of this difference.
5. What is an operations flow diagram, and why is it important?

6. Identify three specific instances in which a business's location is a critical factor in its capability to operate efficiently and effectively.
7. What is a product prototype, and why it is important?
8. Describe what usability testing is and why it is important.
9. To what extent should a startup be candid and transparent regarding the challenges and risks associated with its product development process?
10. What are the four types of intellectual property, and why is it important to address intellectual property issues in a business plan?

Application Questions

1. Fitbit (http://www.fitbit.com) is the name of a company that makes a product called the Fitbit Force, which is a wireless-enabled device that measures data such as the number of steps walked, quality of sleep, and other personal metrics. Spend some time looking at Fitbit's Web site to get acquainted with its product offerings. What do you think were the major "operational" issues that Fitbit included in its business plan?
2. Discuss the manner in which a company like Fitbit can use "operations" as a means of gaining a competitive advantage over its competitors.
3. Imagine that you have invented a new type of backpack for students to carry their books on campus. As part of your business plan, you have decided to "outsource" the actual manufacture of the backpack to a company in China. Do some research to determine how you would locate a company in China to manufacture your backpack, and what type of arrangement you would likely enter into with them. How much information should you include in your business plan about the company and your arrangement with them?
4. Suppose you were working on a business plan for an upscale men's clothing store. What factors should you consider in selecting the physical location of the store? How much attention would you devote to this issue in your business plan?
5. Image you're planning to open a coffee shop named Mountain Fresh Coffee. Your coffee shop will be much like a Starbucks or a Caribou Coffee, and will be located three blocks from the campus of a major Midwestern university. Some of the unique aspects of your coffee shop are as follows: (1) You will only employ people who have a passion for coffee, (2) all the coffee you sell will be fair trade certified, (3) the ambience of your shop will be relaxed and unhurried, and (4) you will give back 10 percent of your after-tax profits to local charities. With these factors in mind, along with your own creativity and business sense, complete both a backstage and front-stage operations model for Mountain Brew Coffee. Make your operations model as extensive as the one for Prime Adult Fitness shown in the chapter.

Endnotes

1. B. Barringer, *Launching a Business: The First 100 Days* (New York: Business Expert Press, 2013).
2. Oopsy Daisy Homepage, available at www.oopsydaisy.com (accessed October 2, 2013).
3. Silpada Design Homepage, available at www.silpada.com (accessed October 2, 2013).
4. P. S. Cohen, *Hungry Start-Up Strategy* (San Francisco, CA: Berett-Koehler Publishers, 2012).
5. S. Rich and D. Gumpert, *Business Plans That Win* (Cambridge, MA: Harper & Row, 1985).
6. S. Shane, *Finding Fertile Ground* (Upper Saddle River, NJ: Pearson Education, 2005).

CHAPTER 10

FINANCIAL PROJECTIONS

INTRODUCTION

The final section of a business plan presents a firm's pro forma (or projected) financial projections. Having completed the previous sections of the plan, it's easy to see why the financial projections come last. They take the plans you've developed and express them in financial terms. As a result, you'll find yourself referring to earlier sections in your business plan frequently while you prepare your financial projections. For example, you prepared your sales forecasts in Chapter 6, a marketing budget in Chapter 7, and a schedule of the salaries of your initial management team in Chapter 8. These numbers, along with others, flow directly to the financial projections you develop in this chapter.

There are three things to be particularly mindful of as you approach this chapter. First, although you may be very passionate about a particular business idea, like starting a fitness center for people 50 years old and older, the people who read your plan will be primarily interested in your business's potential financial results. Investors are normally interested in the size of the returns and how quickly a company can grow, whereas bankers are more interested in the predictability and stability of a company's financial results and how it will minimize risk. As a result, it's important to provide these folks the financial information they need to make their judgments. If your plan is beautifully written, but the financial section is lacking, investors and bankers simply won't have the information they need to offer you financing or funding.

The second thing to be mindful of as you approach this chapter is that your financial statements show whether your business can get up and running successfully. There are many businesses that once started represent viable ongoing businesses. The trick is to get them started. Unless your business is cash flow positive from the beginning, which is rare, there will be a period of time when you'll lose money while you're ramping up the business. For example, as you'll see later in the chapter, Prime Adult Fitness's financial projections look very promising for 2015 and beyond. But its startup year, 2014, is projected to be challenging. Its 2014 income statement projects a $94,570 loss, and its 2014 cash flow statement shows that the company will need to rely on a prearranged line of credit from a bank to avoid running seriously low on cash. The main reason that Prime Adult Fitness's first year will be so tough is that it will open its doors on January 1, 2014, with a fully equipped building and staff (and all the related expenses), but only a handful of members. It will take the entire year for the company to reach its goal of 2,100 membership units. In the meantime, all of its fixed expenses (and most of its variable expenses) march on. In 2015 and beyond, its cash flow improves dramatically because its membership goals are projected to be met. The challenge for Prime Adult Fitness will be to survive 2014 (the year it is building its membership) to get to 2015 and beyond.

Most startups are similar to Prime Adult Fitness—there will be a startup period during which they lose money until they are fully up to speed and reach profitability. A firm's pro forma financial statements, in particular its initial balance sheets and cash flows, show how this period will unfold. Discerning readers will be looking for this information. Very few, if any, investors or bankers will finance a firm that doesn't demonstrate that it has thought through this critical issue. If the statements are missing, or if they are done poorly or incorrectly, the entire plan will be compromised.

The third thing to be mindful of as you approach this chapter is that most students and entrepreneurs are not familiar with how to complete pro forma financial projections. If you fall into this category (as most people do), don't wing it. Get help. The financial statements are too important to not be completed carefully and accurately. A good source for one-on-one help is SCORE (http://www.score.org), an organization of retired businesspeople who will normally provide assistance for free. Small business development centers frequently hold classes and workshops on how to complete financial statements. Approaching an accounting professor in your own college or university to ask for assistance may be another viable option.

This chapter consists of six parts that cover the information normally included in the financial section of a business plan: sources and uses of funds statement, assumptions sheet, income statements, balance sheets, cash flows, and ratio analysis.

Now let's look at the first section in this chapter, the sources and uses of funds statement. The Prime Adult Fitness sources and uses of funds statement is shown in Figure 10-1.

SOURCE AND USE OF FUNDS STATEMENT

The source and use of funds statement is a document that lays out specifically how much money a firm needs (if the intention of the business plan is to raise money), where the money will come from, and what the money will be used for. Normally, a portion of the startup funds is provided by the founders or the initial management team; a portion is contributed by an early investor, such as an angel

FIGURE 10-1   Source and Use of Funds Statement (Prime Adult Fitness Business Plan)

Sources of Funds

Source	Amount
Management Team Investment	$ 325,000
Angel Investor—Timothy Kemp	$ 175,000
Grant from Healthy After 50	$ 60,000
Line of Credit with Oviedo Security Bank	
($100,000 LOC; $50,000 to be disbursed when business opens)	$ 50,000
Total Funds Committed	$ 610,000
Total Funds Required	$ 1,125,000
Total Funds Needed from an Equity Investor	$ 515,000

Uses of Funds

Cost	Item
Retrofit Building (including architect)	$ 750,000
Exercise Equipment—Purchase Outright	$ 50,000
Office and Computer Equipment	$ 60,000
Furniture	$ 30,000
Sales and Marketing	$ 40,000
Attorney Fees	$ 10,000
Initial Inventory	$ 20,000
Other	$ 15,000
Cash (working capital and reserve to cover 2014 losses)	$ 150,000
Total Required Funds	$ 1,125,000

*Approximately $25,000 in additional startup costs have been bootstrapped by founders.

investor, a friend, or a family member of one of the founders; and the remainder is what's still needed. The level of detail, regarding both sources and uses of funds, shown in the Prime Adult Fitness sources and uses of funds statement in Figure 10-1 is appropriate for most new ventures. The items from the sources and uses of funds statement normally become the initial assets and liabilities of the firm. As explained later in this chapter, only certain items qualify to be reflected on a firm's balance sheet. Still, the sources and uses of funds statement is an important starting point in preparing the initial balance sheet for the firm.

If any of the funds you will be receiving come from an unusual source, you should substantiate the source of funding. For example, one of Prime Adult Fitness's sources of funds, as shown in Figure 10-1, is a grant from a nonprofit agency called Healthy After 50. This organization believes in Prime Adult

FIGURE 10-2 Assumptions Sheet (Prime Adult Fitness Business Plan)

The financial statements depend on important assumptions. The key underlying assumptions are as follows:

General (Assumptions)

1. Interest in fitness and exercise will remain strong.
   Sources: Mintel, IBISWorld, International Health, Racquet & Sportsclub Association
2. We assume access to equity capital in the amount of $515,000, consistent with the sources and uses of funds statement in this business plan.

Financial Statements (Assumptions)

Income Statements

1. Sales forecasts are based on the analysis presented in the "market analysis" section of this business plan. Sales are projected to increase 6 percent per year.
2. We assume that our receivables, which will primarily consist of overdue monthly membership fees, will take 30 days (on average) to collect.
3. Officer's compensation based on "Ownership and Compensation" table shown in the "management team" section of this business plan.
4. COGS for each month includes direct labor costs associated with delivering fitness classes and maintaining fitness machines.
5. Employees' benefits figured at 17.5 percent of salary.
   Source: Percentage obtained from Katherine Chen, CPA
6. Marketing expenses based on annual marketing budget in "marketing plan" section of this business plan.

Balance Sheets

1. Accumulation of accounts receivable is consistent with industry norms.
2. The retrofitting of the building and the leasing of fitness equipment are "off the balance sheet" transactions consistent with normal accounting practices.

Fitness's overall mission and has committed $60,000 to help the company get started. Placing a letter from the director or president of Healthy After 50 in the appendix to the business plan to verify that the grant is forthcoming would be appropriate.

The next section of this portion of the business plan presents the assumptions sheet. This section of the Prime Adult Fitness business plan is shown in Figure 10-2.

ASSUMPTIONS SHEET

An assumptions sheet is an explanation of the most critical assumptions that your financial statements are based on. Some assumptions will be based on general information, and no specific sources will be cited to substantiate the assumption. For example, if you believe that the U.S. economy will remain strong, and that's an underlying assumption driving your sales projections, then you should state that assumption. In this instance, you wouldn't cite a specific source—you're reflecting a consensus view. (It's then up to your reader to agree or disagree.) Other assumptions will be based on very specific information, and you should cite the source for your assumption. For example, on its pro forma income statements, Prime Adult Fitness computes employee benefits at 17.5 percent of salary. Primed Adult Fitness obtained that percentage from Katherine Chen, the certified public accountant (CPA) it is working with (and is identified in Chapter 8). Ms. Chen works with businesses that draw from the same labor pool that Prime Adult Fitness will draw from.

In many instances, the assumption sheet references earlier portions of the business plan. For example, Prime Adult Fitness computed its sales projections in the market analysis section of the plan, where a full explanation of where the numbers came from was provided. The explanation doesn't need to be repeated here. Although the assumption sheet is only meant to comment on the most critical numbers used to prepare the financial statements, it's impossible to over-emphasize the importance of conveying to your reader that your statements are built on good data. The online resources shown in Appendix 2.2 at the end of Chapter 2 provide an excellent starting point to look for industry norms and other data. There are two reference books that are also helpful in computing financial statements: *Dun & Bradstreet Industry Norms and Key Business Ratios*[1] and the *Almanac of Business and Industrial Financial Ratios*.[2] Both of these books are usually available in the reference section of a university or major city library. The *Almanac of Business and Industrial Financial Ratios*, for example, reports the average operating costs (for line items such as cost of operations and employee benefits) as a percent of net sales for many lines of business at different sales levels.

In many instances, simple gumshoe labor and inquisitiveness is all that's needed to obtain and report an important financial number. For example, if your business will be occupying a building, a simple call to the electric company or a rental company that manages buildings may be all that's needed to get a good handle on anticipated utility costs. It's fully appropriate to cite these types of sources, as long as you're convinced that they're credible, in the assumptions sheet.

PRO FORMA FINANCIAL STATEMENTS

The pro forma (or projected) financial statements are the heart of the financial section of a business plan. Although at first glance preparing financial statements appears to be a tedious exercise, it's a fairly straightforward process if the preceding sections of your business plan are thorough. If your plan has been built in the manner described in this book, most of the hard work, such as projecting sales and creating a marketing budget, has already been done. The financial statements also represent the culmination or finale of the entire plan. As a result, it's interesting to see how they turn out.

A firm's pro forma financial statements are similar to the historical statements an established firm would normally prepare, except they look forward rather than track the past. Pro forma financial statements include the income statement, balance sheet, and cash flow statement. The statements are usually prepared in this order because information flows logically from one to the next. Most experts recommend three to five years of statements, with the first two years for the income statement and the cash flow statement completed on a monthly basis. If the company you're writing your plan for already exists, you should also include three years of historic financial statements.

The first statements that are normally prepared are the pro forma income statements. The Prime Adult Fitness pro forma income statements for 2014, 2015, 2016, and 2017 are shown in Figure 10-3.

PRO FORMA INCOME STATEMENT

The pro forma income statement reflects the projected results of the operations for a firm for a given period of time. It records all the projected sales and expenses for the given period and shows whether the firms will be making a profit or experiencing a loss (which is why the income statement is often referred to as the "profit and loss" statement). Income statements are typically prepared on a monthly, quarterly, or annual basis. For a startup, it's important to complete the statements on a monthly basis, at least for the first two years. Most pro forma income statements are prepared in a multiyear format, making it easy to spot trends.

The pro forma income statements for Prime Adult Fitness are shown in Figure 10-3. The value of the multiyear format is clear. After a loss in 2014 (its startup year), the company is projected to experience healthy increases in sales and net income for 2015, 2016, and 2017. An income statement also exposes a company's risks. For example, even though Prime Adult Fitness shows a $317,740 net income in 2015, a 15 percent drop in projected sales would turn the $317,740 gain into a $44,736 loss. This scenario illustrates in part why projecting sales as accurately as possible is such a critical issue.

The three numbers that receive the most attention when evaluating an income statement are the following:

- *Net sales.* Net sales consist of total sales minus allowances for returned goods and discounts.
- *Cost of goods sold (COGS).* COGS includes all the direct costs associated with producing or delivering a product or service, including the material costs and direct labor. For Prime Adult Fitness, this includes the direct labor needed to teach the center's classes, run its programs, and maintain the fitness equipment, as well as the materials disbursed to members in classes.
- *Operating expenses.* Operating expenses include marketing, utilities, and administrative costs not directly related to producing a product or service.

In regard to increases in net sales from one year to the next in the pro forma statements, these numbers are normally determined in the "market analysis"

FIGURE 10-3   **Pro Forma Income Statements 2014, 2015, 2016, 2017 (Prime Adult Fitness Business Plan)**

Pro Forma Income Statement 2014 (First Year of Business)

	January	February	March	April	May	June
Gross Sales	60,890	83,000	102,600	123,710	135,360	152,020
(Returned Goods and Discounts)						
Net Sales	60,890	83,000	102,600	123,710	135,360	152,020
(Cost of Goods Sold)	16,740	22,820	28,210	34,020	37,220	41,800
Gross Profit	44,150	60,180	74,390	89,690	98,140	110,220
Expenses—General and Administrative						
Officers' Compensation	25,750	25,750	25,750	25,750	25,750	25,750
Salaries and Wages	16,000	16,000	16,000	17,000	17,000	17,000
Payroll Taxes	3,820	3,820	3,820	3,890	3,890	3,890
Employee Benefits	10,800	10,800	10,800	10,980	10,980	10,980
Professional Services	1,000	1,000	1,000	1,000	1,000	1,000
Building Rent	27,000	27,000	27,000	27,000	27,000	27,000
Utilities	5,850	5,850	5,850	5,850	5,850	5,850
Telephone, Internet, and Web Site	1,300	1,300	1,300	1,300	1,300	1,300
Office Equipment Lease	1,400	1,400	1,400	1,400	1,400	1,400
Insurance	3,000	3,000	3,000	3,000	3,000	3,000
Marketing	10,000	9,000	7,000	4,000	3,000	3,000
Supplies	1,500	1,500	1,500	1,500	1,500	1,500
Interest	500	500	500	500	500	500
Taxes						
Other General and Admin Expenses	3,500	3,500	3,500	3,500	3,500	3,500
Depreciation and Amortization	1,500	1,500	1,500	1,500	1,500	1,500
Total Expenses	112,920	111,920	109,920	108,170	107,170	107,170
Net Income	(68,770)	(51,740)	(35,530)	(18,480)	(9,030)	3,050

	July	August	September	October	November	December	Total
Gross Sales	153,030	159,750	167,200	176,150	185,100	191,540	1,690,350
(Returned Goods and Discounts)							
Net Sales	153,030	159,750	167,200	176,150	185,100	191,540	1,690,350
(Cost of Goods Sold)	42,080	43,930	45,980	48,440	50,900	52,670	464,810
Gross Profit	110,950	115,820	121,220	127,710	134,200	138,870	1,225,540
Expenses—General and Administrative							
Officers' Compensation	25,750	25,750	25,750	25,750	25,750	25,750	309,000
Salaries and Wages	18,000	18,000	18,000	19,000	19,000	19,000	210,000
Payroll Taxes	3,940	3,940	3,940	3,990	3,990	3,990	46,920
Employee Benefits	11,160	11,160	11,160	11,340	11,340	11,340	132,840
Professional Services	1,000	1,000	1,000	1,000	1,000	1,000	12,000
Building Rent	27,000	27,000	27,000	27,000	27,000	27,000	324,000
Utilities	5,850	5,850	5,850	5,850	5,850	5,850	70,200
Telephone, Internet, and Web Site	1,300	1,300	1,300	1,300	1,300	1,300	15,600

FIGURE 10-3 (continued)

	July	August	September	October	November	December	Total
Fitness Equipment							
Lease	1,400	1,400	1,400	1,400	1,400	1,400	16,800
Insurance	3,000	3,000	3,000	3,000	3,000	3,000	36,000
Marketing	2,000	2,000	2,000	2,000	6,000	6,000	56,000
Supplies	1,500	1,500	1,500	1,500	1,500	1,500	18,000
Interest	500	500	500	500	500	7,250	12,750
Taxes							
Other General and Admin Expenses	3,500	3,500	3,500	3,500	3,500	3,500	42,000
Depreciation and Amortization	1,500	1,500	1,500	1,500	1,500	1,500	18,000
Total Expenses	107,400	107,400	107,400	108,630	112,630	119,380	1,320,110
Net Income	3,550	8,420	13,820	19,080	21,570	19,490	(94,570)
Income as a Percent of Gross Sales							

Pro Forma Income Statement 2015 (Second Year of Business)

	January	February	March	April	May	June
Gross Sales	201,400	201,400	201,400	201,400	201,400	201,400
(Returned Goods and Discounts)						
Net Sales	201,400	201,400	201,400	201,400	201,400	201,400
(Cost of Goods Sold)	55,380	55,380	55,380	55,380	55,380	55,380
Gross Profit	146,020	146,020	146,020	146,020	146,020	146,020
Expenses—General and Administrative						
Officers' Compensation	25,750	25,750	25,750	25,750	25,750	25,750
Salaries and Wages	20,000	20,000	20,000	20,000	20,000	20,000
Payroll Taxes	4,070	4,070	4,070	4,070	4,070	4,070
Employee Benefits	11,500	11,500	11,500	11,500	11,500	11,500
Professional Services	1,000	1,000	1,000	7,000	1,000	1,000
Building Rent	27,000	27,000	27,000	27,000	27,000	27,000
Utilities	6,150	6,150	6,150	6,150	6,150	6,150
Telephone, Internet, and Web Site	1,400	1,400	1,400	1,400	1,400	1,400
Office Equipment Lease	1,400	1,400	1,400	1,400	1,400	1,400
Insurance	3,150	3,150	3,150	3,150	3,150	3,150
Marketing	10,000	9,000	7,000	4,000	3,000	3,000
Supplies	1,500	1,500	1,500	1,500	1,500	1,500
Interest	500	500	500	500	500	500
Taxes	5,200	5,200	5,200	5,200	5,200	5,200
Other General and Admin Expenses	3,670	3,670	3,670	3,670	3,670	3,670
Depreciation and Amortization	1,500	1,500	1,500	1,500	1,500	1,500
Total Expenses	123,790	122,790	120,790	123,790	116,790	116,790
Net Income	22,230	23,230	25,230	22,230	29,230	29,230

FIGURE 10-3　(continued)

	July	August	September	October	November	December	Total
Gross Sales	201,400	201,400	201,400	201,400	201,400	201,110	2,416,510
(Returned Goods and Discounts)	-	-	-	-	-	-	-
Net Sales	201,400	201,400	201,400	201,400	201,400	201,110	2,416,510
(Cost of Goods Sold)	55,380	55,380	55,380	55,380	55,380	55,360	664,540
Gross Profit	146,020	146,020	146,020	146,020	146,020	144,750	1,751,970
Expenses—General and Administrative							
Officers' Compensation	25,750	25,750	25,750	25,750	25,750	25,750	309,000
Salaries and Wages	20,000	20,000	20,000	20,000	20,000	20,000	240,000
Payroll Taxes	4,070	4,070	4,070	4,070	4,070	4,070	48,840
Employee Benefits	11,500	11,500	11,500	11,500	11,500	11,500	138,000
Professional Services	1,000	1,000	1,000	1,000	1,000	1,000	18,000
Building Rent	27,000	27,000	27,000	27,000	27,000	27,000	324,000
Utilities	6,150	6,150	6,150	6,150	6,150	6,150	73,800
Telephone, Internet, and Web Site	1,400	1,400	1,400	1,400	1,400	1,400	16,800
Fitness Equipment Lease	1,400	1,400	1,400	1,400	1,400	1,400	16,800
Insurance	3,150	3,150	3,150	3,150	3,150	3,150	37,800
Marketing	2,000	2,000	2,000	2,000	6,000	6,000	56,000
Supplies	1,500	1,500	1,500	1,500	1,500	1,500	18,000
Interest	500	500	500	500	500	7,250	12,750
Taxes	5,200	5,200	5,200	5,200	5,200	5,200	62,400
Other General and Admin Expenses	3,670	3,670	3,670	3,670	3,670	3,670	44,040
Depreciation and Amortization	1,500	1,500	1,500	1,500	1,500	1,500	18,000
Total Expenses	115,790	115,790	115,790	115,790	119,790	126,540	1,434,230
Net Income	30,230	30,230	30,230	30,230	26,230	19,210	317,740
Income as a Percent of Gross Sales							13.1

Pro Forma Income Statement 2016 (Third Year of Business)

Gross Sales	2,561,290
(Returned Goods and Discounts)	
Net Sales	2,561,290
(Cost of Goods Sold)	704,350
Gross Profit	1,856,940
Expenses—General and Administrative	
Officers' Compensation	397,540
Salaries and Wages	254,400
Payroll Taxes	56,110
Employee Benefits	158,560
Professional Services	19,080
Building Rent	324,000
Utilities	78,220
Telephone, Internet, and Web Site	17,800
Fitness Equipment Lease	16,800

FIGURE 10-3 (continued)

Insurance	40,070
Marketing	59,360
Supplies	19,080
Interest	12,750
Taxes	68,820
Other General and Admin Expenses	46,680
Depreciation and Amortization	18,000
Total Expenses	1,587,270
Net Income	269,670
Income as a Percent of Gross Sales	10.5%

Pro Forma Income Statement 2017 (Fourth Year of Business)

Gross Sales	2,716,130
(Returned Goods and Discounts)	
Net Sales	2,716,130
(Cost of Goods Sold)	746,930
Gross Profit	1,969,200
Expenses—General and Administrative	
Officers' Compensation	421,390
Salaries and Wages	269,660
Payroll Taxes	59,470
Employee Benefits	168,070
Professional Services	20,240
Building Rent	324,000
Utilities	82,910
Telephone, Internet, and Web Site	18,860
Fitness Equipment Lease	16,800
Insurance	42,470
Marketing	62,920
Supplies	20,220
Interest	12,750
Taxes	72,950
Other General and Admin Expenses	49,480
Depreciation and Amortization	18,000
Total Expenses	1,660,190
Net Income	309,010
Income as a Percent of Gross Sales	11.3

portion of a firm's business plan and are simply transferred to the pro forma statements. There are two ways to handle year-to-year increases in projected expenses. Some increase in expenses will be known. For example, in 2016, Prime Adult Fitness projects adding a senior vice president of strategic planning to its management team. The salary range for this position is known, so a direct number can be added to the category "officers' compensation," and appropriate adjustments can be made to payroll taxes and employee benefits to reflect the change. For general expense items, many firms use the constant ratio method of forecasting—which increases expense items at the same rate as sales. Prime

Adult Fitness used this method in preparing the expenses portion of its pro forma income statements.

One ratio of particular importance in evaluating a firm's pro forma income statements is a firm's projected profit margins, or return on sales (ROS). This number is computed by dividing net income by net sales. Beyond 2014, its startup year, Prime Adult Fitness's ROS is projected to be 13.1 percent, 10.5 percent, and 11.3 percent for the years 2015, 2016, and 2017, respectively. These are healthy numbers. IBISWorld reported in the "industry analysis" section of this business plan that the average ROS for a sample of 196 fitness centers was 9 percent. Prime Adult Fitness's higher percentages likely reflect the greater scale of its operations than many of the fitness centers in the survey. Any time an apparent discrepancy appears in financial ratios, you should be prepared to explain the discrepancy at a minute's notice. For example, Prime Adult Fitness's projected drop from a 13.1 percent ROS in 2015 to a 10.5 percent ROS in 2016 may require an explanation in an investor presentation. The projected drop is due to the company's plans to add a VP of strategic planning position to its top management team in January 2015, as mentioned previously, at a cost of $70,000 a year plus benefits. The salary and benefits are reflected as a 70,000+ increase in expenses, without a corresponding increase in sales. This is what's causing the drop in 2015 ROS.

Pro forma income statements are useful in envisioning a firm's overall earnings potential and prospective changes from year to year. They don't, however, provide an indication of a firm's cash position. A firm can show excellent sales numbers, but if the sales accumulate as accounts receivable (or are used to build inventory), a firm can run out of cash despite glowing income statements. As a result, enthusiasm for impressive sales and net income figures on pro forma income statements are usually tempered. The sales still have to be realized and the money has to be collected for the results to be meaningful.

Still, Prime Adult Fitness's growth in net sales and net income during the period projected demonstrates the upside potential of the opportunity. If everything goes right, and the company launches as planned, the numbers appear to be realistic and feasible. The key phrase, however, is that everything must go as planned. Ultimately, your reader must have confidence that you and your team have the ability to execute the opportunity.

The second set of pro forma financial statements that are normally prepared are the pro forma balance sheets. Prime Adult Fitness's pro balances sheets for 2014, 2015, 2016, and 2017 are shown in Figure 10-4.

PRO FORMA BALANCE SHEET

Unlike the pro forma income statement, which covers a specific period of time, a pro forma balance sheet is a projection of a firm's assets, liabilities, and owner's equity at a specific point in time. The top of a balance sheet (or the left-hand side, depending on how it is displayed) shows a firm's assets, whereas the bottom (or right-hand side) shows its liabilities and owner's equity. The assets are listed in order of their "liquidity," or the length of time it takes to convert them to cash.

FIGURE 10-4 Pro Forma Balance Sheets 2014, 2015, 2016, 2017 (Prime Adult Fitness Business Plan)

	January 1, 2014 Start of business	December 31, 2014 End of first year	December 31, 2015 End of second year	December 31, 2016 End of third year	December 31, 2017 End of fourth year
Assets					
Current Assets					
Cash and Cash Equivalents	200,000	140,930	317,170	426,840	748,850
Accounts Receivable		50,000	100,000	150,000	150,000
Inventory	20,000	35,000	45,000	50,000	50,000
Other Current Assets	10,000	17,500		25,000	25,000
Total Current Assets	230,000	243,430	462,170	651,840	973,850
Fixed Assets					
Fitness Equipment	100,000	125,000	175,000	185,000	185,000
Vehicles				35,000	70,000
Furniture	30,000	35,000	35,000	55,000	60,000
Office Equipment	60,000	70,000	72,000	100,000	100,000
Less Accumulated Depreciation		(18,000)	(36,000)	(54,000)	(72,000)
Total Noncurrent Assets	190,000	212,000	246,000	321,000	343,000
Other Assets					
Total Assets	420,000	455,430	708,170	972,840	1,316,850
Liabilities					
Current Liabilities					
Accounts Payable		75,000	100,000	125,000	150,000
Accrued Expenses		25,000	25,000	35,000	45,000
Short-Term Notes Payable	50,000	90,000	10,000		
Total Current Liabilities	50,000	190,000	135,000	160,000	195,000
Long-Term Liabilities					
Long-Term Notes Payable	50,000	40,000	30,000		
Mortgages Payable					
Total Long-Term Liabilities	50,000	40,000	30,000		
Total Liabilities	100,000	230,000	165,000	160,000	195,000
Contributed Capital	320,000	320,000	320,000	320,000	320,000
Retained Earnings	0	(94,570)	223,170	492,840	801,850
Total Liabilities and Shareholder's Equity	420,000	455,430	708,170	972,840	1,316,850

The liabilities are listed in the order in which they must be paid. A balance sheet must always "balance," meaning a firm's assets must always equal its liabilities plus owner's equity.

Most startups create a projected opening, or base, balance sheet that shows what the business will look like at a beginning point in time. The Prime Adult Fitness base balance sheet is January 1, 2014, which coincides with the start date for its pro forma income statements and cash flows. The major categories of assets listed on a pro forma balance sheet are the following:

- *Current assets.* Current assets include cash plus items that are readily convertible to cash. It also includes items such as accounts receivable and inventory.

- *Fixed assets*. Fixed assets are assets used over a longer time frame, such as real estate, buildings, equipment, and furniture.

The major categories of liabilities listed on a balance sheet are the following:

- *Current liabilities*. Current liabilities include obligations that are payable within a year, including accounts payable, accrued expenses, and the current portion of long-term debt.

- *Long-term liabilities*. Long-term liabilities include notes or loans that are repayable beyond one year, including liabilities associated with purchasing real estate, buildings, and equipment.

- *Owners' equity*: Owners' equity is the equity invested in the business by its owners plus the accumulated earnings reported by the business after paying dividends.

Balance sheets, regardless of whether they are actual or projected, are somewhat deceiving. Firms spend money on many things that never show up on their balance sheets. For example, many operating leases, like Prime Adult Fitness's lease of fitness equipment, are "off balance sheet" transactions. Similarly, intellectual property, such as patents, trademarks, and copyrights, receive value on the balance sheet in some cases, and in other cases, they don't. In addition, intangible assets, such as the amount of training a firm has provided to its employees or the value of its brand, are not recognized on its balance sheet. Real estate is valued on a balance sheet at its cost rather than fair market value. Although this stipulation doesn't normally affect pro forma balance sheets, it's another facet of balance sheets that needs to be understood. A firm could buy a piece of land for $250,000 and watch its value increase to $1 million over time but would still value the land at $250,000 on its balance sheet.

As a result of these issues, it's important to understand what a set of pro forma balance sheets potentially accomplish. When evaluating a pro forma balance sheet, the two primary questions are whether a firm will have sufficient short-term assets to cover its short-term debts and whether it is financially sound overall. Two calculations provide the answer to the first question. At the end of 2014, Prime Adult Fitness's projected working capital, defined as its current assets minus its current liabilities, is projected to be $53,430. This number represents the amount of liquid assets the firm has available. Its projected current ratio, which equals its projected current assets divided by its projected current liabilities, is 1.28, meaning that it is projecting that it will have $1.28 in current assets for every $1.00 in current debt. This is a tight number and may cause you to pause and wonder if the company will have sufficient current assets to meet its current liabilities. The numbers are stronger in future years, as the company's projected earnings help it build cash reserves. Prime Adult Fitness's current ratio is projected to be 3.42, 4.08, and 5.0 at the end of 2015, 2016, and 2017, respectively. This is a healthy trend.

The second question, will a firm be financially sound overall, is assessed by computing a firm's overall debt ratio. A company's debt ratio is computed by dividing its total debt by its total assets. Prime Adult Fitness is projecting a debt to asset ratio of 50.50 percent at the end of 2014, which is high. Similar to its current ratio, its debt to asset ratio improves over time as its projected earnings build cash and improve its overall financial situation. Its projected debt to asset ratio is 23.30 percent, 16.45 percent, and 14.81 percent for 2015, 2016, and 2017, respectively. This is obviously a healthy trend. Again, although these numbers are impressive, they hinge on Prime Adult Fitness's management team's ability to execute all phases of its business plan.

The numbers across all of a firm's pro forma financial statements are consistent with one another. Note that the profit of $317,740 Prime Adult Fitness reports on its pro forma 2016 income statement shows up as the difference between its 2016 and 2015 pro forma balance sheets.

The final set of pro forma financial statements that are prepared are the projected cash flows. These statements must be prepared last because they rely on data from their corresponding pro forma income statements and balance sheets to be completed. Prime Adult Fitness's pro forma cash flow statements for 2014, 2015, 2016, and 2017 are shown in Figure 10-5.

PRO FORMA CASH FLOW

Many of the readers of your business plan will consider your pro forma cash flows to be the most valuable of your financial statements for the reasons mentioned earlier in the chapter. The cash flow statements provide an indication of whether a firm will be able to maintain a sufficient cash balance to get up and running successfully. This issue is critical enough that you should prepare your cash flow on a monthly basis, at least for the first two years of your firm's existence.

Interpreting and analyzing pro forma cash flow statements takes practice. The entries are intuitively obvious but still cause you to pause and think because there are a lot of unusual additions and subtractions involved. The basic idea behind a cash flow statement is to start with a beginning balance, like the amount of cash you have on hand at the beginning of a month; add your projected monthly income (or loss); and then list all the other transactions that either add or subtract from your cash. To capture items in an organized manner, the cash flow statement is divided into three activities: operating activities, investing activities, and finance activities.

- *Operating activities.* Operating activities include net income (or loss), depreciation, and changes in current assets and current liabilities other than cash.
- *Investing activities.* Investing activities include the purchase, sales, or investment in fixed assets, such as real estate, equipment, and buildings.
- *Financing activities.* Financing activities include cash raised during the period by borrowing money, making payments on loans, or paying dividends.

The best way to visualize how a cash flow works is to spend some time looking at the Prime Adult Fitness pro forma cash flow statements, shown in Figure 10-5. On the statements, the uses of cash are recorded as negative figures (which are shown by placing them in parentheses), and the sources of cash are recorded as positive

FIGURE 10-5 Pro Forma Cash Flow Statements 2014, 2015, 2016, 2017 (Prime Adult Fitness Business Plan)

Pro Forma Cash Flow Statement 2014 (First Year of Business)						
	January	February	March	April	May	June
Cash Balance at Beginning of Month	200,000	133,380	83,790	36,410	8,580	53,700
	(Beginning of Year)					
Cash Flow from Operating Activities						
Net income	(68,770)	(51,740)	(35,530)	(18,480)	(9,030)	3,050
Additions (sources of cash)						
Decrease in accounts receivable						
Decrease in inventory						
Increase in accounts payable	4,000	4,000	5,000	5,000	6,000	6,000
Increase in accrued expenses	2,100	2,100	2,100	2,100	2,100	2,100
Increase in short-term notes payable					50,000	
Decrease in other current assets						
Depreciation	1,500	1,500	1,500	1,500	1,500	1,500
Subtractions (uses of cash)						
Decrease in accounts payable						
Decrease in accrued expenses						
Decrease in short-term notes payable						
Increase in accounts receivable	(4,200)	(4,200)	(4,200)	(4,200)	(4,200)	(4,200)
Increase in other current assets			(5,000)			(2,500)
Increase in inventory	(1,250)	(1,250)	(1,250)	(1,250)	(1,250)	(1,250)
Total Adjustments						
Cash Flow from Investing Activities						
Subtractions (uses of cash)						
Purchase of fitness equipment				(12,500)		
Purchase of vehicles						
Purchase of furniture						
Purchase of office equipment			(10,000)			
Cash Flow from Financing Activities						
Additions (sources of cash)						
Increase in long-term notes payable						
Increase in mortgages payable						
Subtractions (uses of cash)						
Decrease in long-term notes payable						
Decrease in mortgages payable						
Cash Balance at End of Month	133,380	83,790	36,410	8,580	53,700	58,400

FIGURE 10-5 (continued)

	July	August	September	October	November	December	Summary (For Year)
Cash Balance at Beginning of Month	58,400	67,600	81,670	101,140	120,870	135,590	200,000
Cash Flow from Operating Activities							
Net income	3,550	8,420	13,820	19,080	21,570	19,490	(94,570)
Additions (sources of cash)							
Decrease in accounts receivable							
Decrease in inventory							
Increase in accounts payable	7,500	7,500	7,500	7,500	7,500	7,500	75,000
Increase in accrued expenses	2,100	2,100	2,100	2,100	2,100	1,900	25,000
Increase in short-term notes payable							50,000
Decrease in other current assets							
Depreciation	1,500	1,500	1,500	1,500	1,500	1,500	18,000
Subtractions (uses of cash)							
Increase in accounts receivable	(4,200)	(4,200)	(4,200)	(4,200)	(4,200)	(3,800)	(50,000)
Decrease in short-term notes payable						(10,000)	(10,000)
Increase in inventory	(1,250)	(1,250)	(1,250)	(1,250)	(1,250)	(1,250)	(15,000)
Decrease in accounts payable							
Increase in other current assets							(7,500)
Decrease in accrued expenses							
Total Adjustments							
Cash Flow from Investing Activities							
Subtractions (uses of cash)							
Purchase of fitness equipment					(12,500)		(25,000)
Purchase of vehicles							
Purchase of furniture				(5,000)			(5,000)
Purchase of office equipment							(10,000)
Total Adjustments							
Cash Flow from Financing Activities							
Additions (sources of cash)							
Increase in long-term notes payable							
Increase in mortgages payable							

FIGURE 10-5   (continued)

Subtractions (uses of cash)							
Decrease in long-term notes payable						(10,000)	(10,000)
Decrease in mortgages payable							
Cash Balance at End of Month	67,600	81,670	101,140	120,870	135,590	140,930	**140,930**
							(End of Year)

Pro Forma Cash Flow Statement 2015 (Second Year of Business)

	January	February	March	April	May	June
Cash Balance at Beginning of Month	**140,930** (Beginning of Year)	162,960	185,990	208,520	230,550	259,580
Cash Flow from Operating Activities						
Net income	22,230	23,230	25,230	22,230	29,230	29,230
Additions (sources of cash)						
Decrease in accounts receivable						
Decrease in inventory						
Increase in accounts payable	2,500	2,500	2,500	2,500	2,500	2,500
Increase in accrued expenses						
Increase in short-term notes payable						
Decrease in other current assets						
Depreciation	1,500	1,500	1,500	1,500	1,500	1,500
Subtractions (uses of cash)						
Decrease in accounts payable						
Decrease in accrued expenses						
Decrease in short-term notes payable						
Increase in accounts receivable	(4,200)	(4,200)	(4,200)	(4,200)	(4,200)	(4,200)
Increase in other current assets						
Increase in inventory			(2,500)			(2,500)
Total Adjustments						
Cash Flow from Investing Activities						
Subtractions (uses of cash)						
Purchase of fitness equipment						(25,000)
Purchase of vehicles						
Purchase of furniture						
Purchase of office equipment						
Cash Flow from Financing Activities						
Additions (sources of cash)						
Increase in long-term notes payable						
Increase in mortgages payable						
Subtractions (uses of cash)						
Decrease in long-term notes payable						
Decrease in mortgages payable						
Cash Balance at End of Month	162,960	185,990	208,520	230,550	259,580	261,110

FIGURE 10-5 (continued)

	July	August	September	October	November	December	Summary (For Year)
Cash Balance at Beginning of Month	261,110	291,140	321,170	348,700	378,730	362,260	140,930
Cash Flow from Operating Activities							
Net income	30,230	30,230	30,230	30,230	26,230	19,210	317,740
Additions (sources of cash)							
Decrease in accounts receivable							
Decrease in inventory							
Increase in accounts payable	2,500	2,500	2,500	2,500			25,000
Increase in accrued expenses							
Increase in short-term notes payable							
Decrease in other current assets						17,500	17,500
Depreciation	1,500	1,500	1,500	1,500	1,500	1,500	18,000
Subtractions (uses of cash)							
Increase in accounts receivable	(4,200)	(4,200)	(4,200)	(4,200)	(4,200)	(3,800)	(50,000)
Decrease in short-term notes payable					(40,000)	(40,000)	(80,000)
Increase in inventory			(2,500)			(2,500)	(10,000)
Decrease in accounts payable							
Increase in other current assets							
Decrease in accrued expenses							
Total Adjustments							
Cash Flow from Investing Activities							
Subtractions (uses of cash)							
Purchase of fitness equipment						(25,000)	(50,000)
Purchase of vehicles							
Purchase of furniture							
Purchase of office equipment						(2,000)	(2,000)
Total Adjustments							
Cash Flow from Financing Activities							
Additions (sources of cash)							
Increase in long-term notes payable							
Increase in mortgages payable							

FIGURE 10-5   (continued)

Subtractions (uses of cash)							
Decrease in long-term notes payable						(10,000)	(10,000)
Decrease in mortgages payable							
Cash Balance at End of Month	291,140	321,170	348,700	378,730	362,260	317,170	**317,170** (End of Year)

Pro Forma Cash Flow Statement 2016 (Third Year of Business)

Cash Balance at Beginning of Year	317,170
Cash Flow from Operating Activities	
Net income	269,670
Additions (sources of cash)	
Decrease in accounts receivable	
Decrease in inventory	
Increase in accounts payable	25,000
Increase in accrued expenses	10,000
Increase in short-term notes payable	
Decrease in other current assets	
Depreciation	18,000
Subtractions (uses of cash)	
Increase in accounts receivable	(50,000)
Decrease in short-term notes payable	(10,000)
Increase in inventory	(5,000)
Decrease in accounts payable	
Increase in other current assets	(25,000)
Decrease in accrued expenses	
Total Adjustments	
Cash Flow from Investing Activities	
Additions (sources of cash)	
Sale of fitness equipment	
Sale of vehicles	
Sale of furniture	
Sale of office equipment	
Subtractions (uses of cash)	
Purchase of fitness equipment	(10,000)
Purchase of vehicles	(35,000)
Purchase of furniture	(20,000)
Purchase of office equipment	(28,000)
Total Adjustments	
Cash Flow from Financing Activities	
Additions (sources of cash)	
Increase in long-term notes payable	
Increase in mortgages payable	
Subtractions (uses of cash)	
Decrease in long-term notes payable	(30,000)
Decrease in mortgages payable	
Cash Balance at End of Year	426,840

FIGURE 10-5 (continued)

Pro Forma Cash Flow Statement 2017 (Fourth Year of Business)	
Cash Balance at Beginning of Year	426,840
Cash Flow from Operating Activities	
Net income	309,010
Additions (sources of cash)	
Decrease in accounts receivable	
Decrease in inventory	
Increase in accounts payable	25,000
Increase in accrued expenses	10,000
Increase in short-term notes payable	
Decrease in other current assets	18,000
Depreciation	
Subtractions (uses of cash)	
Increase in accounts receivable	
Decrease in short-term notes payable	
Increase in inventory	
Decrease in accounts payable	
Increase in other current assets	
Decrease in accrued expenses	
Total Adjustments	
Cash Flow from Investing Activities	
Additions (sources of cash)	
Sale of fitness equipment	
Sale of vehicles	
Sale of furniture	
Sale of office equipment	
Subtractions (uses of cash)	
Purchase of fitness equipment	
Purchase of vehicles	(35,000)
Purchase of furniture	(5,000)
Purchase of office equipment	
Total Adjustments	
Cash Flow from Financing Activities	
Additions (sources of cash)	
Increase in long-term notes payable	
Increase in mortgages payable	
Subtractions (uses of cash)	
Decrease in long-term notes payable	
Decrease in mortgages payable	
Cash Balance at End of Month	748,850

figures. In regard to operating activities, an item like depreciation is shown as a positive figure because it was deducted from net income on the income statement but was not a cash expenditure. Similarly, an increase in accounts receivable is shown as a negative item because it was added to your net income but wasn't collected as cash. The treatment of investing and financing activities is more straightforward. If you buy a piece of equipment, that subtracts from your cash. If you take out a loan, that adds to your cash. If you make a principal payment on a loan, that subtracts from your cash, and so forth. The closest attention is typically paid to operating activities because it shows how changes in a company's accounts receivable, accounts payable, and inventory levels affect the cash it has available to maintain routine activities.

As stated earlier in the chapter, Prime Adult Fitness's pro forma cash flow shows that it will run low on cash midway during its first year of existence. Anticipating this challenge, the founders arranged for a line of credit from a bank, which the company will use to shore up its cash position during this period. If the founders hadn't completed pro forma financial statements and realized that they will run low on cash in May of 2014, they could have found themselves in a very tight cash position. The time to arrange a line of credit isn't when you're running out of cash. Instead, their 2014 pro forma cash flow alerted them to this challenge, which they prepared for by arranging the line of credit.

In summary, it's extremely important that all of a firm's pro forma financial statement be prepared as accurately and realistically as possible. If your business plan does capture the attention of an investor or banker, your financial statements will be gone over very carefully, as part of the "due diligence" process. Incorrect entries, math errors, exaggerated items, and estimates that are simply off the mark (i.e., the average price to rent warehouse space in your community is $12.00 per square foot, and you're projecting you can rent it for $4.00 per square foot) will be picked up and may compromise your ability to get funding or financing if they are serious enough. Conversely, sharp financials that realistically translate a firm's plans into numbers and are error free can make a very positive impression.

Finally, like the business plan itself, going through the process of preparing your pro forma financial projections may be as valuable as the projections themselves. The numbers will invariably change, but the lessons you're bound to learn through preparing the statements are invaluable. Sometimes, entrepreneurs discount the value of financial analysis, thinking that the numbers are just a guess so they're really not important. Still, demonstrating the ability to prepare financial statements and think through the issues behind them is vital. This point is illustrated through a vignette reported by Rich and Gumpert in their book *Business Plans That Work*. The vignette portrays the reaction an investor had when an entrepreneur claimed that financial projections aren't really that important:

> One entrepreneur who was undergoing some intense questioning by panelists about his company's projections finally said, in exasperation, "I really don't take our projections or any projections more than a year out all that seriously. After all, I don't really know how much business is reasonable to expect three, four, and five years into the future." A panelist's response was swift and certain. "We know you can't say for sure what's going to happen," the panelist observed. "But you must go through the thought process. You must consider best-case and worst-case scenarios. You must demonstrate that you can quantify the marketing, production, and other research and testing you've done. We may not agree with your projections, but we want to see that you've thought about where your company might be in five years and quantified your thinking."[3]

BUSINESS PLAN INSIGHT

Break-Even Analysis: A Simple Yet Very Valuable Calculation

Break-even analysis is a calculation that allows a firm to determine the volume of business it must do to "break even" in terms of profit and loss. It's a form of analysis that's often used by startups and by existing firms to discern whether adding a new product to their existing product line makes sense. Technically, the break-even point for a new company or a new product is where the total revenue received equals the total costs associated with the company or product.

The best way to show how a break-even analysis works is to provide an illustration. Say you're interested in opening a smoothie restaurant. You could use a break-even analysis to determine whether opening the restaurant is feasible. The formula for break-even analysis is as follows:

Total fixed costs/(price – average variable costs)

As a result, if the total fixed costs associated with opening the restaurant is $85,000, the average prices of the smoothies you'll sell is $4.50, and the variable cost for each smoothie is $2.10, then the break point for your restaurant is as follows:

$85,000 (total fixed costs)/($4.50–$2.10) or $2.40=35,417 units

This number means that you'll have to sell 35,417 "units" or smoothie drinks per year to break even. That number breaks down to 98.5 smoothies per day, on average, based on a 360-day year. To determine whether opening the restaurant is feasible and makes good financial sense, that number should be compared to the sales that similar smoothie restaurants experience.

Break-even analysis is also useful in helping entrepreneurs determine whether different business strategies make sense. Assume you're considering moving to a location with more foot traffic to boost your sales. Your rent will be higher, and your total fixed costs will jump from $85,000 per year to $112,000. If your prices and variable costs remain the same, the move will increase your break-even point to the following:

$112,000 (total fixed costs)/($4.50-$2.10) or $2.40=46,666 units.

On a daily basis, the move will increase your break-even point from 98.5 smoothies a day to 130. You'll have to then decide whether moving to the new location will provide you with sufficient increased sales to justify the move.

Another financial instrument that is often used but was not computed for Prime Adult Fitness is the break-even analysis. An explanation of the break-even analysis and how it's used is provided in the Business Plan Insight box.

The next section of this chapter focuses on ratio analysis, which is a standard technique for analyzing pro forma financial statements. This portion of the Prime Adult Fitness business plan is shown in Figure 10-6.

FIGURE 10-6   Ratio Analysis (Prime Adult Fitness Business Plan)

Profitability Ratios

	2014	*2015*	*2016*	*2017*
Return on Assets (ROA)	NA	54%	32%	27%
ROA = net income/average total assets				
Return on Sales (ROS)	NA	13.1%	10.5%	11.3%
ROS = net income/net sales				

Average total assets = beginning total assets + ending total assets/2.
Average shareholders' equity = beginning shareholders' equity + ending shareholders' equity/2.

Liquidity Ratios

	2014	**2015**	**2016**	**2017**
Current ratio	1.28	3.42	4.08	5.00
Current assets/current liabilities				

Overall Financial Stability Ratios

	2014	**2015**	**2016**	**2017**
Debt ratio	50.50%	23.30%	16.45%	14.81%
Total debt/total assets				

RATIO ANALYSIS

The most practical way to interpret or make sense of a firm's historical or pro forma financial statements is through ratio analysis.

In general, ratios are computed by taking numbers out of financial statements and forming ratios with them. Each ratio has a particular meaning in regard to the potential of a business. Your readers will instantly recognize the general picture that a particular ratio conveys. For example, as mentioned earlier in the chapter, Prime Adult Fitness's current ratio is projected to be 1.28 at the end of 2014. That ratio will alert a discerning reader to pay attention to whether the firm has a backup plan (such as a prearranged line of credit) to use if its cash position deteriorates further. It will also alert the reader to look forward to see if the projected cash position improves over time. Another valuable use of ratios is to compare a firm's ratios to industry norms. If a firm's ratios, such as projected return on assets (ROA) and ROS, are consistently better than industry norms, that's probably an indication that the firm's financial projections are too optimistic.

The three most common categories of financial ratios are profitability ratios, liquidity ratios, and overall financial stability ratios. Profitability ratios compare the amount of income earned against the resources used to generate it. Liquidity ratios measure the relationship between a company's short-term assets and its short-term liabilities. Overall financial stability ratios measure the overall financial stability of a firm.

The Prime Adult Fitness projected financial ratios are shown in Figure 10-6. The ROA ratios are high, reflecting in part the company's ability to generate high income in a facility it is leasing. Thus, the value of the facility doesn't show up on the firm's projected balance sheet. If Prime Adult Fitness was purchasing the building it will occupy for $5 million, its ROA in 2015 would be 7 percent.

Chapter Summary

1. The final section of a business plan presents a firm's pro forma financial projections. Having completed the previous sections of the plan, it's easy to see why the financial projections come last. They take the plans you've developed and express them in financial terms.

2. The source and use of funds statement is a document that lays out specifically how much money a firm needs (if the intention of the business plan is to raise money) and what the money will be used for.

3. An assumptions sheet is an explanation of the most critical assumptions that your financial statements are based on.

4. The pro forma income statement reflects the projected results of the operations for a firm for a given period of time. It records all the projected sales and expenses for the given period and shows whether the firms will be making a profit or experiencing a loss.

5. Pro forma income statements are useful in envisioning a firm's overall earnings potential and prospective changes from year to year. They don't, however, provide an indication of a firm's cash position.

6. Unlike the pro forma income statement, which covers a specific period of time, a pro forma balance sheet is a projection of a firm's assets, liabilities, and owner's equity at a specific point in time.

7. Many of the readers of your business plan will consider your pro forma cash flows to be the most valuable of your financial statements. The statements provide an indication of whether a firm will be able to maintain a sufficient cash balance to get up and running successfully.

8. To capture items in an organized manner, the cash flow statement is divided into three activities: operating activities, investing activities, and finance activities.

9. The most practical way to interpret or make sense of a firm's historical or pro forma financial statements is through ratio analysis.

In general, ratios are computed by taking numbers out of financial statements and forming ratios with them. Each ratio has a particular meaning in regard to the potential of a business.

Review Questions

1. Why is the financial plan typically one of the last chapters in a business plan?
2. What is the purpose of a sources and uses of funds statement?
3. What is the purpose of an assumptions sheet?
4. Briefly describe the three pro forma financial statements that should be included in a business plan.
5. How is it possible for a firm to show a sizable net income on its income statements and still be running out of cash?
6. Describe the term "cost of goods sold (COGS)."
7. Why would a current ratio of 1.1 raise concerns?
8. Describe why many people feel that the cash flow statement is the most valuable statement of the three financial statements normally included in a business plan.
9. Describe the purpose of ratio analysis.
10. Briefly describe at least one profitability ratio, one liquidity ratio, and one overall financial stability ratio.

Application Questions

1. Suppose a friend of yours showed you the pro forma income statements for his startup and exclaimed excitedly that during its first three years of operation, his firm will make a net income of $150,000 per year, which is just the amount of money, $450,000, that the firm will need to pay off a three-year loan. Explain to your friend why he might not actually have $450,000 in cash, even though his pro forma income statements say that he will earn that amount of money.
2. Suppose a colleague of yours is gearing up to write a business plan for a business she plans to start. She told you she plans to prepare the financial statements first, to get that job out of the way before she tackles the rest of the plan. Explain to your colleague the flaw in her approach.
3. An acquaintance of yours is looking to invest in a local restaurant. He has narrowed the possibilities to three restaurants. He has requested and received both historical and pro forma income statements, balance sheets, and statements of cash flow from each of the restaurants. He's turned to you for advice in terms of how to use the financial statements to assist him in his investment decision. Provide your acquaintance advice on a systematic approach for using the financial statements to aid in his decision.
4. You have been invited to speak at a small business growth conference. The title of the speech that you've been asked to deliver is "Be Careful What You Wish For: How Growing Too Fast Can Financially Overwhelm A Company." Write a summary of the points that you'll make in the speech.

5. Imagine that you are an investor and that you're leafing through the business plan of a startup that has attracted your interest. You've reached the financial projections section of the plan, glance at your watch, and realize you only have five minutes to make an assessment. List the items you would look at and the order in which you would look at them. Justify why each of these items would be a priority in the five minutes you have available.

Endnotes

1. Dun & Bradstreet, *Industry Norms & Key Business Ratios: Statistics on Over 800 Lines of Business, Desk Top Edition* (New York: Dunn & Bradstreet, 2003).
2. L. Troy, *Almanac of Business and Industrial Financial Ratios* (New York: CCH, Inc., 2007).
3. S. Rich and D. Gumpert, *Business Plans That Work* (New York: Harper & Row, 1985).

CHAPTER 11

PRESENTING THE PLAN WITH CONFIDENCE

INTRODUCTION

If your business plan piques the interest of an investor or banker, or you enter it into a business plan competition, you'll normally be asked to make a verbal presentation of the plan. On these occasions, you'll want to be prepared to present the plan with confidence and poise. If the presentation goes well, it can move you closer to obtaining the funding or financing you need. If it doesn't, it can impede your chances of moving forward and represent a setback in your attempts to get your business off the ground.

This chapter provides a primer on making an effective business plan presentation. Most of us do not routinely make verbal presentations, so careful planning and practice pay off. If you've followed the approach to writing a business plan described in this book, you've put a lot of time and effort into the process. You'll want to cap off your efforts by presenting your plan in a manner that maximizes your chances for success.

This chapter contains two sections. The first section focuses on preparing for and making an effective presentation. Tips and suggestions are provided on steps to take before you make the presentation and how to deliver the presentation effectively. The second section of the chapter focuses on the content of the presentation. This section is augmented by walking you through a 12-slide PowerPoint presentation and making recommendations for what to include on each slide.

PREPARING FOR AND DELIVERING AN EFFECTIVE BUSINESS PLAN PRESENTATION

The first set of issues to think about after you've been asked to make a verbal presentation of your business plan is how to go about preparing for the task and how to deliver an effective presentation. How you present yourself and the manner in which you interact with the people you will be presenting to makes as much difference as the plan itself. As you present your plan, your audience will be judging not only your plan but also you (and your team). The way you carry yourself, your facial expressions, how sharp your PowerPoint slides are, how you handle difficult questions, and similar attributes are all cues to your audience of how effective a business owner you are likely to be. As a result, it's important that you prepare and deliver the presentation in an effective manner.

This section covers two topics: preparing for the presentation and effective presentation techniques.

PREPARING FOR THE PRESENTATION

The initial task in preparing for a business plan presentation is to find out as much as you can about the people you'll be presenting to. This task may require some legwork but is normally well worth it. All venture capital firms have Web sites that include lists of their portfolio companies and bios of their partners, and it's usually easy to find out the backgrounds of business angels via Web searches and discrete inquiries. If you're involved in a business plan competition, it's not inappropriate to ask about the names and backgrounds of the judges.

Knowing this information is important for two reasons. First, if you can tie the business you're proposing into other activities that the people you're meeting are involved with, they may see more value in supporting your efforts. For example, if you were presenting the business plan for Prime Adult Fitness to a group of angel investors and noticed that one of the investors is a heart surgeon that practices at a local teaching hospital, you might mention during the presentation that Prime Adult Fitness would be open to the possibility of collaborating with the hospital. This comment might prompt the heart surgeon to start thinking about the types of studies he could conduct in your facility relating to exercise and cardiovascular health. If you can establish this type of tie-in with one or more of the panelists during the presentation, it might enhance the value of your business in their mind(s).

The second reason it's important to learn about the people you'll be presenting to is to try to find some type of personal connection with one or more of the individuals involved. Any type of common ground you can find, like having the same college or university affiliation or a similar hobby, helps break the ice and build rapport. You'll have to find an appropriate way of working the connection into your presentation, or bring it up during the informal minutes before or after your presentation. As long as you come across as sincere, people normally consider it a compliment that you went to the trouble of learning about their backgrounds.

The other tasks involved in preparing for a business plan presentation consist of a hodgepodge of activities. Any one of the activities, however, could be problematic if not handled correctly. You should make sure to know how much time you have and plan accordingly. The number one rule in making a presentation is to follow the rules. If an angel group tells you that you'll have one hour, but 30 minutes of the hour is reserved for questions and answers, you should carefully time your presentation so it doesn't last for more than 30 minutes—no excuses. You should also dress appropriately. If you're unsure of what to wear, call the receptionist of the firm at which you'll be presenting and ask about attire. If that route isn't practical, it's always better to dress up, by wearing formal business attire, than it is to dress down. The only exception to these rules of thumb is if your business has sharp polo shirts or something similar with your company name and logo on it. In this instance, it might be appropriate for your team members to wear that attire. You should also have business cards, even if you are a very early stage startup. There are many places where you can get generic business cards printed for just a few dollars. It's also advisable for each member of your team to have a LinkedIn account. Investors also prepare for the meetings they have with entrepreneurs. One of the most common things they'll do prior to a presentation is browse the LinkedIn profiles of the people they'll be meeting with.

It's also important to practice your presentation. Many experienced entrepreneurs practice their presentations several times in front of colleagues and others to time the presentation and get feedback. It's also a good idea to watch other people present, to get a sense of what works and what doesn't. There are business plan competitions in many areas, and you should sit in on the competitions if possible. There are also places on the Internet where presentations are posted. For example, firms that are planning to launch an IPO are taken on a "road show" by their investment bank. A road show is a whirlwind tour that consists of meetings in key cities where the firm presents its business plan to groups of investors. These presentations are taped and are available at http://www.retailroadshow.com until the IPO is completed. Another option is to simply type "business plan presentation videos" into Google or another Internet search engine. You'll need to pick and choose carefully, but normally a number of videos will pop up from business plan competitions held on university campuses or in other locations. Many of the videos will include not only the business plan presentation but also the ensuing question and answer period with the judges.

Finally, to the extent that you can, you should try to find out as much as you can about the venue you'll be presenting in. If you'll be in a small conference room, then you usually don't have to make any special adjustments. But if you'll be presenting on a stage or to a large audience, which is sometimes the case in the finals of a business plan competition, then you might want to make the fonts on your PowerPoint slides larger, for example, and find innovative ways to project to a larger audience.

DELIVERING AN EFFECTIVE PRESENTATION

Many books have been written about delivering effective presentations, and you may want to visit your library and browse through several of the books. Two particularly good books are *Presenting with Credibility: Practical Tools and Techniques for Effective Presentations*[1] by Bruna Martinuzzi and *HBR Guide to Persuasive Presentations*[2] by Nancy Duarte. Both of these books contain numerous tips and pointers for making effective business presentations.

The first thing to consider in making a presentation is who will do the presenting. If you're a sole entrepreneur, you'll obviously be doing the presenting, but if you're part of team, the question always arises regarding how many members of the team should talk during the presentation. This issue is a judgment call, but there is a strong case to be made for involving as many team members as possible. If you tag team your presentation and it goes well, it shows that your team members work well together, and there is no one member of your team who is so dominant that he or she wants all the attention. It also helps keep the listener attentive and alert. It varies the pace of the presentation and allows the listener to learn a little bit about each of the individuals involved.

The second thing to consider is the proper role of the PowerPoint slides you're using and your verbal remarks. This is a place where many presenters, whether alone or as part of a group, miss the mark. Your PowerPoint slides are not meant to tell the story of your business. You (and your team) should tell the story, and the slides should provide an overall context and punctuate your remarks. This is a hard rule to follow because the natural tendency is to try to help the listener by making the slides as complete as possible. But that's usually a mistake. Your PowerPoint slides should be brief and contain only major themes and supporting points. Your audience should spend the majority of their time listening to you rather than reading your slides. The only exception to this rule is if you're sending a set of slides for someone to review instead of making a presentation. In this instance, the slides should be more complete because they'll need to tell the story.

There are many rules of thumb about PowerPoint slides in presentations, and you'll need to use your judgment in making various calls. Some experts recommend a 6-6-6 rule when drafting slides: 6 words per bullet, 6 bullets per page, and no more than 6 text slides in a row before a visual break (a slide that includes graphs, tables, or illustrations). All kinds of colorful metaphors are attached to the dangers of trying to fit too many slides into a presentation or making your slides too dense, including "death by PowerPoint" and "PowerPoint Poisoning" (coined first by Delbert). A maximum of 12 PowerPoint slides in a 20- to 30-minute business plan presentation and the 6-6-6 rule are good guidelines to follow. In the mock PowerPoint presentation shown later in this chapter, 12 slides are used.

The final and most important advice about delivering an effective presentation is to make it interesting, upbeat, and heartfelt (to the degree appropriate and fitting). No one wants to listen to a plodding, boring presentation, no matter how much potential the venture has. In addition, although it sounds clichéd, you need to connect with your audience. The following is a brief list of techniques that presenters use to try to accomplish this objective:

- Tell a personal story or anecdote.
- Use humor.
- Show passion through hand gestures and excitement in your voice.
- Involve the audience by asking for a show of hands on key points.
- Demonstrate a prototype of the product.

This is just a brief list—you can use many other techniques as well. A very telling study conducted by MIT validates the importance of these types of techniques. According to the study, communication happens on three levels: 55 percent visual (body language), 35 percent vocal (tone of voice), and 7 percent verbal (words).[3] There are additional techniques that help a presenter connect with an audience, including building pauses into your presentation to ask if anyone has a question, and varying the pitch of your voice and changing your expressions to help keep the listeners engaged.

It's also important to understand that your overarching goal, during a business plan presentation, is not only to educate your audience about your idea but also to fire them up (to inspire). This goal can be accomplished in both overt and subtle ways. A subtle way is to tell a personal story or anecdote, which indicates why you feel your business is important and why you are fully committed to its success. For example, according to Jeremy Ryan's bio (Jeremy is the CEO and cofounder of Prime Adult Fitness), Jeremy's interest in fitness stems from an incident involving his father. At age 49, Jeremy's father survived a heart attack and restored his health by joining a fitness center and exercising regularly. Jeremy's father is now an active 73-year-old retiree. In his business plan presentation, Jeremy could briefly talk about his father and the impact that joining a fitness center has had on extending his life. This type of heartfelt story, as long as it ties in with the business, usually deeply resonates with an audience.

PREPARING THE CONTENT OF AN EFFECTIVE BUSINESS PLAN PRESENTATION

The second component of putting together an effective business plan presentation is to determine the content to present. As important as the issues are that were just covered, the presentation has little to no chance of succeeding if the content is poorly thought out or important elements are missing.

Obviously, you can't convey everything that's in a 25- to 35-page business plan in a 20- to 30-minute presentation. As a result, you have to focus on the parts of the plan that are the most important to your audience. The single biggest mistake that people make in putting together a business plan presentation is focusing on the areas that excite them the most, rather than the areas that will help their audience make a decision. As indicated in Chapter 10, whereas you may be very passionate about your product (or service) idea, like starting a fitness center for people 50 years old and older, the people listening to your plan may have other interests. Although they need to know about your product, your market, your management team, and so forth, they usually have very specific information that they're listening for. For venture capitalists, it's usually how quickly you can grow your business and your anticipated rates of return. For bankers, it's normally how predictable your cash flows are and how you plan to minimize risk. For a business angel, it may be another topic. You'll need to anticipate what the "hot-button" issue is for your audience and structure your presentation accordingly.

A number of authors, and business plan experts, have recommended templates for business plan presentations. The templates spell out the number of slides to include, the order in which to include them, and the content to include on each slide. Although slight variations exist across authors, there is general consensus about what should be included in a 20- to 30-minute business plan presentation. The following plan represents a consensus of various approaches. You should tweak and vary the approach to make it fit your plan and to tailor it to the audience you are presenting to.

The plan presented here contains 12 slides. Many experts figure two minutes per slide (on average), so this number works fairly well for a 20- to 30-minute presentation. Presumably, the people you will be presenting to will have a copy of your business plan. If you're not confident of that, bring several copies of your plan to the presentation. This is particularly important if you're participating in a business plan competition. There may be members of the audience who are hearing your plan for the first time and may be interested in seeing the entire business plan.

SAMPLE BUSINESS PLAN PRESENTATION

The presentation starts with a title slide, which is normally projected on the screen while your audience is assembling and before you start your formal remarks.

Company Name/Logo

Name of Founder(s)
Contact Information of Founder(s)

Acknowledgment of Whom the
Presentation Is Being Made To

Date

Comments: This slide should be sharp and uncluttered. Make sure to include contact information for at least one of the founders. You should also personalize the presentation by putting the correct date on the cover slide and acknowledging to whom the plan is being presented.

Slide 1: Overview

- Brief explanation of your product or service
- Short explanation of the key points that will be conveyed in the presentation
- Short discussion of the potential positive outcomes (business, societal, financial) that will result from the launching of the business

Comments: This slide should give your audience an overview of your business and its potential. It's a good place to include a story, an anecdote, or a statistic that vividly illustrates why the business is important and why you're launching it. It you don't "hook" your listeners here, it's hard to regain their attention. Tailor your remarks specifically to your audience. If one fact about your business is particularly compelling, tell it here.

Slide 2: The Problem

- Explain the problem to be solved
  - What's the pain?
  - Why aren't customers satisfied with current solutions?
  - Will the problem get better or worse over time?
- Validate the problem via research
  - What do your potential customers think?
  - What do the experts say?
- How big is the problem?

Comments: It's always best to first talk about the problem (i.e., no fitness center available that's exclusively for people 50 years old and older), and then present your company (in the next slide) as the solution to the problem. You should validate your assertions via primary and secondary research. Primary research is vital. Prove to your audience that you've talked to potential customers, and they see the problem the same way you do. This is a good place to talk about the results of your feasibility analysis and concept tests. You can also cite industry experts or services such as Mintel, Bizminer, and IBISWorld, but nothing is more convincing than your own data. Convey to your audience the size of the problem. The problem normally has to suggest a large market to get the interest of equity investors.

Slide 3: The Solution

- Present your business as the solution to the problem
  - Describe how your solution is distinctly different from others that are addressing the same problem
- Describe the degree to which your solution makes your customers lives richer or more efficient or effective
- Talk about how you'll erect barriers to entry to prevent others from quickly copying your solution

Comments: Present your business as the solution to the problem. Describe how your solution is better than others. For example, in Prime Adult Fitness's case, there are many all-purpose fitness centers that are starting to offer classes for older people, but Prime Adult Fitness will be the only center *exclusively* for older people. Talk about how much difference your business will make in the lives of your customers. Will your solution help your customers as little, a moderate amount, or a lot? You'll also need to address the imitation issue. How will you keep others from immediately duplicating what you're doing? This is where patents or other intellectual property may come into play. You may also benefit by capturing a strong first-mover advantage.

Slide 4: Opportunity and Target Market

- Articulate your specific target market
  - Talk about business and environmental trends that are providing your target market momentum
- Show, graphically if possible, the size of your target market, your projected sales (three years minimum), and your projected market share
  - Explain how you arrived at your sales figures
  - Be prepared to defend your numbers

Comments: Articulates your specific target market. Show graphically, if you think it's necessary, how you segmented your market. Demonstrate, through your verbal remarks, that you are fully acquainted with the market and the behavior of its customers. Talk specifically about the trends that are providing your market momentum. Show (in dollars) the size of your target market, your projected sales, and your projected market share for at least three years. Graphs work best and break up the tedium of a primarily text-based presentation. Impress your audience by having a solid rationale to support your projected sales. Be prepared to defend your numbers.

Slide 5: Technology

- Talk about your technology, or unique aspects of your product or service, if appropriate
  - Don't talk in an overly technical manner
  - Make your descriptions easy to understand
- Show pictures or descriptions of your product or your product prototype
  - If applicable, bring a prototype to the presentation
- Talk about any intellectual property issues that are involved

Comments: This slide is optional but is normally included. You should talk about your technology or any unusual aspects of your product or service. Make sure to talk in layman's terms. Show a picture of your product or service (an artist's rendition may be sufficient), or a product prototype if applicable. If a working prototype of your product exists, bring it to the presentation. If you're a service business, like Prime Adult Fitness, a sample brochure or daily schedule of the events that will take place in your center is a form of a prototype. Talk about any intellectual property issues that are involved.

Slide 6: Competition

- Discuss your direct, indirect, and future competitors
- Show your competitive analysis grid
- Use the competitive analysis grid as a way to discuss the advantages you will have over your competitors
  - Talk about why you think your points of competitive advantage are sustainable
  - If your exit strategy is to be bought by one of your larger competitors, this is a good place to introduce the possibility

Comments: Lay out your competitive landscape. Don't diminish your credibility by understating the current or future competition. Display your competitive analysis grid, and use it to visually depict your points of competitive advantage. Talk about why you think your points of competitive advantage are sustainable. If your exit strategy is to be bought by one of your larger competitors, this is a good place to introduce the possibility. Show how your points of competitive advantage would benefit your potential acquirer.

Slide 7: Marketing and Sales

- Describe your overall marketing strategy
- Describe your pricing strategy
- Talk about your sales process
  - Explain what motivates people (companies) in your industry to buy
  - Explain how you'll make your customers aware of your product or service
  - Explain how you'll reach your customers
    - Describe whether you'll field your own sales force or will work through intermediaries

Comments: Begin by describing your overall marketing strategy. Describe your pricing strategy and whether you plan to feature cost-plus pricing or value-based pricing. Describe how your price(s) will compare to your competitors. Talk about your sales process, and walk your audience through how people will become aware of your product or service and how you'll sell it to them. If you plan to field your own sales force, talk about how your salespeople will be compensated. If you've administered a buying intentions survey or conducted other primary research regarding how people feel about your product, report the results here.

Slide 8: Management Team

- Describe your existing management team
  - Describe their backgrounds and expertise
  - Describe how their backgrounds and expertise are key to the success of your venture
  - Describe how the team works together
- Discuss the gaps in the management team and how you plan to fill them
- Briefly discuss your board of directors and/or board of advisors

Comments: As emphasized throughout this book, your audience will see your management team as a key element in the potential success of your new venture. Explain how the team came together and how their backgrounds and expertise are keys to the success of your firm. If you've put together a board of directors or a board of advisors, briefly mention the key individuals who are involved. Show the gaps in your team by displaying a skills profile, and explain how you'll fill the gaps. If, overall, you've been able to put together an impressive team (of employees and advisors), talk briefly about how you've been able to "sell" your vision for the firm to these individuals. If your audience sees that you've been able to get good people to commit to your firm as employees and advisors, they'll believe that you can sell your product to paying customers.

Slide 9: Financial Projections

- Show a summary of your income projections and your cash flow projections for the first three to five years
  - Condense the projections as appropriate to fit them onto a single slide
  - If the font appears to be too small, use an additional slide

Comments: Show a summary of your income projections and cash flow projections for the first three to five years. If the font seems too small, use an additional slide. Make sure to have the actual projections available if anyone wants to see more detail. Know your numbers cold. You shouldn't stumble or hesitate if asked about any number in the projections. Be prepared to explain the assumptions behind your numbers. Describe your projected return on sales in the context of industry norms.

Slide 10: Current Status

- Highlight the milestones achieved to data
- Describe how much money the founders, the management team, and any early investors have put into the firm
  - Describe how the money has been spent
- Describe the current ownership structure of the firm
- Describe the firm's form of business ownership (i.e., LLC, Subchapter S Corporation, C Corporation)

Comments: Describe the current status of your firm in the context of the milestones you've achieved. Describe how much money the founders, the management team, and any early investors have put into the firm. Talk about how the money has been spent. Investors, in particular, want to see evidence that you use money effectively. Don't diminish the value of your accomplishments. Talk about the current ownership structure of your firm (a graph works well for this), and describe your business's form of legal ownership.

Slide 11: Financing Sought

- Show a sources and uses of funds statement that leads you to the financing you seek
  - The sources and uses of funds statement should specify, to the extent possible, specifically how you'll use the funds
- Show the milestones you'll be able to accomplish after you receive the funding you're seeking

Comments: This slide lays out specifically how much financing you're seeking and how you'll use the money. Be prepared to talk about how much of your firm you're willing to give up if you're presenting to equity investors or the type of terms you're looking for if you're trying to obtain a bank loan. Show the milestones you'll be able to accomplish after you receive the funding you're requesting.

Slide 12: Summary

- Summarize the strongest points about your venture
- Summarize the strongest points about your team
- Discuss your exit strategy
- Solicit feedback
  - Set up a follow-up meeting if possible

Comments: Bring the presentation to a close. Summarize the strongest points (two to three maximum) about your venture and your team. Discuss your exit strategy. Solicit feedback if you're presenting to equity investors or bankers. If you're presenting in a business plan competition, thank the judges for their participation. Be ready to answer any questions about your new venture.

Chapter Summary

1. If your business plan piques the interest of an investor or banker, or you enter it into a business plan competition, you'll normally be asked to make a verbal presentation of the plan. On these occasions, you must be prepared to present the plan with confidence and poise.
2. Most of us do not routinely make verbal presentations, so careful planning and practice pay off.
3. The first set of issues to think about after you've been asked to make a verbal presentation of your business plan is how to prepare for the task and how to deliver an effective presentation. How you present yourself and the manner in which you interact with the people you will be presenting to makes as much difference as the plan itself.
4. You should make sure to know how much time you have to make your presentation and plan accordingly. The number one rule in making a presentation is to follow the rules.

5. You should dress appropriately for a presentation. If you're unsure of what to wear, call the receptionist of the firm at which you'll be presenting and ask about attire. If that route isn't practical, it's always better to dress up, by wearing formal business attire, than it is to dress down.

6. It's important to practice your presentation. Many experienced entrepreneurs practice their presentations several times in front of colleagues and others to time the presentation and get feedback. It's also a good idea to watch other people present to get a sense of what works and what doesn't work.

7. A strong case can be made for involving as many of the members of your team as possible in a business plan presentation.

8. Your goal, during a business plan presentation, is not only to educate your audience about your idea but also to fire them up (to inspire).

9. An important component of putting together an effective business plan presentation is to determine the content to present. Obviously, you can't convey everything that's in a 25- to 35-page business plan in a 20- to 30-minute presentation. As a result, you have to focus on the parts of the plan that are the most important to your audience.

10. The 12 slides in the mock business plan presentation in this chapter include overview, the problem, the solution, opportunity and target market, technology, competition, marketing and sales, management team, financial projections, current status, financing sought, and summary.

Review Questions

1. Why is it important to carefully prepare and plan for a business plan presentation?

2. What are the most important issues involved with preparing for a business plan presentation?

3. What is meant by the statement, "as you present your plan, your audience will not only be judging your plan, but they will also be judging you?"

4. Why is it important to know about the people you'll be presenting your business plan to?

5. Why is it important to practice your presentation?

6. What is the proper role of PowerPoint slides in a business plan presentation?

7. What are the positive aspects of involving as many of the members of a management team as possible in a business plan presentation?

8. What is meant by the phrase "death by PowerPoint?"

9. What is a reasonable number of PowerPoint slides to include in a 20- to 30-minute business plan presentation?

10. List the title of the slides included in the mock 12-slide business plan presentation included in this chapter.

Application Questions

1. You recently agreed to serve as a judge for a business plan competition at the college or university you attend. A week before the presentation, you received an e-mail from the organizer of the competition with some last minute information. One comment in the e-mail struck you. The organizer of the competition said, "I think you'll be really impressed with the research the students have done to validate the markets for their ideas." If this statement is accurate, what type of research would you expect to hear from the student teams that you listen to?

2. Make a list of 10 mistakes that you could make in a business plan presentation. Next to each mistake, make a brief suggestion for how to avoid the mistake.

3. Josh Peters, a friend of yours, asked you to sit in on a dry run of his business plan presentation. You know that Josh is looking for $200,000 to launch his venture. At the end of the presentation, you ask Josh why he never mentioned how much money he's looking for. He replied, "That's a point of negotiation. I don't want to disclose how much I'm looking for or how much of the company I'm willing to give up, until I know how interested someone is in my venture." Discuss the pluses and minuses of Josh's approach.

4. Suppose you are in the process of raising capital for your startup. You have been asked by a local angel group to present your business plan at their next meeting. Describe how you would go about preparing for the presentation. Make your answer as complete as possible.

5. Imagine you're an investor who is very impressed with a business plan you recently reviewed. The market for the product the business plan is focused on is huge, the founders of the company seemed to have found a real problem that needs to be solved, the management team looks good, and the financial projections are impressive. You just listened to the founders of the firm present the plan, and the presentation was weak at best. The founders seemed poorly organized, the slides weren't sharp, and they only did a so-so job answering questions. You don't quite know what to do next. The written plan is impressive, but the presentation was a disappointment. If the investor asked you for your advice, what would you tell him?

Endnotes

1. B. Martinuzzi, *Presenting with Credibility: Practical Tools and Techniques for Effective Presentations* (New York: Six Seconds, 2012).
2. N. Duarte, *HBR Guide to Persuasive Presentations* (Cambridge, MA: Harvard Business Review Press, 2012).
3. D. DiResta, *Knockout Presentations* (Worcester, MA: Chandler House, 1998).

NAME INDEX

B

Battelle, John, 95
Berkus, David, 9
Bezos, Jeff, 198
Blank, Steve, 60
Boire, Ron, 150
Bratton, Shaun, 5
Buchheit, Paul, 95

C

Charan, Ram, 181
Chen, Katherine, 232
Ciravolo, Tish, 29
Cooper, R.G., 56
Cuban, Mark, 182

D

Druxman, Lisa, 162

G

Goizueta, Roberto, 139
Gumpert, David, 206–207, 235
Gupta, Ujjwal, 27

J

Joos, Bill, 9

K

Kagle, Bob, 186
Kamer, Dean, 11

Kawasaki, Guy, 4, 13,
    89, 106
Ketler, Lorna, 31–32
Keveles, Melanie, 6
Klaus, Rodan, 59
Klause, Sharelle, 58
Koetting, Michael, 31
Kotler, Philip, 28
Kurtzman, Joel, 131, 171

L

Levitt, Susie, 28
Li, Ray, 5

M

Martinuzzi, Bruna, 244
McCracken, Harry, 26
McTasney, Marissa, 6
Mullins, John W., 17

O

Omidyar, Pierre, 185

P

Page, Larry, 96
Patel, 95
Patterson, Tom, 58
Porter, Michael, 114
Price, Robert W., 9

R

Rangneikar, Ashish, 27
Rich, Stanley, 206–207, 235
Rodan, Dr. Katie, 57, 59

S

Sahlman, William A., 7
Sanghani, Gaurav, 31
Schuup, Sarah, 31
Schwartz, Jonathan, 26
Shea, Katie, 28
Skoll, Jeff, 185
Stross, Randall, 185
Sullivan, Stacy, 95
Susan Nichols, 29

U

Udall, Laura, 28, 153, 165,
    183–184, 191–192
Upadhyay, Sid, 31

V

Vitug, John, 5

W

Whiting, Gwen, 2–4
Whitman, Meg, 186
Wieber, Lindsey, 2–4
Wilkins, Barb, 31–32

SUBJECT INDEX

1-800-FLOWERS, 98

A

ABI/Inform, 38
ABIresearch, 27
accountants as management
        teams members, 185
AdhereTech, 28, 40
advertising plans, 161
    See also marketing plans
advisory boards, 183–184
Affordable Care Act
        (Obamacare), 27
aggressive growth
        businesses, 14
*Almanac of Business and
        Industrial Financial
        Ratios,* 219
Amazon, 166, 197
American Factfinder, 39
American Pet Product
        Association, 39–40
annual sales estimates,
        142–145
Anytime Fitness, 32
Apple iPhone, 23, 110, 115
assets, 217, 226
    current, 226, 228
    fixed, 227, 228
    intangible, 227
    intellectual, 209–211
    liquidity, 225, 227, 238
    pro forma balance sheet,
        projection of assets, 225
    short-term, 227, 238
    sources and uses of funds
        statement items as initial
        assets and liabilities, 217
assumptions sheet, 218–219
Athletic and Sporting
        Goods Manufacturing
        (U.S.), 132

attorneys
    form of business ownership,
        retention for, 97–98
    management teams
        members, 185
    patent applications,
        retention for, 210
AXS TV, 182

B

baby boomers, 25
Baby Boot Camp, 130
back stage/front stage
        operations plans, 195
backpacks, 28
balance sheets. *See* pro forma
        balance sheets; ratio
        analyses
bankers, relationship with, 185
barriers to entry, 39, 96, 250
Ben & Jerry's Homemade, 99
Benchmark Venture Capital, 185
BenchPrep, 27
Best Buy, 165
Big and Tall Guys, 98
Bing, 68
BizMiner, 38, 63, 67, 119
BizStats, 38, 67
Blue Nile, 124, 138
boards of advisors, 183–184
boards of directors
    attributes of board, 181
    guidance, 181–182
    inside directors, 179
    legitimacy, 182
    outside directors, 179
Bodacious, 31–32
brainstorming, 33–34
branding
    design elements, 9
    intellectual property,
        209–211

mission statements, 94–96
name selection, 98
niche markets, 39, 111
patents, 96, 99, 209–211
points of differentiation,
        153–154
positioning strategy,
        96–97, 153
public relations, 161–163
taglines, 94
value-based
        pricing, 155–156
    See also marketing plans
break-even analyses, 236
Bug report, 34
business ideas, new
    economic trends, 23–25
    environmental
        trends, 23–26
    gaps in marketplace, 29–32
    new companies, 25
    political and regulatory
        changes, 27
    social trends, 25–26
    technological advances, 26–27
    unsolved problems, 28–29
    See also First Screen
business incubators, 4
business locations, 197
business names
Business Week., 140
brand, 98
    legal issues, 99–100
    types of business, 98–100
business ownership, 178
    types, 97
business plan competitions,
        5–6, 243
business plans, definition, 1, 83
Business Plans That Win (Rich
        and Gumpert), 206
Business Plans That Work (Rich
        and Gumpert), 235